THE ROUSING OF THE SCOTTISH WORKING CLASS

THE ROUSING OF THE
SCOTTISH WORKING CLASS

JAMES D. YOUNG

CROOM HELM LONDON

McGILL-QUEEN'S UNIVERSITY PRESS
Montreal

© 1979 James D. Young
Croom Helm Ltd, 2-10 St John's Road, London SW11

British Library Cataloguing in Publication Data

Young, James D
The rousing of the Scottish working class.
1. Labor and laboring classes — Scotland — History
I. Title
301.44'42'09411   HD8399.S3

ISBN 0-7099-0025-2

McGill-Queen's University Press
1020 Pine Avenue West, Montreal H3A 1A2

ISBN 0-7735-0509-1

Legal deposit 4th quarter 1979
Bibliothèque Nationale du Québec

Printed and bound in Great Britain

CONTENTS

Dedicated to Lorna, Alison,
Agnes, Maggie, David and Alex

No saviours from on high deliver,
No trust have we in prince or peer;
Our own right hand the chains must shiver,
Chains of hatred, of greed and fear.

E. Pottier

PREFACE

The formal work on this book on *The Rousing of the Scottish Working Class* began in 1968 when I undertook the task of preparing a doctoral thesis on Scottish working class history in the nineteenth century. Since then I have researched in libraries in Glasgow, Edinburgh, Dundee, Aberdeen, Falkirk, London, Amsterdam and Madison, Wisconsin, USA, and the world has changed and moved on. As the rise of Scottish nationalism, women's history, social history and comparative labour history intruded on my conceptualisation of Scottish history, the scope and concerns of *The Rousing of the Scottish Working Class* were broadened and enlarged. But the informal ambition to write a book on Scottish labour history began in the late 1940s when James Dick, a veteran rank-and-file radical who lives in the village of Airth, Stirlingshire, won me over to socialism and introduced me to the rich literature of international socialism and some of the oral history of the Scottish working class. If his warmth, compassion, anger at injustice and socialist vision have coloured my portrayal of the Scottish labour movement in the 1920s, we do not subscribe to the fashionable tendency among some historians in academia to glorify the proletarian status *per se*.

In 1974 the Social Science Research Council gave me a grant to research into British Workers' Culture and Attitudes to State Intervention, 1880-1920, and I have incorporated some of my findings into *The Rousing of the Scottish Working Class*. This final product is an attempt to repay my intellectual debt to a small army of individuals who have encouraged me to pursue my interest in labour and socialist history, and particularly the late Provost David Smith, of Grangemouth, my home town, the late Dr Edwin Muir under whom I studied Scottish literature, Professor Arnold and Mary Klopper and David Smith, Dalkeith.

But while *The Rousing of the Scottish Working Class* is permeated with a deep commitment to socialism as a moral ideal and practical necessity in Scotland as elsewhere in the world, it is not written in the sour, destructive spirit that informs some would-be radical 'socialist' historical writing today. The criticisms of the concrete reality of authoritarianism and cultural dependency in the Scottish past and present are motivated by a desire for reform, radical renovation, the need for debate and discussion and the restoration of the full ethical consciousness and humanism of the socialist philosophy. Yet this study, though written from a committed socialist vantage-point, is not a biased one in which unflattering or disconcerting facts are either suppressed or distorted. It is, in fact, an ambitious attempt to chronicle the story of the Scottish working class between 1770 and 1931.

I wish to thank Mrs Nora Glasgow, Mr Hugh B. MacKay, Mrs C.A.G. Rowlinson, Miss E.M.H. Schreuder, Mr John Danks and the other librarians who helped me to locate obscure books and documents in the British Library, the International Institute of Social History, Amsterdam, the State Historical Society, Madison, Wisconsin, the Mitchell Library, the National Library of Scotland, the Scottish Records Office and the Library of Stirling University. I also wish to acknowledge the cheerful good humour with which Miss Margaret Hendry and Miss Betty Neech typed the manuscript of this book; and the University of Stirling and the Carnegie Trust for the Universities of Scotland for giving me grants towards the cost of researching in so many libraries. And finally, and most importantly, I wish to thank my wife, Lorna, and my children, David and Alison, for their patience, tolerance and encouragement.

Polmont, Falkirk,
Stirlingshire, 1979

1 CULTURAL IMPERIALISM, THE SCOTTISH ENLIGHTENMENT AND THE 'LOWER ORDERS'

The ladder of ascent was steep and narrow; differentiations among orders and even within orders were carefully marked and universally acknowledged; the gap between the noble and the peasant or the rich and the poor was a vast gulf in which the one stared at the other almost with disbelief. Far too many men and women remained in the eighteenth century what they had been through all the centuries before: beasts of burden, 'two-footed animals', as Voltaire said, not without compassion, approximating the state of nature.[1]

There is a deep-lying struggle in the whole fabric of society; a boundless grinding collision of the New with the Old. The French Revolution, as is now visible enough, was not the parent of this mighty movement, but its offspring.[2]

Scotland became an English cultural colony after the Reformation, and a certain degree of anglicisation was imposed on the Lowlands before the Union of 1707. Of all the Celtic nations within Britain, Scotland was the only one in which the English possessing classes had local allies who were willing to undertake the process of 'cultural pacification'.[3] The presence of English allies within Scottish civil society persuaded the English elite to concede relative cultural autonomy to Scotland after 1707. As Scottish society was pushed into a subordinate role, a victim of 'internal colonialism', with an economy peripheral to the core of English capitalism and civil institutions dominated by 'the conquering metropolitan elite', a unique situation arose.[4] Scottish history was subsequently rewritten by an intellectual elite in the universities, and a host of paradoxes and complexes sprang up and left a deep impress on the consciousness of outsiders. This became particularly noticeable from the late eighteenth century Enlightenment onwards, and the Scottish elite, who were already feeling insecure and defensive, justified their role in the cultural subordination of the lower orders by developing contradictory but nonetheless important concepts about the 'democratic intellect' of the Scot, Scottish 'democracy' and *capitalist* 'improvement'. Intellectuals' perceptions of Scottish history, the Scottish scene in the eighteenth century, as well as their self-deceptions, have had an enduring influence.

While the history of the advent of every capitalist society in the eighteenth and nineteenth century was unique, it is the purpose of this chapter to explore and analyse the major forces that shaped modern Scotland. By seeking to answer the question, 'How did Scottish working people get to be the way they are today?', we will require to look at history from above as well as history from below. From this perspective the multi-faceted events of the Scottish past are viewed through the lens of the present; and, though it is not the historian's job to attempt to resolve social tensions, history seen through the eyes of the present will bring the *continuity* of authoritarianism, social deprivation, women's oppression, cultural dependency, inarticulacy and our internationally high levels of crime, ill-health and alcoholism into very sharp focus.

As the dominant themes of this chapter are usually played down or ignored in the orthodox textbooks, it is necessary to emphasise the distinctiveness of Scottish capitalist society and the peculiarities of the working class. An exploration of the distinctiveness of the Scottish experience in the late eighteenth and early nineteenth centuries will illuminate the importance of history from below at a time when industrial capitalism was imposing a new mode of production and new social relations from above. Though there is nothing unusual 'in the traditions of the dead generations pressing down like the Alps on the minds of the living', the Scottish working class is clearly more imprisoned by traditionalism than any other working class in Western Europe. The reconstruction of a *social picture* of the past in which the connections between the past and the present are implicit will rehabilitate the 'obscure' events and individuals ignored in the orthodox textbooks. A new focus on the relationships between social and economic forces and individuals in the making of Scottish history will prevent interpretation from being submerged in description.

As the Scottish Enlightenment and capitalism developed side-by-side in the eighteenth and early nineteenth centuries, it is necessary to emphasise the importance of Enlightenment ideas — that is, social values, beliefs and ruling class assumptions — in the making of the Scottish working class. A poor and polyglot society that was taken over by a wealthier and more powerful metropolitan capitalism, the Athens of the North was really a type of gulag society which could not, in the view of the Scottish Enlightenment thinkers, afford the luxury of a democratic outlook, the rule of law or democratic institutions. Since the 'peace and order of society' was, in the opinion of Adam Smith, the high priest of Scottish capitalism, much more important than 'even the relief of the miserable',[5] it is easy to see why simple trade unions among the plebeians or labouring poor were implicitly more revolutionary than the early English trade unions.[6]

An attempt to focus attention on the forces which made the Scottish working class, within the context of a very poor society with a ruling elite, committed to the preservation of peace and social order at the expense of everything else must take account of the absence of a State apparatus. This is why the role of the Presbyterian church as a substitute State and the colonial relationship between Scotland and England compel us to focus on such a series of initial abstractions as cultural imperialism, the Scottish Enlightenment and internal colonialism. If this means that our introductory chapter will be more abstract than the other chapters in this book, it nevertheless provides us with the great advantage of being able to portray the attempts of the Scottish working class to make itself in relation to the interaction of the process of anglicisation and industrialisation. By focusing on a total social situation in which the relationship of the indigenous elite to English metropolitan capitalism vitiated the authenticity of Scottish capitalism as a wholly indigenous development,[7] it will be much easier to appreciate E.P. Thompson's *general* argument that the working class was 'not the spontaneous generation of the factory-system'.[8]

I

As the representative of the major mercantile power in Europe in the eighteenth century, the English gentry was an assertive, successful and self-confident capitalist class.[9] The success, aggression and self-confidence of this class was the outcome of processes which had been at work in English society between 1530 and the onslaught of the Industrial Revolution.[10] The process of anglicisation, though intensified in the eighteenth century, began during the Reformation when the English Bible was circulated throughout the Lowlands and led to 'the split mind that the Scots have had about their native language ever since'.[11]

As the English were aware of their power and superiority and in need of new markets in the eighteenth century,[12] it is not difficult to understand why the Scottish possessing classes were prepared to ape the language and manners of the English. The political dominance and economic and cultural superiority of English capitalism explain why the ambitious and modernising Scottish landed interests, mercantile wealth, the indigenous intellectuals and the Presbyterian church surrendered so completely to English culture before the 'take off' into industrialisation. Such Scots as Sir John Sinclair argued that the political circumstances in which they found themselves made it natural for them to imitate the manners and the language of their wealthier and more powerful neighbours in England.[13] There was thus an interaction between the imposition of English cultural imperialism and the enthusiasm of the Scottish possessing classes in aping the language and manners of the English.

As a result of the 'glorious revolution' of 1688 the English bourgeoisie now possessed the most revolutionary culture in Europe — a culture and world-outlook which placed them in the forefront of the struggle against Absolutism. The English bourgeoisie was therefore able to play out its role of pioneering the most 'progressive', path-breaking culture in Europe until the outbreak of the French revolution in 1789. But if access to English markets and the influence of English culture had been rejected by the Scottish elite of landed interests and mercantile capital in the eighteenth century, Scotland would undoubtedly have ended up as an even more backward country than she was.

By enlarging what was already the largest free trade area in the world, the incorporation of Scotland into the British empire reduced the Jacobite threat — a threat represented by the economic and political strategy of men like Sir James Steuart and Andrew Fletcher — of foreign alliances and competitive hostility towards England. As the Scottish bourgeoisie of agrarian capitalists and merchants was hostile to the Jacobites' dream of restoring Absolutism, the English possessing classes and their Scottish allies had concrete economic and political reasons for inaugurating the Union of 1707. Though the Union of 1707 was not the cause but a necessary pre-condition for the Scottish Industrial Revolution in the 1770s, the long-term effects of the Union were, as Henry Hamilton argued, 'entirely beneficial to the Scots economy'.[14] The Scottish corn and cattle trade to England prospered after 1707; the Scottish linen industry was given encouragement; and English capital was invested in the Lowlands.

However, the investment of English capital in Scotland was inhibited by the threat posed by the exiled Stewarts down to 1745. The aggressive, forward-thrusting, path-breaking motivation of the Scottish Enlightenment to impose cultural improvement on the barbarous Highlands was really inseparable from the anglicisation of the whole of Scotland. Though Christopher Hill traced the process of the anglicisation of Scottish society back to 1530, he argued that 'the defeat of the 1745 brought an *extension of London influence* over the Highlands of Scotland similar to that which the outcome of the civil war had brought to the dark corners of northern and western England a century earlier'.[15] Nevertheless the problem of civilising the Highlands was inextricably tied up with the task of imposing a unique system of planned capitalism on Scotland as a whole. As Michael Hechter puts it: 'While some Lowlanders may have been motivated by altruistic sentiments in their efforts to promote anglicisation in the Highlands, it is evident that many others desired internal peace so as to attract English capital to Scotland for investment'.[16]

As English capitalism and the Scottish Enlightenment were inseparably bound together, the contradictory aspects of the essence of the process of modernisation can only be understood by examining the world-outlook of intellectuals who were, as T.C. Smout puts it, 'so emotionally dependent upon the approval and support of the (Scottish) landed classes that it is scarcely conceivable that the golden age could have taken place if the gentry and nobility had been unwilling to become its patrons'.[17] As the Scottish intellectuals and landed classes sought the total eradication of Absolutism and Jacobitism, it is clear that their still evolving ideology was both radical and revolutionary. And at the same time as they identified themselves with the French philosophes' intellectual critique of European Absolutism, they also developed a sustained intellectual assault on Gaelic, the Scots language and the traditional sexual behaviour and pre-industrial customs and culture of the lower orders.

As there was a perceptible interaction between the extension of English civilisation and the Scots readiness to ape the language and manners of the English, it is clear that the Scottish Enlightenment was not a simple or uncomplicated by-product of English imperialism. This subtle distinction is crucial to an understanding of Michael Hechter's concept of internal colonialism. The representatives of English metropolitan capitalism certainly allowed the Scottish elite a considerable degree of autonomy; and, though the Scottish elite was subordinate *vis-à-vis* England after the 'glorious revolution' of 1688, the Scottish Enlightenment was at least partly indigenous.

Though the process of anglicisation began during the Reformation, England and Scotland did not really begin to enter into relations of cultural and economic life until after 1745. This was summed up by the historian, Henry Graham: 'Intercourse between them was slight, always intermittent, and seldom pleasant even in the higher classes. Dislike of everything English was keen in the North; a contempt of everything Scottish was bitter in the South'.[18] Moreover, as the 'vast bulk of the merchant wealth of Scotland' was contained in the Lowlands in 1745,[19] this was where the English found allies who were prepared to assist the Duke of Cumberland to eradicate Jacobitism. But before the Scottish intellectuals could assist in the process of cultural pacification, they had first to anglicise themselves.

This process of anglicisation was intensified in the 1750s when the Select Society induced 'persons from England, duly qualified to instruct in the knowledge of the English tongue, the manner of pronouncing it with purity, and the art of public speaking' to settle in Edinburgh.[20] Later on Dugald Stewart would attribute the advent of the Scottish Enlightenment in the mid-eighteenth century to the intellectuals' ultimate success in overcoming 'the peculiarities of a provincial idiom' which had previously kept their ideas from gaining a European audience.[21] By the early nineteenth century, however, an anonymous contributor to the *Edinburgh Review* observed that the Scottish Enlightenment had been Scottish in form rather than in content.

> Lord Kames made nearly the first attempt, and a tolerably clumsy one at writing English; and ere long, Hume, Robertson, Smith, and a whole host of followers, attracted hither the eyes of all Europe. And yet in this brilliant resuscitation of our 'fervid genius', there was nothing truly Scottish, nothing indigenous; except, perhaps, the natural impetuosity of intellect, which we sometimes claim, and are sometimes upbraided with as a characteristic of our nation. It is curious to remark that Scotland, so full of writers, had no Scottish culture, nor indeed any English; our culture was almost exclusively French. It was by studying Racine and Voltaire, Batteux and Boilean, that Kames trained himself to be a critic and philosopher; it was the light of Montesquieu and Mably that guided Robertson in his political speculations; Quesnay's lamp that kindled the lamp of Adam Smith.[22]

And yet the advent of the Scottish Enlightenment was inseparable from the Scots' complete surrender to English culture.

It is, moreover, clear that the Scots would not have been able to industrialise in the late eighteenth century if they had not surrendered so completely to English culture. Anglicisation and industrialisation were inseparable and 'the effects of literacy' were, as David Buchan argues, 'intrinsically bound up with the effects of the anglicisation of Scottish life'.[23] These connections were summed up by one observer in 1792 when he wrote: 'It is easy to see that the progress of languages must ever follow that of Refinement, of Opulence, of Knowledge, of the Polite Arts. The wider extent of the English dominions, and the greater wealth of the English must necessarily have continued to render the English court more splendid than the Scottish'.[24] But if this process was historically 'progressive' in so far as it destroyed feudalism in the Lowlands, it also created the 'inarticulate Scot'.

As a result of the Scottish elite's surrender to English culture in the mid-eighteenth century the inarticulate Scot was subsequently found in every 'rank' and 'order'. The Scots who belonged to the lower orders were already known for their uncommunicativeness in the late eighteenth century,[25] though the intellectuals were sometimes prepared to ignore the Scots' dialect and 'the numberless uncouth vulgarisms of the lower classes'.[26] John Millar, the Whig professor of law, saw a connection between 'the fly and cautious temper' of the lower orders and inarticulacy;[27] but the inarticulacy was also discernible in the higher ranks. The Scot of the higher ranks used 'a species of translation, which check[ed] the versatility of fancy, and restrain[ed] the genuine and spontaneous flow of his conceptions'.[28] Not surprisingly, the 'Caledonian English of the college, the pulpit and the bar' amused the English intellectuals; and it was, in the words of James Elphinston, 'a paradox reserved for modern times' that 'any nation should write a language it could neither read nor speak'.[29]

Moreover, if the world-outlook of the Scottish intellectuals was nevertheless 'progressive' and revolutionary, it clearly articulated the civilising and industrialising mission of English metropolitan capitalism. Just as the Lowlanders were now emerging from the ignorance and barbarism of the seventeenth century as a result of the extension of English civilisation,[30] so were the Highlands being incorporated into the British empire and improved in 'industry and civility' in inverse proportion to the decline of the Gaelic language.[31] While the 'intercourse of the Highlanders with the Low Country people' and the assault on the Gaelic language and the Highlanders' culture assisted the process of assimilation,[32] the commonalty in the Highlands had continued after 1745 to defy the authority of the Parliament in London by wearing 'the Highland dress, the bonnet, the philabeg and the tartan hose'.[33] This conflict between the civilising mission of English metropolitan capitalism and the attempts of the Highland Society of Scotland to preserve the language, poetry and music of the Highlands led the *Edinburgh Review* to advocate the destruction of 'those prejudices' which retarded the imposition of the English language and the Highlanders' assimilation into the Empire.[34]

But if the Highlanders were portrayed in the 'conjectural' historical accounts of the philosophes as backward and barbarous, so had the

Lowland Scots been subjected to a similar fate before they were rescued by the 'glorious revolution' of 1688. This English revolution of
1688 marked the beginning of civilisation, enlightenment, refinement
and improvement in what had previously been a very barbarous society.
As the Scottish philosophes and, later on, the novelists Walter Scott
and John Galt, portrayed Scottish history as the story of darkness
and unmitigated rudeness before the English revolution ushered in
the beginning of refinement, they argued that the subsequent diffusion
of English light and learning depended on the Union of 1707 and the
destruction of the clan system after the Jacobite rebellion of 1745.

As the writings of the philosophes and novelists were permeated
with assumptions of a clear and in their view self-evident relationship
between Scottish economic prosperity and the imposed diffusion of
English light and learning, there is clear evidence to support Hechter's
concept of internal colonialism. What made the Scottish philosophes'
case such a strong one was the contrast between the legislation passed
in the old Scots Parliament before 1707 and the sometimes obviously
'progressive' nature of the subsequent legislation passed in the English
House of Commons. For if the Scottish lower orders were the victims
of cultural genocide, there can be no doubt that the imperial Parliament
imposed some progress on its more backward internal colony. The
collier-serfs, who had been enslaved by the legislation of the old Scots
Parliament in the sixteenth century, were subsequently emancipated
by successive laws passed in the English House of Commons. Another
example of the modernisation being imposed in the teeth of Presbyterian
opposition was cited by the American historian, Matilda J. Gage, when
she argued thus: 'Notwithstanding two hundred years of such experience
when by an Act of Parliament in 1784, the burning and hanging of
witches was abolished, the General Assembly of the Calvinist Church
of Scotland "confessed" this Act "as a great national sin" '.[35]

This visible and concrete success in imposing modernisation and
capitalist improvement on their own society through the medium of
the English Parliament confirmed the philosophes in their patrician
and elitist assumptions. As improvement was already seen to be working in so far as Scotland now enjoyed some of the economic prosperity
of the British empire in the late eighteenth and early nineteenth
centuries, the philosophes and such novelists as Walter Scott and John
Galt waged ideological war on the nationalism and latent nationalism
of the lower orders by deepening and intensifying their intellectual
critique of the rudeness and backwardness of their own society. Walter
Scott, a novelist who always articulated the modernising ideas of the

Enlightenment, used his novels *and* factual accounts of Scottish history to emphasise the crucial importance of eradicating the 'seeds of disunion' within 'the bosom of Scotland' even after 1745 and 'all marks of distinction between the Highlander and the Lowlander' which inhibited the growth of 'the useful arts', agriculture and industry.[36]

However, the survival of Jacobite sentiments in the Lowlands as well as in the Highlands long after 1745 kept the English possessing classes suspicious, hostile and sometimes contemptuous of the Scottish commonalty. As the Scottish provincial elite was well aware of this English suspicion and contempt down to 1820, they responded by waging ideological war on the Absolutist outlook of Jacobitism and the folk-memories of the Scottish past before the advent of the 'glorious revolution' of 1688. This was the major theme of many of the novels of Walter Scott and John Galt and the socio-historical writings of such philosophes as John Millar, Dugald Stewart, Lord Kames and William Robertson. As Scotland and America were still, in the words of John Clive and Bernard Bailyn, 'England's cultural provinces' in the eighteenth century,[37] it is not surprising to find evidence of the English possessing classes' contempt for the Scottish lower orders in the Lowlands as well as in the Highlands. This olympian superiority of the English possessing classes towards the inferior Scots was articulated by Henry Skrine in 1795 when he wrote:

> It must be confessed, however, that the common people of Scotland
> are more than a century behind the English in improvement; and
> the manners of the Lowlands in particular cannot fail to disgust
> a stranger. All the stories that are propagated of the filth and
> habitual dirtiness of this people are surpassed by the reality . . .
> Their manners are equally unpleasant, being uncommunicative
> and forbidding in the extreme.[38]

As the spokesmen for the social and cultural values of English capitalism were seldom convinced that the progress of commerce and cultivation in the Lowlands would necessarily remove the existing 'idleness' and ignorance,[39] the Scottish elite became even more hostile towards their own lower orders. The constant condescending social criticism of Scottish backwardness led the philosophes in Edinburgh and Glasgow to portray – and to try and make – their own lower orders more docile and better behaved than the English plebeians. Far from the Scottish philosophes being either compassionate or socially sensitive towards the commonalty, the social and cultural pressures that emanated from English metropolitan capitalism forced the Scottish possessing classes to be even more ruthless than the English in their attempts to make their own plebeians conform and obey the higher ranks.

Under the enormous social, cultural and psychological pressures of an aggressively self-confident and assertive metropolitan capitalism, the Scottish philosophes were much more directly involved in the process of industrialisation than any comparable group of intellectuals in Europe. As there was clearly a causal connection between their identification with the landed interests and their 'lack of social and political iconoclasm',[40] it is very difficult to accept George E. Davie's denial that 'the radical thinkers south of the border faced up to the problem of democraticising industrial society with a consistency and boldness which puts the Scottish school of philosophy to shame'.[41] Far from the indigenous elite contributing to the growth of democracy, it persistently abused the rule of law and did nothing to challenge the authoritarian ethos of Scottish society.

As the Scots philosophes were so much more directly involved in helping to impose industrialisation on their own society than the English, they could not possibly have produced a Voltaire, a Rousseau, a Tom Paine or even a John Wilkes or a John Cartwright. What horrified William Cobbett when he analysed the role of Dr Black and 'the Scotch feelosofers' in imposing capitalism in Scotland was their ruthless disregard for the 'rights' or feelings of 'the poor' and their readiness to solve 'distress in the farming districts' by sending the surplus 'hands' into the towns to become industrial workers without their consent.[42] But if the lack of a democratic outlook in the thought of the Scottish philosophes was seen in, for example, Dugald Stewart's intellectual justification for excluding 'women from political privileges' and the vote,[43] it was the ruthless social insensitivity towards 'the poor' which infuriated William Cobbett when he wrote:

The 'Instructor' gives us a sad account of the state of the working classes in Scotland. I am not glad that these poor people suffer: I am very sorry for it; and if I could relieve them, out of my own means, without doing good to and removing danger from the insolent boroughmongers and tax-eaters of Scotland, I would share my last shilling with these poor fellows. But I must be glad that something has happened to silence the impudent Scotch quacks, who have been for six years past, crying up the doctrine of Malthus, and railing against the English poor laws. Let us now see what they will do with their poor.[44]

This overall social and intellectual climate seems to have contributed to the political iconoclasm of the lower orders, though the Scottish Enlightenment had a quite devastating cultural influence on the formation of the industrial proletariat.

II

But what precisely were the ideas, cultural products and consequences of the interaction of English capitalism and the Scottish Enlightenment which had such a devastating influence on the making of the Scottish working class in the late eighteenth and early nineteenth centuries? First of all, the Scots linguistic insecurity can be seen during the centuries following the Reformation when the Presbyterian contempt for the arts created the cultural vacuum that subsequently worried such Scots as Eric Linklater and Edwin Muir; and secondly, the sexual repression which began at the Reformation and later merged in an industrial society with what William Power called 'the inhibitions of Gradgrind Calvinism'. Thirdly, the Scottish lower orders were influenced by a total culture in which an insecure and authoritarian elite articulated an obsessive awareness of its own provincial inferiority and backwardness.

While the Scottish elite's sense of provincial inferiority strengthened their determination to catch up with the superior culture and manners of the English, and as the Enlightenment occurred in a society with a centuries-old history of extreme backwardness and authoritarianism,[45] they saw causal connections between the progress of commerce and the modernisation of sexual behaviour. Thus John Millar argued that 'the indiscriminate gratification of the propensity between the sexes' was being 'further obstructed by the general improvements of society'.[46] In the world-outlook of the Scottish philosophes modernisation did not only entail anglicisation with the social consequences of inarticulacy and linguistic insecurity, but also involved the codification of correct sexual attitudes which, if not required by an evolving industrial society, were certainly useful in keeping some working people 'quiet', 'docile' and oppressed. It is, however, important to emphasise that there was a mingling of old and new modernising attitudes towards sexual behaviour.

The roots of sexual repression were planted at the Reformation when the Calvinist attack on erotic poetry consisted of only one aspect of what G. Legman depicts as a war against 'the mariolatric remnants of sex worship then called "witchcraft" '.[47] This was the historic background against which the Presbyterian pulpits in the eighteenth century 'rang with denunciations' of the 'seductive temptation to sin', 'lust', 'worldliness' and 'promiscuous dancing'; and from the standpoint of the semantic value judgments of Gradgrind Calvinism, Henry Graham was not lacking in perception when he observed that Scottish social life in 'some of its moral aspects stands out conspicuously pure compared with that of England'. Moreover, if adultery 'brought down social disgrace' on offenders in Scotland,[48] no social class escaped the wrath of the Presbyterian clergy. And if the Scottish philosophes were at odds with the clergy on a whole range of questions, the former were also determined — in the name of progress, enlightenment, improvement and modernisation — to eradicate illegitimacy, irregular marriages and sexual pleasure in all ranks and orders.

However, if the devastating influence of the sexual attitudes of the Scottish philosophes is to be understood, they must be seen in the perspective of what was happening elsewhere in Europe. In a provocative and influential book, *The Making of the Modern Family*, Edward Shorter has argued that the greatest achievement of industrial capitalism in Western Europe was the sexual emancipation of the women of the lower orders. From this historical perspective a sexual revolution began in the late eighteenth century when the advent of market capitalism gave birth to 'a revolution in sentiment'. This was the context in which 'mentalities were undergoing the historic shift towards individualism and affection'. Thus 'the burial of chastity before marriage commenced in 1750, not 1900'; and the perceptible increases in illegitimacy in the West at large and the 'surge of affection' were an automatic consequence of economic change. Moreover, and most important, industrial capitalism weakened traditional community controls against fornication and pre-marital pregnancies and enabled large numbers of lower class women to 'undertake sexual experimentation'.[49]

While Shorter's novel, original and provocative views on the so-called causal connections between the advent of industrial capitalism and the sexual emancipation of lower class women, might have some validity for women in other industrialising countries in the late eighteenth and early nineteenth centuries, Scottish industrialisation actually intensified the existing sexual and social enslavement of working women. As the traditional sexual repression which sprang from the Reformation merged with the modernising sexual attitudes of the Scottish Enlightenment the cultural formation of the Scottish working class was overshadowed by a sustained intellectual critique of illegitimacy, sexual pleasure and adultery. The Scottish philosophes did not question existing sanctions against fornication, adultery, illegitimacy and pre-marital sexual gratification, and it is not surprising to find this ideology impinging on the consciousness of trade unionists. For even the trade unionists formulated rules committing themselves to expel any members found guilty of adultery, fornication, drunkenness or swearing.[50]

From the standpoint of the Scottish Enlightenment the existence of high levels of illegitimacy and the absence of chastity amongst unmarried persons were signs of backwardness; and Lord Kames deplored the fact that illegitimacy was not always regarded by the lower ranks as a 'disgrace'.[51] As the lower orders experienced a very low social status within a patriarchal society, James Logan simply noted the fact that 'a Scottish bride was expected to show reluctance and require a certain degree of violence, which was neither thought unbecoming in the man, nor a hardship to the woman'.[52] But if the Scottish Enlightenment was attempting to regularise and modernise sexual attitudes, Lord Kames argued that sexual intercourse ought to be restricted to the purpose of procreation. Moreover, he quoted the case of a Highland woman who destroyed her illegitimate child in flames to 'conceal her fraility' or moral weakness as evidence of the spread of sexual enlightenment.[53] As traditional Presbyterian sexual attitudes coalesced with the new Scottish Enlightenment sanctions against existing sexual behaviour,[54] the formation of the Scottish working class was coloured by inarticulacy and the authoritarianism of the total environment they inhabited. Furthermore, it was a paradox that sexual repression and high levels of illegitimacy existed side-by-side in the nineteenth century. But in the midst of appalling housing conditions a rural proletariat of farm workers and coal miners, who still clung to their *natural* sexual attitudes and codes, made an inordinate contribution to the illegitimacy statistics.

As a result of a very complex interaction between Scottish and English political, cultural and economic relationships from the early eighteenth century onwards and what were really *disparate* elements in the world-outlook of the Scottish philosophes, the cultural forma-tion of the Scottish working class was influenced by the convergence of the devastating influence of inarticulacy, linguistic insecurity, drunkenness, women's oppression, sexual repression, the heterogeneity of the pre-industrial labour groups and the problems of Highland emigration and, later on, immigration and migration.[55] Yet some of these disparate factors were a direct consequence of the Union of 1707. For if the inarticulacy of the lower ranks sprang from an interaction of English cultural imperialism and the enthusiasm of the Scottish elite in aping their superiors, the serious social problem of drunkenness in 'the middling and lower ranks' arose from the malt tax which led the Scots to substitute whisky for beer drinking.[56] As some of these factors coalesced in the nineteeth century with the problem of sexual repression, A.S. Neill could detect a situation many working-class Scots must have experienced when he asserted:

> When I spoke dialect outside the house, I shared the villagers'
> open view of sex; when I spoke English and became respectable
> upon crossing the threshold of the schoolhouse, I had to put away
> all openness of mind concerning sex language and practice.[57]

In contrast to the English situation where legislation to imprison adulterers 'floundered' because it might have discriminated against 'the amusement of the rich as well as the poor',[58] the Scottish elite was much more consistent and puritanical. Moreover, while the sanctions against adultery and fornication in Scotland were imposed by the Presbyterians, sexual repression was often internalised by the lower ranks. Nevertheless, bawdy sexual attitudes survived the onslaught of the Reformation amongst many Scots, and in a factual note at the end of her long novel, *Discipline,* Mary Brunton described the sexual attitudes of the lower orders in a Scottish town in 1795: 'About twenty years ago, it happened in a remote town that two persons of the lower ranks were accused of adultery. The charge, whether true or false, had such an effect, that the man was driven like a wild beast from human converse. The very children pelted him with mud, crying out, "There goes the adulterer" '.[59] But if the English Methodists were beginning to engage in the task of eradicating fornication and adultery,[60] the Scottish Presbyterians already had a long record of imposing sexual repression before they received assistance from such philosophes as Lord Kames and John Millar.

The extreme general backwardness of Scottish society motivated the ruthlessness of the Enlightenment philosophes and strengthened their determination to rescue their country from rudeness and barbarity. It is important to understand this context if we are going to borrow and apply E.P. Thompson's concept of class to the making of the Scottish working class with its distinctive experience and peculiarities. Since 'class happens when some men, as a result of common experiences (inherited or shared), feel and articulate the identity of their interests as between themselves, and as against other men whose interests are different from (and usually opposed to) theirs',[61] the 'conditioning' as well as the 'agency' of the Scottish working class in the process of being made and making itself cannot be separated from the Presbyterian milieu in which they lived and worked.

Yet some of the customs and remnants of the culture of diverse and heterogeneous pre-industrial groups in Scottish society survived the onslaught of the modernising and civilising mission of English metropolitan capitalism. The conditioning to which the Scottish working class was subjected during its formative period in the late eighteenth and early nineteenth centuries certainly resulted in the particular class peculiarities of inarticulacy, drunkenness, provincial insecurity, sexual inhibitions and ethnic prejudices.[62] But in comparative European terms this working class was unusually well-educated, literate, politically aware, sympathetic to republicanism and a 'primitive' socialist belief in the need for the equality of property.[63] It was, moreover, the pre-industrial traditions and mentalities of the past — for example, widespread Jacobite sympathies in the Lowlands as well as in the Highlands — which helped to make the Scottish weavers, artisans and peasants the most politically aware and progressive in Europe. In contrast to the situation in England, where 'the traditional anti-French bias of John Bull's beef-fed contempt for the starveling continentals' inhibited mass support for Jacobinism,[64] the historic bonds with Scotland's 'hereditary ally' made working-class Jacobinism a more powerful, popular and outward-looking force.[65]

The existence of widespread Jacobite sentiments in the consciousness of the pre-industrial labour force in the Lowlands as well as in the Highlands was of crucial importance in fashioning the character of Scottish working class radicalism in the late eighteenth and early nineteenth centuries. As the lower orders tried to push the radical side of the Enlightenment to a political conclusion by agitating for the doctrine of the equality of property in both Lowlands and Highlands,[66] they thereby created serious tensions within the hitherto unified elite of agrarian capitalists, merchants, embryonic industrialists and intellectuals. But as the philosophes, whether Whig or Tory, were committed to the prosecution of the Clearances in the Highlands, they had a vested interest in deliberately undervaluing the Highlanders' culture and traditional way-of-life as well as in suppressing a general awareness of the Highlanders' resistance to the Clearances.

As the 'Scottish scholarly mind' was 'an outstandingly historical or history-conscious mind',[67] the 'conjectural' history of the philosophes — and the reason why they were so instrumental in formulating the ideology of bourgeois society — sprang from the concrete reality of the split between the backward Highlands and the relatively prosperous Lowlands. It is somewhat ironical that the Scottish philosophes who occupied a comparatively backward country played *the* major role in the formulation of the British bourgeois ideology about the origins of European industrial capitalism. For if 'the social science of the Enlightenment [was] seen in its most mature and sophisticated form in Scotland', where an emerging 'commercial civilisation' had begun to 'change the face of Scotland so dramatically',[68] the concrete Lowland/Highland division provided the evidence which enabled the philosophes to contribute so significantly to the genesis of marxist thought. In an essay on 'Town and Country in the Transition to Capitalism', John Merrington has vividly described this relationship between Scottish backwardness, the Lowland/Highland split and the philosophes' contribution to bourgeois ideology: 'The centrality of the town-country relation in the transition to capitalism in the West and more basically the equation of urbanism and capitalism and progress were already explicitly formulated in the earliest theories of the origins of capitalism — those of eighteenth century political economy. For the proponents of the new and revolutionary 'conjectural' history of civil society — Smith, Stewart, Ferguson and Millar — the origins of the division of labour and the market in the "commercial stage" of civilisation were to be sought in the separation of town and country'.[69]

However, if the Scottish Enlightenment was historically 'progressive' in so far as it promoted a sustained intellectual assault on Absolutism and the pre-industrial world until at least 1789, it had a quite devastating influence on the making of the Scottish working class and society as a whole. This was at least partly because the philosophes' indoctrination and conditioning of the emerging working class forced them to relate their interpretation of the Scottish past to the process of modernisation, improvement and the exorcism of those memories of the past which kept many of the lower orders sympathetic to Jacobitism. Incredibly backward as the Highlands were, the philosophes exaggerated the barbarity of the Highlands and the Highland/Lowland split in order to rationalise their support for the cultural genocide they were engaging in.

It is instructive, for example, to examine the case of James Loch as evidence of the philosophy of the Scottish Enlightenment in action north of the Highland line. Known as the 'Sutherland Metternich', this lawyer had been a prominent member of the Whig student elite at Edinburgh university in the 1790s. Yet the one historian who claims that Loch was 'no reactionary' in relation to Parliamentary reform in the early nineteenth century overlooks Loch's commitment to the total destruction of the Highlanders' culture — that is, their songs, poetry and language — and traditional way-of-life.[70] The crucial question in deciding whether he was a reactionary or not rests on how historians evalute the Clearances rather than on his attitude to Parliamentary reform. For if liberal and even some socialist historians are going to persist in justifying what happened in the Highlands in the name of modernisation and 'progress' while regretting the odd example of brutality here and there, they ought to recognise that we cannot criticise an inevitable historical process.

As the Scottish elite was determined to eradicate the memory of Jacobitism and the world-outlook of the pre-industrial labouring peoples of the Highlands and the Lowlands by opting for a form of obscurantist thought-control after the outbreak of the French revolution in 1789, it was inevitable that they would also exaggerate the 'passiveness' of the Highlanders in resisting the Clearances.[71] However, if the Highlanders' resistance to the Clearances existed even before the early nineteenth century episodes documented by James Hunter in *The Making of the Crofting Community,* the philosophes' ideological assault on the backwardness of the Highlanders certainly vitiated solidarity between the lower orders in both parts of Scotland. But though the Highlanders' resistance was always played down by the Scottish elite from the late eighteenth century onwards, it was sufficiently real to compel the authorities to send troops in to repress riots against the Clearances in 1792 and again in 1813.[72]

As the Scottish elite exploited existing prejudices between the Highlanders and the Lowlanders by exaggerating stories about the so-called ineradicable hatred between Gael and Gaul, it is surprising that rank-and-file Friends of the People in the north and south of Scotland agitated for a new division of private property. For if the propaganda and 'conjectural' history of the philosophes vitiated the emergence of large-scale solidarity between the lower orders in different ethnic groups, the writings of Tom Paine found an enthusiastic audience amongst grieves, farm labourers, peasants, weavers and artisans. As early as the 1770s the commonalty in the Highlands and the Lowlands articulated their sympathy for the rebellious colonists in America; and in 1819 the Lord Advocate spoke out against the 'unnatural union between the Radical reformers and the gallant, brave Highlanders'.[73] And the Highlanders' memories of the Clearances — memories they took into the mills, coal mines and factories in the early nineteenth century — were of crucial importance in subsequent Lowland social and political action over the land question.[74] It was, in fact, the land question itself in the late eighteenth century which pushed the artisans, weavers, grieves, orra men and peasants to agitate for equality of property and a new division of the big estates.

III

English/Scottish relationships were of decisive importance in shaping the radicalism of the lower orders in the Athens of the North. For if 'the distant State that dominated Scotland was not the standard European Absolutism', and though the Scots 'were lucky enough to have been *taken over* by a dynamic bourgeois culture instead of a stagnant late-feudal one',[75] the social and economic backwardness of Scottish society enabled the lower orders to develop a 'primitive' socialist ideology and a democratic outlook. In the face of formidable difficulties, artisans, weavers, peasants and grieves in the Lowlands and in the Highlands read the writings of Tom Paine and agitated for a new division of property, though the barrier of language must have inhibited communication between them. But it was the past traditions and social outlook in the Highlands which almost certainly made the peasants and grieves so sympathetic to the new radicalism of the times; for there is a law of combined and uneven development in the 'explosion' of ideas as well as in the economic and social development. Thus W.F. Skene wrote in his history of *Celtic Scotland* in 1888 as follows:

> Yet though the conscious socialist movement be but a century old, the labouring folk all down the ages have clung to communist practices and customs, partly the inheritance and instinct from the group and clan life of our forefathers and partly because these customs were their only barrier to poverty; and because without them social life was impossible.[76]

But if the poverty and economic backwardness of Scottish society reinforced the radicalism of the Scottish working class in its formative phase, the English possessing classes were determined to keep the Scots politically and culturally dependent, subordinate and conscious of their inferior past and present. It was precisely because Scotland was *taken over* by a superior metropolitan capitalist culture that the Scottish philosophes were so history-conscious and determined to eradicate all those memories of the past which might lead the lower orders to question their patrician and elitist assumptions about the origins of property and the inequality of ranks. As the Scottish philosophes were committed to the task of persuading the English possessing classes of the docility, obsequiousness and good behaviour of the Scots, they also emphasised the extent to which 'the common people' had always been 'dependent upon the higher classes'.[77]

A distinctive feature of the overall Scottish experience was the absence of a bourgeois revolution through which the middle ranks and philosophes might have expressed their *own* authentic confidence, mission and path-breaking role comparable to what the English were already doing. In contrast to the English and the French the Scots still had not experienced a bourgeois revolution in the nineteenth century,[78] and the historical actuality of the Scots being taken over by 'a superior kingdom' in 1707 has obscured the question of the origins of capitalism in Scotland.

In a brilliant, wide-ranging survey of the history, impact and consequence of Absolutism and the Absolutist State, Perry Anderson concludes thus: 'In the West, the Spanish, English and French monarchies were defeated or overthrown by bourgeois revolution from below; while the Italian and German principalities were eliminated by bourgeois revolution from above, belatedly'.[79] But if Anderson treats the question of whether there was a Scottish bourgeois revolution or not as an open-ended one, the same openness is absent in the writings of his co-thinker, Tom Nairn. From Nairn's historical perspective, the Reformation was not the Scottish revolution on the model of 1640 or 1789. Thus he is forced to argue that the Enlightenment was *the* Scottish revolution in which the creativity and the genius of the Scottish philosophes enabled the elite of agrarian capitalists, merchants and Presbyterian clergymen to prevent the English possessing classes from imposing a *crude* form of colonialism and cultural imperialism on what was one of the oldest nations in Europe in the 18th century.[80]

While it is obvious that the Scottish Enlightenment was not a by-product of a crude English cultural imperialism in a way comparable to the Irish experience described by James Connolly in *Labour in Irish History*,[81] the indigenous elements in the Scottish Enlightenment were nevertheless subordinate to a superior, self-confident and aggressive metropolitan capitalism. Moreover, if the philosophes played a crucial and indispensable role in the process of modernising and industrialising Scottish society, they did so within a context in which their surrender to English culture created 'a general dichotomy so pronounced in eighteenth century Scotland as to be dubbed a "national schizophrenia" '.[82] The authentic indigenous effort that was evident in the process of rescuing Scottish society from social and economic backwardness was inextricably tied to a superior metropolitan culture; and the devastating influence of the Enlightenment on Scottish society and the formation of the industrial proletariat cannot be understood in isolation from the dominant and domineering presence of English capitalism at the moment of its world ascendancy.

In fact the Scottish Enlightenment began to articulate the civilising mission of English metropolitan capitalism in the 1750s when the latter was beginning to take off into world economic ascendancy. As the Scottish economy became peripheral to the core of English capitalism, Michael Hechter asserts that economic dependency was 'reinforced through juridical, political and military measures'.[83] Though the process of British industrialisation 'developed gradually in a highly "empirical" and de-centralised fashion',[84] the problem of understanding the complex relationships between English capitalism and the Scottish Enlightenment is obscured by the fact that the actual process of industrialisation was a predominantly indigenous affair. However, what was much less indigenous in content (as distinct from form) was the Scottish Enlightenment itself.

As the Scottish Enlightenment owed its breakthrough to the philosophes' willingness to ape the manners and the language of the English, Scotland became culturally even more of an English colony from about 1762 when William Robertson's management of the University of Edinburgh coincided with 'the start of its international reputation as a centre of learning'.[85] But while the problem of anglicisation first emerged in the Scottish universities in 1690 when the Revolutionary Settlement Act excluded Jacobites and Episcopalians from teaching in the Scottish universities,[86] the advent of the Enlightenment was inseparable from the Scots' complete surrender to the influence of English metropolitan culture. Colonial relationships were therefore interwoven into this complex social and industrial process – and these colonial relationships were expressed through a variety of instruments down to 1820.

As the Scottish philosophes increasingly identified with the 'glorious revolution' of 1688, the House of Hanover and the English constitution, and sought to impose the language and manners which they assumed were indispensable for the progress of commerce and manufacturing (i.e., industrialisation), they were forced into a schizophrenic attitude towards their own native society, their own nation's history and in a sense themselves. But this schizophrenia was induced by the self-confident, aggressive metropolitan capitalism of London and the Scots' cultural dependency on the English. For the Scots did not only ape the language and the manners of the English, but they also felt compelled to denounce and denigrate the inferiority, rudeness and simplicity of their own lower orders.[87] This overall social situation was summed up by John Clive and Bernard Bailyn:

> The provincial's view of the world was discontinuous. Two forces, two magnets, affected his efforts to find adequate standards and styles; the values associated with the simplicity and purity (real or imagined) of nativism, and those to be found in the cosmopolitan sophistication . . . The complexity of the provincial's image of the world and of himself made demands upon him unlike those felt by the equivalent Englishman. It tended to shake his mind from the roots of habits and traditions.[88]

But while the Scottish philosophes made an enormous theoretical contribution to the genesis of marxist thought, it ought to be emphasised that they were psychologically and culturally dependent on English metropolitan capitalism. This cultural dependency was spelt out by Robert Mudie in his fascinating book, *The Modern Athens*: 'Even Jeffrey, it he had not had his fees to bear him out, and if his journal had not been patronised in London, might have written his review in vain; ay, and Scott, who persevered longer in writing in obscurity than any other author of the present time, would ere now have been mute or a maniac, had he not been a fierce and forward party-man'.[89] This cultural dependency nevertheless allowed them to put themselves in the forefront of European intellectual life, and it was the colonial situation in which they operated which produced a sort of schizophrenia.

However, if the colonial relationships in which the Scottish elite functioned were certainly not crude colonial ones, the colonial relationship between England and Scotland defined the context in which industrialisation and the making of the Scottish working class occurred. For at the same time as the Scottish elite aped the language and manners of the superior metropolitan capitalism and utilised native capital and entreprenurial skill in the process of industrialising a very backward country, they also articulated their distorted 'nationalist' criticisms of the English.

Not surprisingly, perhaps, the conflicts between the two countries were cultural rather than economic; for the essence of this particular relationship has been defined by Michael Hechter as follows:

> One of the defining characteristics of the colonial situation is that
> it must involve the interaction of two cultures — that of the
> conquering metropolitan elite (cosmopolitan culture) and of the
> indigenes (native culture) — and that the former is promulgated
> by the colonial authorities as being vastly inferior for the
> realisation of universal ends. One of the consequences of this
> denigration of the indigenous culture is to undermine the natives'
> will to resist the colonial regime.[90]

But as the colonial relationships between England and Scotland had
not sprung from any serious economic competition between them, the
Scottish philosophes could actually engage in the luxury of literary
polemics with the English about whether the English or the Scottish
universities were the more democratic, austere, practical or superior.
When the Scots did discuss the role of their universities in British
history, they were at their most schizophrenic.

In a powerful book on *The Democratic Intellect*, George Elder
Davie argues that the eighteenth century Scots 'congratulated themselves
on the advantage of a common market with England' and 'equally
congratulated themselves on the advantage of their well-ordered progressive system of law and education [and religion too] compared with the
stagnant and ill-ordered state of affairs in the South'.[91] But if the
Scottish universities undoubtedly made 'a uniquely important contribution to the development of a provincial, bourgeois culture' by pioneering
such disciplines as political economy,[92] it is hard to see any democracy
in them except in so far as the admission of students was comparatively
open. The Scots believed that their universities were unique and they
always sought evidence for their intellectual superiority to compensate
for their inferior, provincial status in other aspects of British life.
Thus in reply to criticisms that an academic in Oxford had made, the
Edinburgh Review lashed out at their Southern critic in an aggressively
'nationalistic' and — given their sustained comments about the backwardness and rudeness of their own country — schizophrenic tone:

> It is the case of all universities originating in Catholic times, and
> constructed on the principles of a church that claimed infallibility,
> that they either retain their original constitution, or have been but
> slightly reformed. The Scottish universities happily have not retained
> this pernicious structure; and perhaps from the greater extent to

which the Reformation was carried out in our northern part of the island, or, still more, from the poverty of the establishment that had no means of distinction but those derived from exertion, they are without those artificial impediments which, in the south, have so effectively resisted the progress of improvement. Hence it is that our universities have been so rapid in following, and so instrumental in forwarding the improvement of knowledge . . . It is the fashion with such writers as our author to characterise the universities of Scotland by the ephithet of Northern, to which a large portion of demerit is, in their opinion, attached. But so long as Northern is synonymous with Free, so long as it is applied to schools — no salaries to reward sloth and inactivity — and no offers bound by duty or interest to refuse admission to the truth — we shall hold it superior to all other titles to honour; and should sorely grieve to see it exchanged for the riches, the dignities, or even the climate of the south.[93]

But the Scottish universities were, in Dugald Stewart's phrase, 'priest-ridden', and obscurantist;[94] and in a country lacking liberal institutions and liberal traditions the philosophes and novelists as well as the possessing classes generally gave top priority to eliminating the folk-memories of the Scottish past rather than developing a free press, respect for the rule of law or even the 'democratic' outlook of a Voltaire, a Rousseau, a Paine, a Wilkes or a Cartwright.[95]

IV

Moreover, the domineering presence of a thrusting and self-confident metropolitan capitalism extending English civilisation to the Lowlands and the Highlands was of decisive importance in the process by which the Scottish working class was made within a colonial context and yet simultaneously made itself in the late eighteenth and early nineteenth centuries. The transition to industrial capitalism in Scotland was visibly unique, and, in turn, led to unique problems and a unique working class. However, it is important to emphasise that in the context of the beginning of global industrialisation, there had never been any single type of 'the transition'. This problem is well summed up by E.P. Thompson when he argues: 'The stress of the transition falls upon the whole culture; resistance to change and assent to change arise from the whole culture. And this culture includes the systems of power, property-relations, religious institutions, etc., inattention to which merely flattens phenomena and trivialises analysis. Above all, the transition is not to "industrialism" *tout court* but to industrial capitalism or (in the twentieth century) to alternative systems whose features are still indistinct'.[96]

It is significant that the Scottish philosophes boasted about the superiority (sic!) of such abstract phenomena as their austere, practical universities, their education, their law, their religion and the *docility* and the *passiveness* of *their lower orders*. But as there were obvious contradictions between the reality of the Scottish scene and what the philosophes sometimes said about it, they sought to close the gap between this reality and their goals by urging pre-industrial groups to assimilate quickly and face a quiet but sure extermination. As 'the first modern movement' of Irish immigrants into Scotland was 'initiated by the Irish rebellion of 1798 and the number of Irish-born inhabitants increased rapidly after 1815',[97] the Scottish elite was able to attribute their unique social problems to the heterogeneity of their lower orders.

Furthermore, at a time when folk-memories, minority languages and the survival of Jacobite sentiments constituted a major stumbling-block to the progress of the juggernaut of capitalist improvement and modernisation, the Scottish elite sought to eliminate irregular marriages, handfasting and pre-industrial customs and practices.[98] In England 'a new Puritan discipline and bourgeois exactitude' began some centuries before the take-off into industrialisation and the assault on pre-industrial customs and 'working-class morals' was a long-drawn out process;[99] but in Scotland capitalism was imposed much more abruptly on a more heterogeneous labour force. As the Scots offered much more resistance to the invitation to work in the early cotton mills and manufacturing enterprises,[100] there was a recurrent tension between indigenous and immigrant workers even before the Irish and Highland blacklegs were brought to work in the west of Scotland in the early nineteenth century.

As there was a constant influx of culturally diverse pre-industrial groups into the Scottish Lowlands during and after the classic period of the Industrial Revolution, it seems clear that the Scottish experience of industrialisation is much more comparable to the American than to the English experience. What Herbert G. Gutman has argued about the American experience in *Work, Culture and Society in Industrialising America* seems to be equally applicable to the Scottish one: 'In quite a different connection and in a relatively homogeneous country, the Italian Antonio Gramsci concluded of such evidence that "for a social elite the features of subordinate groups always display something barbaric and pathological". The changing composition of the American working class may make so severe a dictum more pertinent to the United States than to Italy. Class and ethnic fears and biases combined together to worry elite observers about the diverse worlds below them and to distort gravely their perceptions of these worlds'.[101] But the cultures and the customs of pre-industrial peoples were not easily eliminated in America and England; and in Scotland the colonial relationship with the superior culture of an expanding metropolitan capitalism created unique problems for the Scottish working class.

Just as the process of American industrialisation was really inseparable from the destruction of folk-memories,[102] so did the Scots persist in their sustained intellectual critique and indoctrination of pre-industrial peoples who were already in or who came into the Lowlands, belatedly. This led to a recurrent problem of national identity amongst the lower orders, and the attempts of diverse Lowland and Highland groups to come together by agitating for a new division of private property and the big estates, reaffirmed the beliefs of the Scottish elite about the barbaric and pathological features of the subordinate groups below them. If we may borrow Herbert G. Gutman's insights, it would seem that this same process of a constant influx of culturally diverse peoples into the Lowlands might explain why the attempts of Gradgrind Calvinism to *alter the habits and behaviour* of the Scottish working class lasted much longer than in most other industrial countries including America.[103]

There were nevertheless important differences between the making of the American or the English and the making of the Scottish working class. The whole ethos of Scottish society was much more authoritarian than the ethos of American or English society; and the Scottish working class made itself in conditions where there was a total absence of Parliamentary democracy in the English sense. And for all the much vaunted superiority of Scottish law, objective observers of the Scottish scene were appalled by what they saw. As Robert Mudie put it: 'The judges, and more especially the crown lawyers, have a power over the people, at which Englishmen would stand aghast. The judges (no matter whether they exercise it or not), have directly or indirectly, the power of nominating every one of the jury by which a Scotsman is tried'.[104] Moreover, there was practically no Scottish radical press, and the suppression of the orthodox press was 'made possible by the judicial system'.[105]

It was therefore inevitable that the Scottish working class would be influenced by this total social situation in which the negative features of cultural imperialism, inarticulacy and sexual repression were quite devastating. As liberal-positivist and metropolitan socialist historians have treated industrialisation and modernisation as being inherently 'progressive' and an unqualified blessing, they have usually ignored what was lost in the process of destroying the traditions, customs, songs and poetry of pre-industrial peoples. This particular contradiction in the socialist tradition of analysing the role of industrialisation has been brilliantly summed up by Raymond Williams, the New Left literary critic, in his book *The Country and the City*:

> The great indictments of capitalism, and of its long record of misery in factories and towns, have co-existed, with a certain historical scheme, with this repeated use of 'progressive' as a willing adjective about the same events. We hear again and again this brisk, impatient and as it is said realistic response: to the productive efficiency, the new liberated forces, of the capitalist breakthrough; a simultaneous damnation and idealisation of capitalism, in its specific forms of urban and industrial development.[106]

And in the Scottish experience the working class paid a particularly heavy price for being rescued from what Karl Marx called 'rural idiocy', and it is very useful to keep Williams' strictures in mind.

It was against this background of an authoritarian social ethos — a background in which English radicals like William Cobbett criticised the tight-fisted Poor Laws of the possessing classes and 'Scotch feelosofers' and their attempts to destroy folk-memories — that the labour movement fashioned its own form of puritanism, temperance and self-help. The puritanical outlook of the early Scottish labour movement cannot be understood in isolation from the harsh, unsympathetic and unfavourable milieu out of which it came; and while the negative features of Presbyterian 'respectability' were impressed on the consciousness of the working class and the labour movement in their formative years, the working class adaptation of these social values was often double-edged. For just as Robert Q. Gray has documented the different meanings of the concept of 'respectability' and the compatability of bourgeois self-help, class solidarity and mutual aid in Victorian Scotland, so was a similar pattern discernible in the late eighteenth and early nineteenth centuries when the first Scottish labour 'movement' began to crystallise.[107]

Notes

1. Peter Gay, *The Enlightenment: An Interpretation* (London, 1970), vol. 2, pp. 517-18.

2. Thomas Carlyle, 'The Signs of the Times', *Critical and Miscellaneous Essays* (London, 1889), vol. 2, p. 82.

3. Michael Hechter, *Internal Colonialism. The Celtic Fringe in British National Development, 1536-1966* (London, 1975), p. 115.

4. Ibid., p. 33.

5. Adam Smith, *The Theory of Moral Sentiments,* edited D.D. Raphael and A.L. Macfie (Oxford, 1976), p. 226.

6. A. Aspinall, *The Early English Trade Unions* (London, 1949), *passim.*

7. 'Scotland packed into about thirty years of crowded development between 1750 and 1780 the economic growth that in England had spread itself over two centuries.' Rosalind Mitchison, *A History of Scotland* (London, 1970), p. 345.

8. E.P. Thompson, *The Making of the English Working Class* (New York, 1966), p. 194.

9. E.P. Thompson, 'The Peculiarities of the English', *The Socialist Register* (London, 1965), p. 317.

10. Christopher Hill, *From Reformation to Industrial Revolution* (London, 1967), p. 28.

11. David Murison, *The Guid Scots Tongue* (Edinburgh, 1977), p. 5.

12. 'The Union of England and Scotland in 1707 greatly increased what was already the largest free trade area in the world. Adam Smith thought this was one of the main reasons for England outstripping France,' Hill, *From Reformation to Industrial Revolution,* p. 182.

13. John Sinclair, *Observations on the Scottish Dialect* (London, 1792), pp. 8-9.

14. Henry Hamilton, *The Industrial Revolution in Scotland* (London, 1966), p. 8.

15. Hill, *From Reformation to Industrial Revolution,* p. 183.

16. Hechter, *Internal Colonialism,* p. 115.

17. Christopher Smout, *A History of the Scottish People, 1560-1830* (London, 1969), p. 506.

18. Henry Graham, *The Social Life of Scotland in the Eighteenth Century* (London, 1899), pp. 1-2.

19. Ian Ross Simpson, *Lord Kames and the Scotland of his Day* (Oxford, 1972), p. 45.

20. Ibid., p. 351.

21. Dugald Stewart, *Collected Works,* Sir William W. Hamilton (ed.) (Edinburgh, 1854-60), vol. X, pp. 346-7.

22. *Edinburgh Review,* no. XCVI, vol. 48, 1828, p. 288.

23. David Buchan, *The Ballad and the Folk* (London, 1972), p. 69.

24. Robert Herron, *Observations Made in a Journey through the Western Counties of Scotland* (Perth, 1792), p. 474.

25. Henry Skrine, *Three Successive Tours in the North of England and a Great Part of Scotland* (London, 1795), p. 71.

26. Hugh Mitchell, *Scotticisms, Vulgar Anglicisms and Grammatical Improprieties Corrected* (Glasgow, 1799), p. viii.

27. John Millar, *An Historical View of the English Government* (London, 1803), vol. 3, p. 96.

28. John Leyden (ed.), *Scottish Descriptive Poems* (Edinburgh, 1803), pp. 13-14.

29. James Elphinston, *The Contrast. A Specimen of the Scottish Dialect* (Edinburgh, 1779), pp. 5-6.

30. William Robertson, *The History of Scotland* (London, 1759), vol. 1, p.260.

31. Herron, *Observations Made in a Journey*, pp. 350-1.

32. Thomas Newte, *Prospects and Observations on a Tour in England and Scotland* (London, 1791), p. 246.

33. *First Statistical Account* (Edinburgh, 1792), vol. 9, p. 190.

34. *Edinburgh Review*, no. VII, 1804, pp. 65-6.

35. Matilda J. Gage, *Woman, Church and State* (New York, 1893), p. 273.

36. Walter Scott, *Tales of a Grandfather* (London, 1836), vol. V, p. 410 and p. 436.

37. John Clive and Bernard Bailyn, 'England's Cultural Provinces: Scotland and America', *William and Mary Quarterly*, vol. IX, no. 2, 1954, p. 212.

38. Skrine, *Three Successive Tours*, p. 35.

39. Ibid., p. 71.

40. Smout, *A History of the Scottish People*, p. 505.

41. George E. Davie, *The Social Significance of the Scottish Philosophy of Common Sense* (Edinburgh, 1973), p. 9.

42. William Cobbett, *Rural Rides* (London, n.d.), vol. 2, p. 83.

43. *Edinburgh Review*, vol. 36, no. 121, 1821, p. 251.

44. Cobbett, *Rural Rides*, vol. 2, pp. 92-3.

45. Hugh Seton-Watson, *Nations and States* (London, 1977), p. 26.

46. Millar, *An Historical View of the English Government*, vol. 4, p. 820.

47. G. Legman, *The Horn Book* (London, 1970), p. 364.

48. Graham, *The Social Life of Scotland in the Eighteenth Century*, pp. 107-8.

49. Edward Shorter, *The Making of the Modern Family* (New York, 1975), *passim*.

50. Raymond Postgate, *The Builders' History* (London, 1923), p. 18.

51. Lord Kames, *Sketches in the History of Man* (Edinburgh, 1778), vol. 2, p. 179.

52. James Logan, *The Scottish Gael* (London, 1831), pp. 360-1.

53. Kames, *Sketches in the History of Man*, pp. 180-1.

54. David Craig, *The Real Foundations* (London, 1973), pp. 39-54.

55. Michael Flinn, etc., *Scottish Population History* (Cambridge, 1977), *passim*.

56. Newte, *Prospects and Observations*, p. 336 and p. 376.

57. A.S. Neill, *Neill! Neill! Orange Peel* (New York, 1970), p. 82.

58. Thompson, *The Making of the English Working Class*, p. 403.

59. Mary Brunton, *Discipline* (Edinburgh, 1815), vol. 3, p. 291.

60. Thompson, *The Making of the English Working Class*, p. 408.

61. Ibid., p. 9.

62. See below.

63. William Aiton, *A History of the Rencounter at Drumclog* (Hamilton, 1821), p. 7.

64. E.J. Hobsbawm, *The Age of Revolution* (New York, 1964), p. 103.

65. See Chapter 2.

66. Herron, *Observations Made in a Journey*, p. 432 and David Stewart, *Sketches of the Character, Manners, and Present State of the Highlands of Scotland* (Edinburgh, 1822), vol. 2, pp. xxxviii-xxxix.

67. William C. Lehmann, *Henry Home, Lord Kames and the Scottish Enlightenment* (The Hague, 1971), p. 180.

68. Duncan Forbes, Introduction to Adam Ferguson's *Essay on the*

History of Civil Society (Edinburgh, 1966), p. xiii.

69. John Merrington, 'Town and Country in the Transition of Capitalism', *New Left Review,* no. 93, 1975, p. 71.

70. Eric Richards, *The Leviathan of Wealth* (London, 1973), p. 27.

71. James Hunter, *The Making of the Crofting Community* (Edinburgh, 1976), p. 89.

72. Stewart, *Collected Works,* vol. 1, p. 394 and RH 2/4, vol. 102, Scottish Records Office, Edinburgh.

73. *The Military Register,* 29 December 1819.

74. See the letters from Henry George's Scottish correspondents in the 1880s. Microfilm in the Library of the London School of Economics and Political Science.

75. Tom Nairn, *The Break-up of Britain* (London, 1977), pp. 137-8.

76. Quoted in P. Berresford Ellis and Seumas Mac A' Ghobhainn, *The Scottish Insurrection of 1820* (London, 1970), pp. 88-9.

77. Millar, *An Historical View of the English Government,* vol. 3, p. 93.

78. John Foster, 'Capitalism and the Scottish Nation', *The Red Paper on Scotland,* Gordon Brown (ed.) (Edinburgh, 1975), pp. 141-6.

79. Perry Anderson, *Lineages of the Absolutist State* (London, 1974), p. 431.

80. Nairn, *The Break-up of Britain,* passim.

81. James Connolly, *Labour in Irish History* (Dublin, 1910), pp. iv-xiv.

82. David Buchan, *The Ballad and the Folk* (London, 1972), p. 68.

83. Hechter, *Internal Colonialism,* p. 33.

84. Nairn, *The Break-up of Britain,* p. 138.

85. N.T. Philipson, 'Culture and Society in the 18th century Province: The Case of Edinburgh and the Scottish Enlightenment' in *The University and Society* (ed.) Lawrence Stone (London, 1975), p. 410.

86. Alexander Grant, *The Story of the University of Edinburgh* (London, 1884), vol. 2, p. 87.

87. See the writings of William Robertson, Dugald Stewart and John Millar.

88. John Clive and Bernard Bailyn, 'England's Cultural Provinces: Scotland and America', *William and Mary Quarterly,* vol. IX, no. 2, 1954, pp. 212-3.

89. By a Modern Greek (Robert Mudie), *The Modern Athens* (London, 1825), p. 239.

90. Hechter, *Internal Colonialism,* p. 73.

91. George Elder Davie, *The Democratic Intellect* (Edinburgh, 1961), p. xv.

92. See Royden Harrison 'Afterword' in Samuel Smiles, *Self-Help* (London, 1968), p. 264.

93. 'Calumnies Against Oxford', Edinburgh Review, vol. 13, no. XXXI, 1810, p. 168.

94. Dugald Stewart, vol. X, *Collected Works,* p. cxxxviii.

95. Smout, *A History of the Scottish People,* p. 506.

96. E.P. Thompson, 'Time, Work-Discipline, and Industrial Capitalism', *Past and Present,* no. 38, 1967, p. 80.

97. R.H. Campbell, *Scotland Since 1707. The Rise of an Industrial Society* (Oxford, 1965), p. 180.

98. G. Legman, *The Horn Book* (London, 1970), p. 364.

99. Thompson, Time, Work Discipline and Industrial Capitalism, *Past and Present,* p. 56, and Sidney Pollard, *The Genesis of Modern Management* (London, 1965), pp. 192-7.

100. Alfred, *The History of the Factory Movement from the Year 1802 to the Enactment of the Ten Hour Act in 1847* (London, 1857), p. 19, G.J. Holyoake, *Self-Help a Hundred Years Ago* (London, 1882), pp. 129-31, and

R.W. Cooke Taylor, *The Modern Factory System* (London, 1891), pp. 203-4.

   101. Herbert G. Gutman, *Work, Culture and Society* (Oxford, 1977), pp. 72-3.

   102. Ibid., p. 75.

   103. Ibid., p. 69.

   104. By a Modern Greek, *The Modern Athens,* p. 175.

⚓ 105. W.M. Roach, 'The Radical War in Scotland 1820', *Bulletin of the Society for the Study of Labour History,* no. 27, 1973, p. 17.

   106. Raymond Williams, *The Country and the City* (London, 1975), p. 50.

   107. Robert Q. Gray, *The Labour Aristocracy in Victorian Edinburgh* (Oxford, 1976), pp. 136-43.

2 THE MAKING OF THE SCOTTISH WORKING CLASS, 1770-1820

The question of the lower orders is the great unexamined political question of the Enlightenment. It is not that the philosophes preserved silence on the issue; they never preserved silence on any issue. Their writings, and even more, their private correspondence, abound in references to the common people, the *gemeine Pobel*, the *peuple*, the *canaille*, the vulgar. What is missing is a serious attempt at working out the logic implicit in the philosophes' view of the Enlightenment, which, as I have said, was in essence pedagogic.[1]

Up as far as Kinraddie came the poison and the young laird of that time, and he was called Kenneth, he called himself a Jacobin and joined the Jacobin Club of Aberdeen and there at Aberdeen was nearly killed in the rioting, for liberty and equality and fraternity he called it. And they carried him back to Kinraddie a cripple, but he would still have it that all men were free and equal and he set to selling the estate and sending money to France, for he had a right good heart. And the crofters marched on Kinraddie Castle in a body and bashed in the windows of it, they thought equality should begin at home.[2]

The colonial relationship imposed by a powerful and assertive English metropolitan capitalism was of decisive importance in shaping the radicalism of the Scottish working class. It was not the crude type of colonial relationship that English capitalism was imposing on large parts of Africa and Asia; and the very *subtlety* of the mediating role of the indigenous elite of agrarian capitalists, merchants and intellectuals in assisting the English to impose cultural imperialism on the Scottish populace has obscured its importance in dictating cultural, political and economic developments down to 1820. This relationship was further obscured by the functioning of the indigenous Presbyterian church as a substitute State;[3] and in the constant attempts to eradicate the popular culture including Jacobite and nationalist sentiments, the Church regarded its chief role as one of disciplining the Scottish plebeians.

As the trade union and political links between the Scots and the English were 'impermanent and immature' down to 1820,[4] the colonial relationship and the distinctive experience of the two labour movements actually reinforced the deep-rooted and extensive nationalism of the Scottish plebeians. Though the traditional cultures and 'moral economy' of Scotland and England were being transformed under the impact of industrialisation, the Scottish elite was faced with the task of eradicating a popular culture in which the world-outlook of the lower orders in the Lowlands and Highlands was accommodating traditional Jacobite sentiments with new-fangled notions of the equalisation of property. It is therefore significant that in the trials of the Scottish radicals in 1792 and again in 1820 the controversial question of national independence emerged as one of the dominant issues of working-class politics. As the Scottish radicals' agitation for national independence contributed to the failure of a unified British labour movement to emerge before the Chartist period, it is significant that the most fundamental question on which the rank-and-file of the Scottish and English radical movements differed was the one of private property.

In contrast to the English experience where 'the Leveller challenge' had been 'altogether dispersed' long before the American War of Independence, the Scottish plebeian radicals first began to demand an equalisation of property in the 1770s.[5] The 1770s were, therefore, *the* transitional years in the emergence of a new class consciousness amongst the Scottish plebeians. In 1771 defenders of what E.P. Thompson calls the traditional 'moral economy' issued a seditious advertisement to 'the whole inhabitants and others' in Dumfries who had been engaged in: 'ingrossing, forestalling, and transporting of corn and meal from this port ... under the penalty of having their houses burnt to the ground, and punished in their persons in proportion to the office they bear, viz., if a magistrate with mutilation; and if a tradesman, to have his ears cut off at the cross'.[6] By 1773 some Scots had opted for more open forms of social struggle, and many of their struggles were characterised by violence and coercion.

In 1773 'a great number of sailors defiantly assembled at Greenock and Port Glasgow in a riotous and disorderly manner, peremptorily insisted for an increase of their wages'; and soldiers of the 15th regiment, who had been called in to 'assist the civil power in putting a stop to such illegal proceedings, were immediately surrounded by a vast number of sailors and most incessantly pelted with stones, bricks, etc.'. The allegedly 'uninflammable' Scots of T.C. Smout's conceptualisation of Scottish history were armed with guns and swords; and, though their uprising was quelled within a few days, the authorities had already sent for an additional force of 'two troops of dragoons'.[7] A few months later, when violence had erupted around a group of weavers in Paisley who had entered into illegal combination, the civil authorities were sufficiently worried to commit three men to prison for one month and four others for eight days.[8] The sailors had come together from several ships, and they had probably been influenced by what was happening in the American colonies. At approximately the same time as the strike of weavers in Paisley, there was an 'uprising' of journeymen weavers in Glasgow who had combined to demand higher wages. The Glasgow weavers had been inspired by the example of American republicanism, and they had threatened to emigrate to American *en masse* unless their demands were met. In a confidential letter to the Earl of Suffolk, Thomas Millar, the Lord Justice Clerk of Glasgow, boasted that he had prevented the migration of the weavers by handing out light sentences to the ring-leaders and by speaking with 'tenderness' to all of the men who had been engaged in the wages agitation.[9]

In a Scotland where the State allegedly 'expected and exacted greater obedience' not even the army was immune from the seditious spirit of the 1770s,[10] and in 1778 and 1779 three army mutinies shook the fragile stability of Scottish society. In September 1778, there was a mutiny in the Earl of Seaforth's Highland regiment, and in Edinburgh, where three army mutinies occurred, the mutinies were supported by 'the lower class'.[11] This seditious outburst was soon followed by a mutiny of about fifty soldiers in the 42nd and 71st regiments at Leith in April 1779 and in October 1779 by five companies of the West Fencible regiment quartered at Edinburgh castle.[12] If these army mutinies were sometimes sparked off by economic and other grievances peculiar to Highlanders who were touchy about their traditional customs and cultural values, they also expressed the widespread radical sentiments of many rank-and-file soldiers. While middle-class writers, spies and judges sometimes saw sedition everywhere, it ought to be emphasised that there was often a discrepancy between newspapers' analyses of seditious agitations and the confidential assessments written for the guidance of the authorities in the Home Office in London. In the *Caledonian Mercury* the mutiny of the West Fencible regiment was attributed to ignorance rather than 'mutinous disposition',[13] yet General J. Adolphus Oughton wrote to Weymouth: 'I should think it highly advisable to withdraw all the Fencible regiments from *this country,* replacing them with an equal number of English; as I discover too many seeds of discontent, especially among the lower people. Great numbers of dissenting Ministers, and several of the Established clergy are avowedly Republicans and Americans'.[14] Though these comments emphasised the colonial status of the Scots, they also suggested that, if the maintenance of law and order depended on the loyalty of indigenous troops, Scottish society was very unstable.

If the late-eighteenth century artisan culture of the English and French radicals was inspired by the egalitarian philosophy of Rousseau and Paine,[15] Rousseau's egalitarianism was not the levelling egalitarianism of a Babouef.[16] In contrast to the ideological orientation of the English and the French, the rank-and-file Friends of the People in the Lowlands and Highlands were advocates of a passionate levelling egalitarianism. Though there is no solid evidence to establish the fact that the abruptness with which capitalism developed in Scotland may have catapulted 'the lower orders' somewhat 'primitive' communist attitudes towards private property into the complex process by which the Scottish working class was made and yet made itself, the levelling egalitarianism of many Scottish plebeians was real and tangible. For at a time when the London Corresponding Society was carefully denying that it had any intention of 'invading the property of other men',[17] the Scottish plebeians were agitating for a levelling equalisation of private property.

A minority of peasants rejected the notion that the lairds and proprietors were entitled to own the land and the estates in the Highlands. A Highland peasant told one big landowner that the lairds 'and their families had had these lands long enough, their old notions were not fit for the new times, therefore they must all quit, and make way for the new system and new order of things'.[18] In the Lowlands the plebeian members of the Friends of the People also agitated for a new order of things. A writer who made a 'grand tour' of the western counties of Scotland in 1792 reported on his experience in the town of Kirkintilloch. 'Asking their news, I was answered that their chief news, was the hope of the new division of property to be obtained by the exertions of the Friends of the People. They were readier in quoting Paine's writings, than I should possibly have found them in their Bible. They spoke with exultation of a Society of Friends to the People which had been formed in the town.'[19]

But at the same time as they demanded the equalisation of property, they also challenged the notion of the Scottish possessing classes that it was unnatural to attempt to raise the price of their labour. The French revolution had had a big impact on Scottish society, and the same observer of the Kirkintilloch scene explained why the possessing classes in Glasgow were very concerned over the rise of 'Jacobinism'. 'The bustle made by the Friends of the People filled the minds of the labouring and trading parts of the community with ideas of their skill in legislation and government, which raised them above assiduous application to labour or the negotiations of business. The labourers were, in consequence, obliged to demand higher wages for that little labour which they sulkily performed.'[20] There was, moreover, an unbroken continuity of 'working class' support for the 'necessity of an equalising of property'; and the plebeian Lowland radicals who were involved in the Radical war of 1820 wanted to abolish taxes and divide private property among 'the many' by taking it from the 'few'.[21]

While a class-conscious working class began to emerge in a new context of industrialisation, the colonial relationship between the two countries was a decisive factor in shaping the social and cultural formation of the Scottish working class. As some of the distinctive features of Scottish society were either destroyed or assimilated to the English system, the nationalism of the lower orders was increasingly seen by the English government as evidence of a threat to the stability of the Empire. English capitalism and the Scottish Enlightenment were inextricably bound together; and 'the Lords of Human Kind', who imposed British imperialism on large parts of Africa and Asia, also influenced the shape of Scottish cultural and political life. As A.C. Chitnis puts it: 'English economic domination soon came to mean at the very least modification of areas of Scottish life apparently far removed from the subject of the economy'.[22] Karl Marx was certainly aware of this colonial relationship, too; and, though he attributed the intensity of Scottish economic crises to the 'ruthlessness' of the Highland Clearances, he recognised that English law was frequently 'forced' upon the Scots.[23]

This colonial relationship overshadowed the conditions in which the Scottish working class had to make itself. From a marxist standpoint which emphasises the importance of the complex relationships between economics and culture, the crucial factor in the Scottish experience was the rapidity with which industrial capitalism was imposed from above on recalcitrant plebeians. As Rosalind Mitchison puts it: 'Scotland packed into about thirty years of crowded development between 1750 and 1780 the economic growth that in England had spread itself over two centuries'.[24] This is why the rigid periodisation, the imperial boundaries and the narrowly classificatory approach of cultural historians of the Scottish Enlightenment are much less useful to a historian attempting to chronicle and analyse the story of the Scottish working class between 1770 and 1820.

It is certainly customary for orthodox historians to make rigid distinctions between the 'golden age' of the Scottish Enlightenment in the eighteenth century and what they characterise as the post-Industrial Revolution period of the early nineteenth century. Far from being helpful to those of us who are grappling with the problems of trying to understand the complicated relationships between Scottish industrialisation and the process of anglicisation, the imperial boundaries and rigid periodisation of orthodox historians really obscure our vision of what happened historically. However, it is somewhat paradoxical that those historians who usually insist on seeing the Enlightenment in Edinburgh as a 'golden age' in the eighteenth century are nevertheless willing to emphasise the importance of 1789 as a watershed in the British experience when they want to blur or eliminate Scottish/English differences by insisting that police repression was just as intense and as common in England after the outburst of the French Revolution. And yet 1789 was of great importance in the Scottish experience.

I

The dramatic expansion of the productive forces in Scottish society in the late eighteenth century impressed most observers. There were, in fact, few towns or villages where manufacturing industry was not changing the face of the countryside;[25] and the popular politics which first emerged in the 1770s were clearly influenced by the new context of an industrialising society. But the popular politics of the sans-culottes and artisans in France, England and Scotland were, as Gwyn Williams puts it, 'essentially pre-industrial in a deeper sense than the merely technical'.[26] And this very important point is relevant to the argument of those 'marxist' historians who see an expansion of the productive forces as being innately progressive.

There has long been a tendency among some 'marxist' historians to portray any expansion of the productive forces as being the key to human emancipation from either nature or feudal oppression. The objection to this sort of abstractionism has been put very sharply by Lewis Coser and Irving Howe: 'Now it may readily be granted that a certain expansion of productive capacities is a necessary condition for the emergence of a more humane society. But it is a gross error to assume that for attaining such a society the mere expansion

of the productive forces is a sufficient condition. What matters most
is the relationship between the expansion of the productive forces and
the quality of the human (or class) consciousness that accompanies
it'.[27] However, some 'marxist' historians are not really impressed by
such arguments, and they sometimes cite Antonio Gramsci's conviction
of the innate need for an industrialising society to impose the sort of
moral restraints and discipline that resulted in the Scottish philosophes'
intellectual assault on the folk-memories, natural sexual attitudes and
national language of the |plebeian| Scots. What they ignore as the con-
tradictions in Gramsci's thought which led him to advocate 'civilising'
and emancipating the workers from 'vicious habits like alcoholism'[28] at
the same time as he sought to use populism, social banditry, mysticism
and millenarianism as weapons in the struggle to overthrow capitalism.[29]

By fracturing rigid periodisation and viewing the Scottish Enlightenment as a phenomenon which lasted from 1750 to 1820, we ought
to be able to identify what was distinctive in Scottish radicalism.
Moreover, if we regard the Scottish Enlightenment as part of a cosmo-
politan phenomenon and recognise the crucial importance of 1789 as
a watershed in modern politics, we ought to bear in mind that 'the
communist fantasies' of European authors could be tolerated by
monarchs as an irrelevance provided they did not 'criticise the inhuman
conditions in the mines'.[30] As the expansion of the productive forces
did not exist in isolation from the political attitudes of those Scottish
plebeians who could not conceive of themselves as 'hands', a 'labour
force' or 'things', the most tangible attempt to rescue Scottish society
from its 'picturesque' medieval squalor was made by men who now
regarded themselves as agents rather than objects of history.

Yet the Scots were not just the passive recipients of a modernising
English metropolitan capitalism; for they gave England at least as
many ideas as they borrowed. If there was 'a class struggle without
class' in late eighteenth century England,[31] the Scottish philosophes
in their capacity as the spokesmen for a nascent bourgeoisie played
a major role in the theoretical formulation of the ideology of British
bourgeois society between 1750 and 1820. As Scottish knowledge
was subsequently used to cope with the problems — for example,
social control and political economy — facing an English society undergoing a much slower process of industrialisation, it is only too easy
to overlook the 'totalitarian' or 'Asiatic despotism' in which the Scots
systematised their experience and perception of rapid and forced
industrialisation.[32]

Nevertheless 1789 marked a turning-point in the development of

Scottish politics. Though it could be argued that the eighteenth century French philosophes were much more interested in influencing and utilising Absolutism than in attempting to get rid of it, the Scottish philosophes had no difficulty in emotionally identifying with French social and political thought before the outbreak of the revolution in 1789. Whether the French philosophes had intended to unleash the social and political forces which led to the overthrow of Absolutism or not, the French revolution had a profound impact on British society as a whole.

The radicalism of the Scottish weavers and the vicious witch-hunting authoritarianism of the Justiciary were already foreshadowed in 1787 when hundreds of weavers in Glasgow cut the webs of the looms of the master manufacturers. As troops were called in and killed five weavers before peace and order were restored, the authorities were determined to put down the radicalism of the same weavers who were circulating a pamphlet entitled 'A Plague of Locusts'.[33] Moreover, as Scottish trade unions had already been made illegal under common law as early as 1776, it is clear that the authorities did not have any illusions about the new problems they now faced.[34] Thus James Granger, one of the leading figures in the weavers' agitation, was sentenced to be whipped through the streets of Edinburgh to *'correct those feelings by way of example* for the benefit of society'.[35] From the viewpoint of the Scottish philosophes such repressive behaviour was necessary in a country struggling to free itself from backwardness and inferiority.

Moreover, the Scottish philosophes were all advocates of authoritarian methods of social control; and they would have agreed with Voltaire's comment that the Enlightenment was not for 'our tailors and bootmakers'.[36] In the 'golden age' of the Scottish Enlightenment the colliers were still serfs; and the philosophes were indifferent to the inhuman conditions in the coal mines in the Athens of the North. This applies to all of them, and the Scottish reality of forced industrialisation persuaded them to frown upon trade unions, 'democratic' rights and any questioning of the sacred rights of property and capital. It is important to understand the world-outlook of the philosophes, whether Tory or Whig, and their shared enthusiasm for the English constitution and the 'glorious revolution' of 1688 if we are to grasp the divisions that arose within the Scottish elite after 1789 and their contribution to the ideology of British capitalism.

As the Scottish members of Parliament were 'chosen by a few aristocratic houses' in conditions where the franchise was 'corrupt and little heeded',[37] an alliance of landed aristocrats, a nascent industrial bourgeoisie, weavers and other workers was soon formed to agitate for Parliamentary reform. But in contrast to England, where 'the "natural" alliance between an impatient radically-minded industrial bourgeoisie and a formative proletariat' was 'broken' by 'the counter-revolutionary panic of the ruling class',[38] the alliance of Parliamentary reformers in Scotland was broken by the leaders of the Friends of the People who feared that their own rank-and-file might impose an equalisation of property. This tension within the movement for Parliamentary reform was already foreshadowed in 1790 when the Whig Club in Dundee qualified their support for the French revolution by adding: 'We observe, for the honour of the age and nation, that your renovation has been effected without a civil war, and that neither the superfluous domains of the Prince, nor the possessions of the church, have been divided among rapacious subjects, but both converted to the use of the State, to which they belong'.[39]

Moreover, the 'lower ranks' were increasingly paying attention to public affairs,[40] and the first convention of the Friends of the People was attended by one hundred and sixty delegates from eighty local societies. As the membership fee was only three pennies quarterly, it is not surprising that most of the Friends of the People were plebeians. In most of the major towns the 'lower classes' rioted and shouted 'Liberty, Equality and No King';[41] and these riots triggered off the witch-hunt within the universities. Far from giving the radical movement any effective leadership in the localities, the middle-class leaders retreated and made widespread repression inevitable.

As the leaders of the Friends of the People took fright, they issued a statement of their intention to expel all their members found guilty of participation in the riot in Edinburgh on the King's birthday. Moreover, they depicted these riots as 'seditious';[42] and then Thomas Muir, Hugh Bell and William Skirving inserted a paid advertisement in the *Caledonian Mercury* in which they tried to reconcile themselves to the established social order. In a declaration of the leaders of the Friends of the People, they created a gulf between themselves and their rank-and-file when they argued against the equalisation of property.[43]

The suppression of academic freedom within the Scottish universities and the witch-hunting of the Whig philosophes and students coincided with the riots and political intervention of the lower orders in the streets of the major towns and cities. In 1793 the Speculative Society within Edinburgh university was the chief institutional target of the Tory witch-hunters; for, though Francis Jeffrey lectured his fellow students on 'Nobility: A Defence of Inequality of Ranks', the authorities under the leadership of the dictatorial Tory political manager, Henry Dundas, regarded the universities as hot-beds of sedition and irreligion.[44] Then the Senate of Edinburgh university sent a loyal address to King George III in which it praised the English constitution established by the glorious revolution of 1688 and promised to labour 'with increased assiduity' to instil into their students 'just sentiments with respect to the nature of society'.[45] As the Whig students in Edinburgh were discussing the 'inequality of ranks' in their debating societies a conflict developed between 'the youthful votaries of learning and the votaries of established order'. In the ensuing one-sided conflict, a 'species of proscription' was imposed on the discussion of 'political' questions.[46]

The witch-hunting and suppression of academic freedom were not just confined to the Whig philosophes, however. In a total of more than fifty letters that he sent to one correspondent between 1793 and 1805, Adam Ferguson, a politically independent philosopher, did not make a single reference to the sedition trials or the Scottish Jacobins. If Adam Ferguson's most recent biographer had been aware of the suppression of academic freedom within the Scottish universities, he would not have been so puzzled by Ferguson's silence.[47] If the philosophes refused to preserve silence elsewhere in Europe, the situation in the Scottish universities was quite different. For though he did not refer to the denigration of Adam Smith until much later, Dugald Stewart could not in his lecture on Adam Smith before the Royal Society of Edinburgh even mention the doctrine of political economy in 1793.[48]

Then in 1794 Lord Craig and Lord Abercromby wrote private letters to Dugald Stewart in which they accused him of egging on the lower orders by publishing his essay on 'the Use and Abuse of General Principles in Politics'. In his reply to Lord Craig, Stewart retracted a whole number of his public utterances; and he praised 'the peculiar excellencies of the English constitution of 1688', disapproved of 'sudden changes in established institutions' and criticised Condorcet.[49] But if the witch-hunting and obsessive schizophrenic British 'patriotism' of the Tories was most articulate and vicious in Edinburgh, it found expression in Glasgow university too.

Far from the Scottish universities being beacons of light and learning during the period between 1793 and 1820, they were transformed into partisan bastions of the status quo. In Glasgow university in 1798 the governing body resolved to subscribe £300 of the institution's funds for 'the defence of Great Britain' against the threat of outside Jacobin intervention. At the same time they decided that they would not admit any of the nineteen Irish students who had been expelled from Trinity College, Dublin, for being active members of 'treasonable societies'.[50]

The witch-hunting within the universities and even in such public places as restaurants, where the Tory authorities were themselves spying on Whig philosophes and lawyers,[51] reflected the insecurity of a native elite whose real source of political power was located in faraway London. Bearing in mind, too, that they were alienated from the plebeians by language as much as political attitudes, the causal connection between their predicament as colonial administrators and the development of their 'paranoid' style of political behaviour becomes increasingly clear. For Richard Hofstader, the American historian, depicted the comments in John Robinson's famous anti-Jacobin book as evidence of their 'paranoid style' in politics.[52]

A scientist in Edinburgh university, Professor Robinson packed his book with 'facts' about the existence of an international conspiracy of French Jacobinism; but as Hofstader put it, 'the singular thing about all this laborious work is that the passion for factual evidence does not, as in most intellectual exchanges, have the effect of putting the paranoid spokesman into effective two-way communication with the world outside his group'.[53] This refusal to encourage a two-way communication between the Tory and Whig philosophes — and between them and the plebeians — was the most important single factor responsible for alienating men like Dugald Stewart, Francis Jeffrey and John Millar from the colonial administrators in Edinburgh.

The message of John Robinson's book, *Proofs of a Conspiracy Against All the Religions and Governments of Europe, carried on in the Secret Meetings of Free Masons, Illuminati and Reading Societies,* was simple and clear. As circulating libraries were 'Nurseries of Sedition and Impiety', he wanted books to be kept from the lower orders, public meetings banned, the maintenance of the unreformed British government and the proscription of irreligion.[54] As the Whig philosophes passionately believed in their ability to influence the lower orders by means of circulating libraries (and as Adam Ferguson resented the 'brute force' on which the power of the dominant faction rested),[55] the alienation between the Whigs and Tories had reached its maximum potential.

The Whig philosophes were just as hostile to the political aspirations of the lower orders as the Tory intellectuals like John Robinson. As it became increasingly clear that private property was being interfered with in France in the 1790s, Professor John Millar's enthusiasm for the French Jacobins began to cool.[56] Moreover, he 'neither wept over the imaginary miseries of the lower orders nor shuddered at the imputed vices of the higher';[57] but, though Dugald Stewart modified some of his earlier views, he was not 'cordially received in the city he adored'.[58] He was not allowed to lecture on political economy as the discipline itself was equated with Jacobinism;[59] and in 1807 his second wife, Helen D'Archy Stewart, wrote a letter to Dr William Drennan, Belfast, in which she described the effects of the witch-hunt he had been subjected to:

> I venture to say, you will find him much the same as you left him. His few hairs are indeed grey, and perhaps the sad history of the last twenty years may have made his manner more serious and reserved in company than it was when you knew him, but it is only in company.[60]

In contrast to such early Scottish Enlightenment figures as David Hume who were 'uncertain just how much light the untutored common man could bear',[61] the Whig philosophes' image of themselves rested on their capacity to diffuse light and learning amongst the lower orders.[62] In a situation where 'the pulpit, the bench, the bar, the colleges, the parliamentary electors, the press [and] the magistrates' were dominated by a dictatorial Tory elite, the Whigs found it impossible to formulate a proper account of the Scottish scene. Later on Henry Cockburn would try to account for the timidity of the Whigs by arguing that 'with the people put down and the Whigs powerless' the State was 'master of nearly every individual in Scotland'.[63] In reality the Scottish scene had been much more complex than that; and, when the lower ranks had again come on to the political scene in the 1790s, the United Scotsmen had created the material foundations for the Tories' paranoid style of politics.

In contrast to their English counterparts the Scottish Jacobins were able to attract mass popular support; and they were much more outward-looking and republican. As the Whig philosophes allowed themselves to be witch-hunted without offering any resistance, the later Whig and Liberal historians who inherited that legacy could not conceive of the possibility of serious working class political activity in those years. Moreover, as few of the trials of the United Scotsmen were reported in the Scottish press, and as the evidence pointing up

the existence of their political ballads and pamphlets couched in the
Scots' dialect is buried in the justiciary records in Edinburgh, it is
not really suprising that historians have overlooked their deep, nation-
alist-cum-Jacobin sentiments.[64]

The interaction of a whole complex of factors led the metropolitan
elite to treat the Scottish radicals as colonial subjects. One of the
specific charges against the leaders of the Friends of the People was
that they had read from an 'Address from the Society of United Irishmen in Dublin to the Delegates for promoting a Reform in Scotland
in which the following statement appeared: "We rejoice that you
do not consider yourselves as merged and melted down into another
country, but that in this great national question you are still
Scotland" '.[65] Moreover, Jacobites like John Crome who were violently
opposed to the ruling dynasty of Great Britain found no difficulty
in making the transition to the revolutionary politics of Jacobinism;[66] and
even in the early nineteenth century the authorities in Scotland would
identify the very threatening coalescence of Jacobite and Jacobin
political sentiments among industrial workers.

The agitation for Scottish independence was certainly an important
issue in the trial of Thomas Muir and the other middle-class radicals
in 1793-4, and it is important to emphasise the role of the English
government in the process of driving Scottish radicalism underground.
As E.P. Thompson puts it: 'Braxfield and the mysteries of "Scottish
law" have received too much credit for these verdicts at the hands of
English historians. It was as much a verdict of the English government
as of the Scottish judiciary'.[67] And as a precedent for using English
law to deal with the treason of the Scottish Jacobites had already
been set in 1748 and 1749, the two Jacobins, David Downie and
Robert Watt, were also tried by an English Commission of Oyer and
Terminer in 1794.[68]

The Scottish possessing classes were shaken by the French revolution
and their touchiness was reflected in a variety of ways. In 1792 the
sailors who were engaged in the wages agitation took possession of
every ship in the harbour at Aberdeen;[69] and in 1794 some of the
Presbyterian clergy used their pulpits to prove that 'French equality'
had resulted in 'an equality of misery'.[70] Such obsessions with prevailing
notions of equality led one contributor to the *Scots Magazine* to argue
that: 'A perfect equality, however, in rank and fortune has seldom
been contended for except by the most ignorant enthusiasts'.[71] And
in 1798 another writer argued that property was the key to the natural
inequality of mankind: 'Wherever property is established, all men

endeavour to obtain it; but as they are not all equally strong, healthy, nor endeavour with the same capacity, they cannot all be equally successful'.[72] But beneath the social surface of a repressive, authoritarian society, there were 'ignorant enthusiasts' who were dreaming of an egalitarian society.

The justiciary records are full of the formidable evidence relating to the substantial support the United Scotsmen had gained in far-flung working-class communities as well as in the army.[73] Moreover, a witness at the trial of George Mealmaker described the secret meetings where the United Scotsmen had decided to 'go by themselves, and the common people by themselves' instead of relying on the gentry.[74] The organisation was, as T.C. Smout says, 'a small and shadowy' one advocating annual parliaments and universal suffrage; but it was a secret organisation of necessity and that fact has obscured the considerable support it had won in many working-class communities. In 1798, for example, Robert Jeffray, a weaver in Cambusbarron, Stirling, was put on trial for proposing a seditious toast in a community where such toasts were common, and his comparatively light sentence of three months' imprisonment was almost certainly due to the widespread Jacobin sympathy in parts of Stirlingshire.[75] Such working-class communities had their own sub-cultures; and, contrary to Smout's view, the anti-Militia riots were not only inspired by revolutionary ideas but also quasi-insurrectionary.[76]

The working-class Jacobins[77] were certainly driven underground, and their 'extinction' (sic!) was, in Smout's opinion, followed by 'a decade and a half of silence'. This conclusion rests on the assumption that Jacobin political activity was sealed off from trade union agitation, and that the different sections of the working classes were not aware of any common identity of interests. However, there were some individuals who were simultaneously involved with trade unions and the United Scotsmen. Moreover, the indigenous elite did not distinguish between the two forms of agitation, and George Mealmaker was tried under a law which regarded sedition and combination as indistinguishable;[78] and combinations to raise the price of labour were denounced as 'alterations in the natural order of society'.[79]

II

What had been done quite openly before the trials of 1793-4 was now done secretly. The colonial situation in which the Scottish radicals functioned was significantly different from that of the English radicals and reformers. This point has been summed up by E.P. Thompson:

'Even in the 1790s, each attempt to introduce a "continental" spy system, each suspension of Habeas Corpus, each attempt to pack juries, aroused the outcry beyond the reformers' own ranks. If any — faced by the records of Tyburn and the repression — are inclined to question these limits, they should contrast the trials of Hardy and his colleagues with the treatment of Muir, Gerald, Skirving and Palmer in 1793-1794 in the Scottish courts'.[80]

The underground United Scotsmen were clearly involved in the widespread anti-Militia riots from which not even the Highlands were immune;[81] and in 1797 the indigenous elite in Edinburgh asked the authorities in Whitehall to withdraw all the Scottish troops and replace them with English regiments. In September 1797 the *Scots Magazine* reported that: 'In consequence of the late riots for opposing the Militia Act, several regiments have been marched from England. The Shropshire militia, commanded by Lord Clive, have arrived at Dalkeith and Musselburgh. This is the first English regiment that has served in Scotland. Another has arrived in Glasgow'.[82] And if Scottish historians have minimised the republican commitment of many of the anti-Militia rioters, the authorities were certainly aware of the dangerous situation they found themselves in. For even in the small village of Campsie, the anti-Militia rioters, who were antagonistic to the Rev. Lapsley for the role he played in helping to frame Thomas Muir, set his manse on fire.[83]

W.W. Straka, the Canadian historian, claims that the spontaneous working-class movement against the Militia Act actually facilitated the spread of the United Scotsmen throughout Scotland: but spies soon penetrated the secret 'brotherhood of affection' and reported to the authorities.[84] Trials of the leaders of the United Scotsmen were held in all of the circuit courts between 1797 and 1801. By imposing savage sentences of imprisonment or transportation, the colonial administrators crushed this republican movement for a few years. However, one of the most interesting aspects of the precognitions in the Scottish Record Office is the evidence indicating that they were waiting for the French Jacobins to come over and assist them to 'boot any King's men out of Scotland'[85] and their penetration of Scottish regiments as well as the Volunteers.[86]

At every critical point in the relationship between England and Scotland, the authorities in London made it crystal clear that Scotland was an internal colony. As Scotland was often a troublesome and expensive colony for the English government to hold down between 1773 and 1820, the problems were exacerbated by the Scottish possessing classes' repeated complaints about the violations of the financial and economic aspects of the Treaty of Union of 1707.[87] This was why the Lords of the Treasury poured £15,000 into the Highlands in 1783 for the relief of the poor.[88]

However, the authorities in London were not always so sensitive to economic distress or the unstable political situation in Scotland; and the social tensions which arose from the problems of internal colonialism sometimes found expression in the House of Commons. Thus in 1819, at a time when there was widespread destitution amongst the working classes, Lord Castlereagh doubted whether 'they could take measures to relieve it by public money *without injustice to the whole Empire*'. Indeed, the English government took the view that it would have been unfair to 'burden the proprietors' of England for the relief of the Scottish poor since their own proprietors were exempt from the poor laws; though in 1818 the Chancellor of the Exchequer had granted the Church of Scotland £100,000 to build churches.[89]

Though the Hamilton Presbytery petitioned the House of Commons in 1819 for financial aid to relieve widespread destitution, the Scottish colonial administrators (whether church 'Moderates' or dissidents or Tory or Whig intellectuals) were still propagating the virtues of self-help. As early as the 1780s the Scottish labouring poor regarded begging as a 'disgrace' conflicting with their social values, and they helped each other before being driven in times of economic distress to ask for charity.[90] By 1813 the self-help of the labouring poor was well-known;[91] and it had been strengthened earlier on by the tight-fisted attitudes of the possessing classes.[92]

The oppressive policies of the metropolitan elite impinged on every aspect of Scottish life; and such intensely Scottish problems as drunkenness and alcoholism were at least partly a consequence of the Union of 1707.[93] As a result of the imposition of the malt tax,[94] the Scots substituted whisky for beer drinking even before the take-off into industrialisation.[95] Literary life, too, was subservient to the London publishing houses. In fact the literary activities of Scottish novelists and Whig and Tory intellectuals were influenced by the needs, fashions and financial support of the metropolitan elite; though the Unionist elements in Scottish society were schizophrenic in their attitudes to the two cultures rather than insincere. Even a minority of Scottish trade unionists supported the 'glorious revolution' of 1688 as a bulwark against Popery.[96]

The Scottish trade unionists who supported the settlement of 1688 were a small minority, however; for most of the labouring poor were deeply nationalistic and hostile to the established social order. Even after the United Scotsmen were put down plebeian political activity occurred in a context where Tories and Whigs were hostile to combinations of working people. Scottish trade unionists were declared illegal at common law before industrialisation got underway; and even the Whig lawyers like Francis Jeffrey condemned combinations of working people in principle.[97]

But if the witch-hunting of the Whig intellectials in the universities was still sustained, there is no evidence that the rising bourgeoisie wanted Parliamentary reform badly enough to disturb the status quo. For when he was ostensibly lecturing on political economy in Edinburgh university in 1808, Dugald Stewart refused to discuss taxation as he was 'always unwilling to touch upon any questions which are connected with the political discussions of the time'.[98] And in a private letter written in 1808, where he seemed to anticipate the situation which would arise in 1820, Francis Jeffrey wrote a prophetic passage: 'Let the friends of liberty and the constitution join with the people, assist them to ask, with dignity and with order, all that ought to be granted, and endeavour to withhold them from asking more. But for both purposes let them be gracious and cordial with them, and not by distrust, and bullying, and terror, exasperate them, and encourage the Court party to hazard a contest that will be equally fatal, however it issue'.[99]

A number of strikers who begged for 'cheap meal' in Glasgow in 1812 were actually shot by soldiers;[100] and as trade unions were illegal under common law, anyway, strikes and even combinations were put down with great ferocity.[101] In 1812 Walter Scott looked around him in 'dismay at the power of Scottish trade unionism';[102] and in 1817 the *Edinburgh Annual Register* (with which Scott was associated) attributed the need for the proscription of certain views in the universities to the fact that 'talent' was 'naturally democratic'.[103] But if the Whig talent in the universities was 'democratic', then the Whig 'votaries of learning' were also hostile to plebeian radicalism.

Nonetheless working people did challenge 'the natural order of society' by combining to raise the price of their labour, and they occasionally displayed a tangible hatred of industrialism by attacking machinery during the Luddite period. A professional historian has already chronicled some Luddite activity in Scotland: 'The Finlays did not suffer as some other firms, but the damage was real enough to make Kirkman Finlay urge Buchanan, in 1812, to have cavalry or artillery at a short distance. At Deanston there was an actual attempt to wreck the machines and arms were kept in readiness'.[104] There were violent riots in Glasgow in 1816,[105] and at approximately the same time a number of cotton spinners 'instigated the mob' to destroy the steam looms at the Dalmarnock dye-works.[106] Even in 1813 there had been a mutiny of the Renfrewshire militia,[107] and yet officials in the justiciary had just argued that the Scots were more docile and less prone to crime than their English counterparts.[108] The cotton spinners subsequently engaged in violent strikes, physical assaults on property and attacks on scabs and employers, and the threatening letters they sent to knobsticks — letters signed 'Captain of the Blood-red Knights', 'A Thraster' and 'Arthur Thistlewood' — provided evidence of the class-consciousness linking trade union and political agitation.[109]

From the perspective of the later Whig and Liberal historians the Whig philosophes who lived at that time could not have spoken out without inviting victimisation. As Henry Cockburn put it: 'Nor was the absence of a free public press compensated by the freedom of public speech. Public political meetings could not arise for the elements did not exist. I doubt if there was one during the twenty-five years that succeeded the year 1795. Nothing was viewed with such horror as any political congregation not friendly to existing power. No one could have taken a part in the business without making up his mind to be a doomed man'.[110] While this vivid and colourful description captured the mood and ethos of Scottish society at that time, it ignored the mass activity of the Scottish working-class movement.

Even in circumstances where public meetings were banned and the press censored, the working classes mounted a mass campaign for Parliamentary reform, freedom of speech and assembly and a Scottish republic. The first major sign of the working classes' new pugnaciousness came in 1814 when 15,000 men and women celebrated the Battle of Bannockburn at the 'famed spot' under the shadow of the Scottish flags.[111] As old Jacobite sentiments coalesced with the working-class Jacobin republicanism of the 1790s the colonial administrators again lost their composure. An innocent sermon given by a scholar of known Whig sympathies was enough to set another witch-hunt in motion. When James Mylne, the professor of moral philosophy, conducted services in the chapel of Glasgow university on 26 March 1815, just as news reached the town of Napoleon's escape from Elba, the Sheriff soon arrived to take precognitions. Though Mylne was found to be innocent before trial proceedings were started against him, the Lord Advocate supported the Sheriff's determination to ensure that there was 'no violation of the law within the walls of the college'.[112]

In 1815 Gavin Hamilton, a retired army officer in Strathaven, organised a meeting of the tailors, masons and weavers' trade union benefit societies. As the hopes of thousands of the 'democratic' working people in the surrounding towns and villages were 'then much elevated by the return of Bonaparte' from Elba to France, it was decided to organise a mass demonstration to 'celebrate the victory gained by the Covenanters over the King's troops at Drumclog, on 13 June 1679'. On 13 June 1815, over ten thousand of the 'democratic people' − men, women and children − marched, as William Aiton, the Sheriff-substitute of Lanarkshire put it, 'to the place where the Covenanters defeated Claverhouse, and from thence to a cairn of stones or tumulus, on the farm of Allanton, Ayrshire, about two miles from the field of Drumclog, and where they imagined Sir William Wallace had fought his first battle with the English'.[113]

But if the Scottish working-class movement was identifying with Sir William Wallace, the Covenanters and the French Jacobins, it was also outward-looking. This was why it co-operated with the agitations of the English working-class movement for Parliamentary reform. In 1816 a meeting attended by forty thousand of the 'lower classes' in Glasgow demonstrated for Parliamentary reform; and they elected a committee to present their grievances to the Prince Regent.[114] This radical movement was, moreover, nation-wide; and in Dunfermline the Provost informed the Home Office that several of the working-class radicals who 'were particularly active in the seditious practices of 1793 have been the first to step forward on this occasion'.[115]

A network of secret societies called Union societies was set up in the counties of Ayr, Dumbarton, Lanark, Renfrew and Stirling. With a similar organisational structure to the United Scotsmen and a commitment to Parliamentary reform and a Scottish republic, they were soon penetrated by spies and government agents.[116] However, as they were articulating mass discontent, the spies were powerless to render them ineffective. In Glasgow in 1817, where Neil Douglas, a universalist preacher of recent Highland origin, possessed a large congregation of the 'lower orders', Jacobin sentiments were frequently articulated before his arrest.[117] In that year alone thirty-seven men were arrested upon charges of treasonable practices or administering unlawful oaths; and they included twenty-one weavers, two school masters, four cotton spinners, two manufacturers, a writer's clerk, a web mounter, a carpenter, a vintner and a porter.[118]

However, the Scottish mass movement was too strong and too confident to be stifled by government penetration, and in 1819-20 the mounting plebeian discontent challenged the very foundations on which Scottish society rested. Later on it created formidable problems for Tory historians who had to emphasise the dangers posed by the growth of this movement and for the Liberal historians who had to deny its existence. One historical account was written by William Aiton, the Sheriff-substitute of Lanarkshire, in 1821, when he already denied a Whig claim that the 1820 'conspirators were all deceived and led into the net by the agents of the Government'.[119]

In village, town and city the radicals were not 'wholly occupied with marching and speechifying'; they were also busy collecting arms and 'casting bullets and compounding gunpowder'.[120] In Glasgow thousands of men were parading the streets in 'military order' demanding employment or bread;[121] and the weavers sent a nationalistic, class-conscious petition to the Prince Regent.[122] Then in February English troops under the command of Colonel A. Norcott were 'insulted and pelted with stones';[123] and even in Ross-shire two hundred armed Highlanders, who were threatened with dispossession, attacked fifty special constables.[124] And in the middle of March 1820, the scene for the Radical rebellion was set when soldiers in Paisley inflicted 'a good many bayonet wounds' on working-class demonstrators.[125] This was soon followed by a general strike of sixty thousand working people – the first general strike in British history.

In Airdrie the working-class radicals were again demanding the equalisation of property,[126] and in towns like Paisley 'training after nightfall' was common and widespread.[127] And if William Aiton subsequently blamed the Whig intellectuals for setting 'the simple peasantry and illiterate mechanics' and others 'agog with politics', he was not just chronicling what really happened.[128] He was also fighting to influence future interpretations of those events. It is interesting, though, that in a country depicted by John Galt as 'wrong-resenting', and, where scholarly sheriffs possessed 'history-conscious minds', historical accounts were being written less than a year after these anti-authoritarian events.

For in so far as there was a two-way exchange of views between the Tory and Whig intellectuals, it was restricted to conflicting interpretations of past events. But when they discussed Scottish history or literature rather than contemporary affairs, they could not totally ignore the presence of the radical, republican working-class movement. When James Hogg published a massive two volume collection of Jacobite poetry and songs, he discussed and approved of the survival of Jacobite *sentiments* in the Lowlands as well as in the Highlands.[129] In a long review of Hogg's book, *The Jacobite Relics of Scotland,* where the 'nationalism' of John Galt and Walter Scott was seen as a source of working-class discontent, the *Edinburgh Review* was forced into a recognition of Scottish working-class republicanism:

> Yet we do find a strange sort of spirit lately sprung up — a sort of speculative Jacobitism, not wholly romantic, neither, we are afraid, but connected with the events of the times, and a sort of twin brother to the newfangled doctrine of legitimacy.[130]

Then in 1824 in a brief introduction to a collection of poetry entitled *Scotch Nationality: A Vision,* an anonymous Scottish poet lambasted the anti-Jacobinism of the Whig *Edinburgh Review* during the years when Napoleon had been detained at St Helena.[131] In the absence of important records,[132] the full story of the Radical rebellion of 1820 will never be told. However, a major revolutionary movement was planning to set up a Scottish republic; and it is possible that the authorities' capture of the leading members of the secret Union societies' central committee provoked the secondary leaders into a premature and unco-ordinated 'insurrection'. This would also help to explain why forty armed men entered Kirkintilloch, but threw away their pikes and arms when the town did not rally to their call to action.[133] Whatever really happened, there can be no doubt that an insurrection was being planned by the working-class radicals.

A worker at Carron ironworks, Falkirk, was known to have attended the central committee meeting of the Union societies on 15 January 1820;[134] and in their secret communications to the Home Office the military authorities in Scotland denied that cannon could be made at Carron ironworks without the knowledge of the management. They claimed that there were only a few condemned and large cannon at Falkirk;[135] but after the premature rising at the beginning of April the *Dundee Advertiser* carried the following report:

> About sixty carronades, and a considerable quantity of ammunition, were lately brought down from Carron, and safely lodged in Leith Fort, beyond the reach of the radicals.[136]

On 4 April Colonel Norcott wrote a confidential letter to Henry Monteith, the Lord Provost of Glasgow, informing him that 'few realise how close to rebellion the country is';[137] and even on 12 April when most of the radicals in Glasgow were driven underground, eight hundred colliers in Airdrie tried to take ammunition from the local Volunteers, shouting 'seize the powder'.[138] The revolutionary situation that existed was later described by the *Edinburgh Annual Register* with undramatic accuracy: 'It was in Scotland, after all, that rebellion stalked with the most open front'.[139]

In diverse parts of Scotland the old Jacks were waiting for Marshall MacDonald, one of 'Bonaparte's bravest generals', to come over the water from France with troops to set up a Scottish republic;[140] but the premature 'insurrection' was put down with great ferocity. Only fifty-one of the ninety-six leading activists were caught by the authorities;[141] and some of them lived long enough for their tales and stories to impinge on the 'history-conscious' Scots. Moreover, this oral history, together with other independent evidence, throws serious doubt on the Tory and Whig versions of what happened in 1820.

If the Whigs perpetuated the myth that the working-class radicals were innocent, passive and constitutional reformers who were caught up in an elaborate Tory plot, and that the placards proclaiming a Republic were put up by the government spies, there is no real evidence to support their interpretation of these events. For the Monteith correspondence shows that the King was asked about the 'propriety of issuing a Proclamation to discover the author and printer of the Treasonable Placard, which was posted in Glasgow on Sunday last'.[142] An important consequence of the persistence of oral history was the subsequent publication of an anonymous article in which it was revealed that William Black, an apprentice printer involved in printing the treasonable placard, was, though wounded, hidden by villagers near Bonnymuir after the group led by James Baird and Andrew Hardie came into conflict with the military.[143]

A Commission of Oyer and Terminer was sent down from London for the trial of the Scottish rebels (one of whom carried the flag of the Strathaven Union Society bearing the words 'Scotland free or a desart');[144] Scottish law was contemptuously pushed aside; and John Hullock, an English sergeant, was sent down from London to keep the Scottish Whig lawyers 'right on the [English] law of treason'.[145] As Hullock displayed a bitter contempt for everything Scottish, a fierce conflict developed between Hullock, the English lawyer, and Francis Jeffrey who had offered to defend the radicals. As Jeffrey knew that his 'defence' was a forlorn hope, James Baird, Andrew Hardie and James Wilson were doomed men.[146]

Towards the end of 1820, and once the danger of a 'proletarian' republic had passed, the Edinburgh Whigs organised a mass meeting of solid, middle-class citizens to 'implore the King to dismiss the Ministry and re-assemble Parliament'. This was the famous Pantheon meeting held on 16 December a few weeks after the trial of Queen Caroline; and the Pantheon meeting was so important that Henry Cockburn argued that it resulted in 'a new day' dawning 'on the official seat of Scotch intolerance'.[147] But the new tolerance was for the Whig philosophes, and not for the proletarian radicals.

III

The strength and intensity of Scottish working-class radicalism presented the provincial elite with formidable problems from the 1770s onwards. In 1778 the Presbyterian church 'appointed a fast day on account of abounding sin and present melancholy state of public affairs';[148] and in 1792 a thousand plebeians planted 'a Tree of Liberty' in the market place in Dundee.[149] In *A History of the Rencounter at Drumclog,* William Aiton articulated his distress over the visible continuity of radicalism from the American War of Independence through to the Radical War of 1820. From the 1770s, when the lower orders began to 'study politics', 'too many of them' had shown 'an inclination to notice and bring into view every occurrence whether recent or ancient, where successful resistance has been opposed to any regular and established Government'.[150] It was the *history-conscious radicalism* of the Scottish plebeians which played an important role in sustaining the thought-control and re-writing of history which preoccupied the provincial elite of philosophes and novelists. This was why such an Establishment-minded Scot as Colonel David Stewart of Garth was criticised by an anonymous pamphleteer for publishing his book on *Sketches of the Character, Manners and Present State of the Highlands of Scotland:* 'The best disposed are perhaps the easiest misled in such matters; and the evil is, that when feelings of this sort are indulged in the publications of the day, the people at large are liable to be led astray, and their minds gradually seduced from a due sense of the advantages they have derived from our glorious Revolution'.[151]

Moreover, as the Scottish elite was engaged in a lop-sided 'primitive accumulation of culture',[152] it is necessary to emphasise three very important factors in the unique behaviour of the philosophes and literati. Firstly, they accepted and perpetuated the repressive habits they had inherited from the Scottish past; secondly, they did not challenge their cultural dependency on the metropolitan elite in London; and thirdly, they refused to develop the radical implications of the free and critical thought of the European Enlightenment. As they were determined to put Scottish society on a par with the superior and wealthier 'commercial civilisation' of their southern neighbours, the process of cultural accumulation led the Whig philosophes to advocate the extensive spread of mass education as well as the assimilation of the English language and technology. As the colonial relationship between Scotland and England dominated the tempo and intensity of rapid industrialisation, it is not difficult to see why the Scottish Enlightenment was accompanied by the suppression of the finer and more complex 'democratic' values and social awareness of the European Enlightenment.[153]

As a glaze of obscurantism covered the social and religious life of a polyglot country which lay besotted in backwardness before the Scottish Enlightenment got under way, it is clear that authoritarianism and insensitivity towards human suffering ante-dated the rise of capitalism. But far from the cultural awakening of the Scottish Enlightenment creating a new social conscience amongst the philosophes and literati, the indigenous Tories and Whigs were committed to the maintenance of social peace and order at the expense of everything else. In contrast to the Tories, who were always prepared to use naked force in times of acute social tension, the Whigs preferred to maintain social peace and order by using a mixture of repression and indoctrination.[154]

While the French philosophes like Voltaire criticised the barbarous penal code of an Absolutist monarchy, Scots from Adam Smith to Walter Scott exalted law and order and approved of repression to put down any challenge to the status quo. In a *Life of Napoleon Bonaparte*, Scott blamed the French revolution on the 'naive garrulousness' of the literati. By inflaming the 'popular mind' and 'flattering' the lower orders, they had been responsible for allowing the 'inferior ranks' to impugn the existing social order.[155] And this was why the Scots were determined to prevent anything similar happening in their own country.

But the most striking feature of Scottish experience was that the working class had to make itself within an evolving bourgeois society where the indigenous bourgeoisie did not exercise political rule. As the indigenous bourgeoisie was weak and timid, the Scots produced no bourgeoisie thinkers comparable to Adam Wishaupt who set up an Illuminati in Bavaria in 1776 to 'free nations from the tyranny of princes and priests and as a first step to free peasants and workers

from serfdom, forced labour and guilds'.[156] As the most advanced
thinkers in other European countries were, in the phrase of Lucio
Colletti, 'the interpreters of the rights and reasons of rising bourgeois
society',[157] the absence of Scots who were prepared to fulfil a comparable role was responsible for the dominance of a repressive feudal
mentality within the possessing classes.

Yet the Scottish philosophes and literati were very aware of the
new social tensions — and the new social problems — created by rapid
industrialisation. For if Walter Scott refused to 'flatter' the lower
orders by putting them into the novels where he 'portrayed' his own
society, he did already in 1820 anticipate a part of the socialist critique
of modern capitalism when he observed in the secrecy of a private
letter that: 'Formerly obliged to seek the sides of rapid streams for
driving their machinery, manufacturers established themselves in
sequestered spots and lodged their working people around them. Hence
arose a mutual dependence on each other between the employer and
the employed for in bad times the Master had to provide for their
people's sustenance else he could not have their services in good and
the little establishment naturally looked up to him as their head. But
this has ceased since the manufacturers have been transferred to the
great towns where a Master calls together a hundred workmen this
week and pays them off the next with far less interest in their future
fate than in that of as many worn-out shuttles'.[158] The unique problems
created by an exceptionally advanced, left-wing working class movement gave the Scottish elite an opportunity to formulate an ideology
for British capitalism[159] at a time when the Scottish plebeian radicals
shared Robert Burns' vision of a new epoch in man's struggle for
freedom:

>   Proud Priests and Bishops we'll translate
>   And Cannonise as Martyrs;
>   The guillotine on Peers shall wait;
>   And Knights shall hang in garters.
>   Those despots long have trode us down,
>   And judges as their engines;
>   Such wretched minions of a Crown
>   Demand the people's vengeance!
>   Today 'tis theirs. To-morrow we
>   Shall don the cap of Libertie.

The Golden Age we'll then revive;
    Each man will be a brother;
In harmony we all shall live,
    And share the earth together;
In virtue train'd, enlighten'd Youth
    Will love each fellow-creature;
And future years shall prove the truth
    That man is good by nature;
Then let us toast with three times three
The reign of Peace and Libertie!

Notes

1. Peter Gay, *The Enlightenment: An Interpretation* (London, 1970), vol. 2, p. 517.
2. Lewis Grassic Gibbon, *A Scots Quair* (London, 1974), p. 17.
3. 'Moreover, the kirk retained the power which in England had slipped from the church to the state. The kirk punished immorality and faithlessness: it conducted education both at the lowest and highest levels. In short, real power in Scotland lay in the elective authoritarian councils of the church and not in the hands of the state.' J. Steven Watson, *The Reign of George III, 1760-1815* (London, 1960), p. 280.
4. E.P. Thompson, *The Making of the English Working Class* (New York, 1966), p. 13.
5. Ibid., p. 23 and 'When the States of America declared themselves independent of Great Britain, an opinion prevailed among a certain description of people, that the lands were to be divided into lots of 200 acres to each adult male inhabitant'. *Caledonian Mercury,* 26 November 1792.
6. *Scots Magazine,* 1771, p. 325.
7. Ibid., 1773, p. 331. Book of Adjournal, JC 13/18, Scottish Records Office, Edinburgh.
8. Hector, *Judical Records of Renfrewshire* (Paisley, 1878), pp. 196-205 and *Caledonian Mercury,* 16 October 1773.
9. See T.C. Smout, *A History of the Scottish People, 1560-1830* (London, 1972) and my critique of his interpretation of Scottish history entitled 'The Making of the Scottish Working Class', *Bulletin of the Society for the Study of Labour History,* no. 28, 1974, pp. 61-8.
10. SO 54/46, Public Records Office, London.
11. *Scots Magazine,* 1779, p. 219.
12. Ibid., 1779, p. 593.
13. *Caledonian Mercury,* 9 October 1779.
14. J.A. Oughton to Weymouth, 1779. S.P. 54/47.
15. Gwyn A. Williams, *Artisans and Sans-Culottes* (London, 1968), p. 32.
16. Lucio Colletti, *From Rousseau to Lenin* (London, 1972), p. 190.
17. *Annual Register for 1792* (London, 1793), p. 165.
18. David Stewart, *Sketches of the Character, Manners and Present State of the Highlands of Scotland* (Edinburgh, 1822), vol. 2, pp. xxxviii-xxxix.
19. Robert Herron, *Observations Made in a Journey through the Western*

Counties of Scotland (Perth, 1792), p. 432.

20. Ibid., p. 425.

21. Janet Hamilton, *Poems, Sketches and Essays* (Glasgow, 1885), p. 412.

22. Anand Chitnis, *The Scottish Enlightenment* (London, 1976), p. 85.

23. Karl Marx, *Grundrisse* (Harmondsworth, 1973), p. 133.

24. R. Mitchison, *A History of Scotland* (London, 1970), p. 345.

25. David Loch, *A Tour Through Most of the Trading Towns and Villages of Scotland* (Edinburgh, MDCCLXXVIII), *passim*.

26. Williams, *Artisans and Sans-Culottes*, p. 114.

27. Lewis Coser and Irving Howe, 'Authoritarians of the Left', *Voices of Dissent* (New York, 1958), p. 95.

28. Martin Clark, *Antonio Gramsci and the Revolution That Failed* (Yale, 1977), p. 52.

29. Carl Boggs, *Gramsci's Marxism* (London, 1976), p. 64.

30. Leszek Kolakowski, *Main Currents of Marxism. The Golden Age* (Oxford, 1978), p. 157.

31. E.P. Thompson, *The Poverty of Theory* (London, 1978), p. 238.

32. For if governmental repression did not lead to 'totalitarian' or 'Asiatic despotism' in England, the contrary was the case in Scotland. Thompson, *The Making of the English Working Class*, p. 724.

33. *Annual Register for 1787* (London, 1789), p. 216 and Harry McShane, *Calton Weavers' Memorial 1787* (Glasgow, n.d.), p. 9.

34. *An Introduction to Scottish Legal History* (Edinburgh, 1958), p. 142.

35. *Annual Register for 1788* (London, 1790), pp. 209-10.

36. S.S. Prawer, *Karl Marx and World Literature* (Oxford, 1976), p. 348.

37. Watson, *The Reign of George* III, p. 281.

38. Thompson, *The Making of the English Working Class*, p. 178.

39. 'Address of the Whig Club of Dundee to the President of the National Assembly of France', *Scots Magazine*, 1790, p. 457.

40. *Old Statistical Account* (Edinburgh, 1792), vol, XIV, p. 483.

41. W.W. Straka, 'Reform in Scotland and the Working Class', *Scottish Tradition*, vol. 2, no. 2, 1972, p. 37.

42. Ibid., p. 38.

43. 'To give security to property, against the fraudulent pretences of those whom caprice, interest, ambition might instigate to swindle it from them — and not to violate themselves by the public robbery of an equal division.' *Caledonian Mercury*, 6 December 1792.

44. Henry Cockburn, *Life of Lord Jeffrey* (Edinburgh, 1852), vol. 1, pp. 54-5.

45. D.B. Horn, *A Short History of the University of Edinburgh* (Edinburgh, 1967), p. 40.

46. Notes on the situation in the 1790s in *Edinburgh Annual Register for 1817* (Edinburgh, 1821), p. 146.

47. David Kettler, *The Social and Political Thought of Adam Ferguson* (Ohio, 1965), p. 96.

48. 'The doctrine of a Free Trade was itself presented as of a revolutionary tendency; and some who had formerly prided themselves on their zeal for the propagation of his (Adam Smith's) liberal system, began to call in question the expediency of subjecting to the disputations of philosophers the arena of State policy, and the unfathomable wisdom of the feudal ages.' Dugald Stewart, *Collected Works*, William Hamilton (ed.) (Edinburgh, 1860), vol. X, p. 87.

49. Ibid., *passim*.

50. James Coutts, *A History of the University of Glasgow* (Glasgow, 1909), pp. 304-6.

51. Henry Cockburn, *Memorials of His Time* (Edinburgh, MCMX), p. 83.

52. Richard Hofstadter, *The Paranoid Style in American Politics* (London, 1964), pp. 10-11.

53. Ibid., pp. 37-8.

54. J.B. Morrell, 'Professors Robinson and Playfair, and the Theophis Gallica: Natural Philosophy, Religion and Politics in Edinburgh, 1789-1815', *Notes and Records of the Royal Society of London,* vol. 26, no. 1, pp. 48-9.

55. Kettler, *Adam Ferguson,* p. 97.

56. John Millar, *The Origins of the Distinction of Ranks. To which is prefixed An Account of the Life and Writings of the Author by John Craig* (Edinburgh, 1806), p. cxiii.

57. *Edinburgh Review,* no. v, 1803, p. 158.

58. Cockburn, *Memorials,* p. 95.

59. Ibid., p. 169.

60. Letter dated 31 December 1807, MS. Dc. 100^2, f.4, Edinburgh University Library.

61. Gay, *The Enlightenment,* vol. 2, p. 453.

62. 'Wherever the lower orders enjoy the benefits of education, they will be found to be sober and industrious, and, in many instances, the establishment of a small library in the neighbourhood of a manufactory, has been known to produce a sensible and rapid improvement in the morals of the work people.' Stewart, *Sketches,* vol. II, pp. 346-7.

63. Cockburn, *Memorials,* p. 78.

64. Criminal processes, JC 26/298, Scottish Records Office.

65. Peter MacKenzie, *The Life of Thomas Muir* (Glasgow, 1836), p. 5.

66. J.L. Baxter and F.K. Donnelly, 'The Revolutionary "Underground" in the West Riding, Myth or Reality', *Past and Present,* no. 64, 1974, p. 126.

67. Thompson, *The Making of the English Working Class,* p. 128.

68. Henry W. Meikle, *Scotland and the French Revolution* (Glasgow, 1912), p. 150.

69. HO 102, vol. 66, Scottish Records Office.

70. *Scots Magazine,* 1794, p. 116.

71. A.C., 'On the Necessity of Distinction of Ranks', Ibid., 1794, p. 24.

72. T. Bryson, 'On Distinction of Rank', Ibid., 1798, p. 817; and 'A State of Liberty without Property', *Aberdeen Magazine,* June 1791, pp. 321-5.

73. Criminal Processes, JC 26/294, JC 26/295, JC 26/298.

74. The United Scotsmen had cells in the army and navy, and it is somewhat surprising that earlier Scottish historians ignored the suggestive observations in the newspapers of the time. *Caledonian Mercury,* 13 January 1798.

75. The toast proposed by Robert Jeffray was: 'The old Dog's head cut off, the bitch hanged, and all the whelps drowned, thereby meaning death and destruction to the King, Queen and Royal family'. Criminal Processes, JC 26/294 and *Caledonian Mercury,* 10 September 1798.

76. Straka, *Reform in Scotland,* p. 39.

77. JC 26/298, Scottish Records Office.

78. *Caledonian Mercury,* 11 January 1798.

79. T. 'Strictures on Combinations', *Scots Magazine,* 1808, p. 734.

80. Thompson, *The Making of the English Working Class,* p. 80.

81. *Scots Magazine,* 1797, pp. 705-6.

82. Ibid. The Jacobin 'underground' was involved in the anti-Militia riots in Tranent in 1797. Thompson, *The Making of the English Working Class,* p. 167.

83. *Scots Magazine,* 1797, p. 704.

84. Straka, *Reform in Scotland,* p. 39.

85. Criminal Processes, JC 26/298.

86; Criminal Processes, JC 26/294 and *Scots Magazine,* 1802, p. 782.

87. Young, 'The Making of the Scottish Working Class', *Bulletin of the Labour History Society*, no. 28, 1974, p. 62.

88. *Scots Magazine*, 1783, p. 502.

89. *Hansard*, vol. XLI, 1819-20, p. 1399.

90. Thomas Newte, *Prospects and Observations upon a Tour of England and Scotland* (1791), p. 339.

91. A French Traveller, *Journal of a Tour and Residence in Great Britain during the Years 1810 and 1811* (Edinburgh, 1815), p. 283.

92. Thomas Sommerville, *Sermons* (Edinburgh, 1813), p. 486.

93. Michael Hechter, *Internal Colonialism* (London, 1975), p. 33.

94. Newte, *Prospects*, p. 376 and William L. Mathieson, *Church and Reform in Scotland* (Glasgow, 1916), p. 288.

95. 'In 1708 there were 51,000 gallons of spirituous liquors distilled in Scotland; in 1791, 1,696,000 gallons; in 1720, 520,478 barrels of beer were brewed; and in 1784, only 97,577.' A French Traveller, *Journal of a Tour*, p. 268.

96. See the resolution of the Kilmarnock journeymen shoemakers, *Glasgow Mercury*, 28 January 1799.

97. Francis Jeffrey, *Combinations of Workmen* (Edinburgh, 1825), *passim*.

98. Stewart, *Sketches*, vol. IX, p. 253.

99. Cockburn, *Life of Jeffrey*, vol. 1, p. 197.

100. Peter MacKenzie, *Old Reminiscences of Glasgow and the West of Scotland* (Glasgow, 1890), vol. 1, p. 108.

101. *Glasgow Courier*, 3 June 1815.

102. Thompson, *The Making of the English Working Class*, p. 185.

103. *Edinburgh Annual Register for 1817* (Edinburgh, 1821), pp. 146-50.

104. *James Finlay and Company 1750-1950* (Glasgow, 1951), pp. 63-4.

105. *Scots Magazine*, 1816, p. 633.

106. Ibid., p. 793.

107. Ibid, 1813, p. 234.

108. Ibid., 1808, p. 906; Ibid., 1812, p. 799.

109. A.A.W. Ramsay, 'The Glasgow Outrages, 1820-1825', *Quarterly Review*, April 1927, pp. 326-38.

110. Cockburn, *Memorials*, p. 80.

111. *Edinburgh Evening Courant*, 30 June 1814 and Charles W. Thomson, *The Scottish Lion* (Glasgow, 1820), p. 44.

112. Coutts, *A History of the University of Glasgow*, pp. 349-52.

113. William Aiton, *A History of the Rencounter at Drumclog* (Hamilton, 1821), pp. 97-9.

114. Straka, *Reform in Scotland*, p. 41.

115. Provost of Dunfermline to the Lord Advocate, 9 December 1816, HO 102, vol. XXVI, Public Records Office, London.

116. See the Deposition of 'A.B.', HO vol. XXXII, Ibid.

117. *Edinburgh Evening Courant*, 29 May 1819.

118. *Accounts and Paper*, Parliamentary Papers, vol. XVI, 1818, pp. 126-9.

119. Aiton, *Rencounter at Drumclog*, p. 126.

120. Hamilton, *Poems, Sketches and Essays*, p. 406 and *Caledonian Mercury*, 25 March 1820.

121. George MacGregor, *The History of Glasgow* (Glasgow, 1881), p. 407.

122. 'Memorials of the Glasgow Weavers to the Prince Regent', *Caledonian Mercury*, 26 June 1819.

123. Letter from Col. A. Norcott to the Lord Provost Henry Monteith, 23 February 1820; Monteith correspondence, Letter 11, G1.2, Glasgow City Archives.

124. *Edinburgh Evening Courant*, 11 March 1820.

125. Ibid., 22 March 1820.

126. Hamilton, *Poems, Sketches and Essays,* p. 412.

127. *Life and Opinions of Arthur Sneddon,* John Parkhill (ed.) (Paisley, 1860), p. 74.

128. Aiton, *Rencounter at Drumclog,* p. 124.

129. James Hogg, *The Jacobite Relics of Scotland* (Edinburgh, 1819), vol. 1, p. xiv.

130. *Edinburgh Review,* no. XXXIV, 1820, p. 149.

131. *Scotch Nationality. A Vision* (London, 1824), pp. 61-2.

132. P. Berresford Ellis and Seumas Mac A' Ghobhainn, *The Scottish Insurrection of 1820* (London, 1970), p. 267.

133. 'The men had generally the appearance of factory men, such as spinners, etc.' *Edinburgh Weekly Journal,* 11 April 1820.

134. Delegate's deposition, 7 March 1820, RH 2/4, vol. 131.

135. Major General Bradford to Sidmouth, 31 December 1819, RH 2/4, vol. 128.

136. *Dundee Advertiser,* 21 April 1820.

137. Letter 37, Monteith correspondence.

138. *Edinburgh Evening Courant,* 15 April 1820.

139. *Edinburgh Annual Register for 1820* (Edinburgh, 1823), p. 20.

140. Peter MacKenzie, *James Wilson's Trial* (Glasgow, 1832), pp. 40-1.

141. G.W.T. Omond, *The Lord Advocates of Scotland* (Edinburgh, 1863), p. 262.

142. Mr Hobhouse for Lord Sidmouth to Henry Monteith, 7 April 1820; Monteith correspondence.

143. 'Shortly after Baird's execution there was a female child born to him by a young woman in Paisley, and when the lassie grew up she wrought in my charge as a power loom weaver.' Extract from a letter from John Campbell, *North British Daily Mail,* 12 September 1885.

144. MacKenzie, *James Wilson's Trial,* p. 21.

145. Cockburn, *Life of Jeffrey,* vol. 1, p. 261.

146. Ibid., p. 259.

147. Omond, *Lord Advocates,* pp. 263-5.

148. *Annual Register for 1778* (London, 1780), p. 209.

149. Ibid., 1792, p. 49.

150. Aiton, *Rencounter at Drumclog,* p. 7.

151. Remarks on Col. Stewart's Sketches of the Highlanders (Edinburgh, 1823), p. 3.

152. I have borrowed this phrase from Isaac Deutscher, *The Prophet Unarmed* (Oxford, 1959), p. 199.

153. By a Modern Greek (Robert Mudie), *The Modern Athens* (London, 1925), p. 239.

154. As a typical Whig, Dugald Stewart was regarded as 'timid in action'. Vietch's Memoir in Stewart, *Collected Works,* vol. 10, p. 1.

155. Walter Scott, *Life of Napoleon Bonaparte* (Edinburgh, 1835), vol. 1, pp. 42-5.

156. Archibald Robertson, *The French Revolution* (London, 1949), pp. 12-3.

157. Colletti, *From Rousseau to Lenin,* p. 169.

158. David Daiches, 'Scott and Scotland', *Scott Bicentenary Essays,* Allan Bell (ed.) (Edinburgh, 1973), p. 42.

159. 'More quickly and to a greater extent than most of their English counterparts, influential Edinburgh Whigs seem to have been aware of the need to take account of the emergent forces of the early nineteenth century – as early as 1809 Jeffrey was urging them to "infuse their spirit" into "the Democrats", who are almost for rebellion – and they were more zealous than the English exponents of political economy.' A. Tyrell, 'Political Economy, Whiggism and the Education of working-class adults in Scotland, 1817-1840', *Scottish Historical Review,* vol. 48, 1969, p. 154.

3 NATIONALISM, RADICALISM AND CHARTISM IN 'SLEEPY SCOTLAND'

But unfortunately for Scotland, for a long period after the union, it seems to have been doomed to entire neglect; or, if the attention of the government was occasionally directed to that country, it was in the spirit of vengeance, to devise the means of chastising its pride and subduing its spirit. This period was, emphatically, the dark age of Scotland, during which its energies slumbered; and it appeared to the world, not so much an integral part of the British Empire, as one of the most inert and unwilling appendages.[1]

Steam has added thousands, nay millions to the annual income of Glasgow. It has augmented the resources of Great Britain to such an extent that it saves seventy millions of dollars in the matter of motive power alone. No pen can describe the additions which it has made in other parts of the world to their manufactures and commerce. It has brought all nations into more intimate relations, and is yet destined, in many respects, to revolutionise the world.[2]

Glasgow is the great emporium of the commerce and manufacture of Scotland. All around the city is planted cotton, iron, and paper mills, coal-pits and whatever else is attendant on the grand system of commerce. The country may be said to be fairly mill-ridden, subjugated, lamed and touzled by the demon of machinery.[3]

As Scotland and England entered increasingly into relations of exchange in cultural and political life after the Radical War of 1820, it is clear that a conceptual framework of colonialism is not very useful for understanding Scottish history between 1820 and 1850. But if a distinctive Scottish working class emerged and challenged the Establishment between 1820 and 1850, it did so within a total social situation which is best characterised as one of 'internal colonialism'. As internal colonialism (as distinct from 'internal colonialisation') consisted of 'the political incorporation' of a culturally distinct group by 'the core', this goes a long way towards explaining the particular external and internal forces which influenced the peculiarities of the

Scottish working class.

Just as the Scottish economy was forced into 'complementary development to the core' and dependency on external markets, so was economic dependency reinforced through 'judicial, political and military measures'. Moreover, as members of the peripheral group were, in Michael Hechter's language, distinguished by 'a lower standard of living and a higher level of frustration when measured by such indicators as alcoholism', Scottish working-class movements displayed an instinctive awareness of the problems of alcoholism, inarticulacy and poverty by developing their own counter-culture.[4]

The Scots complex sense of provincial inferiority, English cultural imperialism, inarticulacy, the dispossession of Highland peasants, migration, a lower standard of living, mass drunkenness, high levels of illegitimacy and literacy and the didactic novel were all interwoven into a social situation in which the rule of law was seen as an unrealistic luxury.[5] Moreover, the management of Scottish affairs was 'thrown upon the Lord Advocates'[6] whose complex sense of provincial identity led them to justify the parsimonious nature of Scottish poor relief,[7] the intensification of repressive measures against working-class radicals and trade unionists and the repudiation of the rule of law.[8]

I

The most important consequence of the Radical War of 1820 was the 'liberalisation' of Scottish political life. For after the failure of the radical revolt in April 1820, the Edinburgh Whigs organised their famous Pantheon meeting at which they implored 'the King to dismiss the Ministry and re-assemble Parliament'. This led, as Henry Cockburn put it, 'to the dawn of a new day on the official seat of Scotch intolerance'. What motivated the Scottish Whigs to take this unusual stand of opposing the Scottish Tory administration in conditions of near-dictatorship was explained by the historian William L. Mathieson: 'Jeffrey, who was the principal speaker, followed the lead of the *Scotsman* in emphasising the cleavage between the upper and middle ranks as "the great radical evil which now threatens this country. It is to fill up this chasm, to occupy the middle ground, and to show how a large proportion of the people are attached to the constitution, while they lament its abuses, that such meetings as this should be assembled" '.[9]

But if the failure of the Radical War forced the working-class radicals 'underground', they still remained active in the cause of reform and democracy. The trial of Queen Caroline a few weeks before the Pantheon meeting gave the Edinburgh 'mob' the opportunity to reiterate their challenge to the status quo. The Edinburgh 'mob' displayed a solidarity and 'organisation which, with arms and perseverance, would have made them formidable to a large military force'; and they had kept their plans 'so secret' that 'the legal and local authorities' had not been able to penetrate their organisations.[10] By challenging the Tory dictators in Edinburgh, the Whigs helped to create a new situation in which the metropolitan elite in London decided upon a new programme of 'liberalisation'. The most obvious sign of this was the visit of George IV to Edinburgh in 1822.

At the time of 'the great Sutherland clearings', when evicted peasants comparable to 'a secondary German state' were driven from their homes by 'armed force',[11] George IV came on his historic visit to Scotland and put an end to 'our party squabblings and animosities'.[12] The most significant features of George IV's visit to Scotland were the sustained attempts to portray him as 'every inch a Scottish king' and the identification of the British monarchy with a romantic conception of the Highlands.[13] By contributing a hundred guineas for the support of the Gaelic schools in the Highlands and by dressing himself in Highland garb, George IV assisted Walter Scott to manufacture myths about the 'romantic' Highlands.[14]

Though George IV's visit to Edinburgh laid a new milestone in what Tom Nairn calls 'the Jekyll-and-Hyde physiognomy of modern Scottishness', John Galt, the Tory novelist, was soon to criticise him for not visiting 'the charnel houses' and making himself 'acquainted with the inevitable lot of humanity'.[15] But if Galt also ridiculed the unintelligibility of the Glasgow bourgeoisie who tried to 'speak exquisite English' before George IV,[16] he betrayed his own Jekyll-and-Hyde mentality when he criticised the Glasgow radicals for displaying their republicanism.[17] However, the most telling criticism of the royal visit to Scotland came from J.G. Lockhart who described the myths that were being manufactured about the Highlands as a 'cruel mockery'.[18]

From 1820 onwards the provincial elite in Edinburgh co-operated with the metropolitan elite in London in the common task of imposing their ideas and ideology on the Scottish commonalty. As both the provincial and metropolitan elites saw Scottish society as poor, backward and lacking in liberal institutions and liberal traditions, and with an unstable and potentially explosive working class, they set about the business of indoctrinating the working classes. With the gradual encroachment of the English language and the attainment of high levels of literacy among working people, even 'the most fashionable and aristocratic London publishers' were flooding the important 'book market of the west of Scotland' with *cheap* publications.[19] At the same time encouragement for the didactic novel 'having for its object to counteract some of the prejudices prevalent among the middle and lower classes' meant that the battle for the mind of the 'lower ranks' was being given top priority.[20]

Far more than their counterparts elsewhere in the United Kingdom, the Scottish working-class radicals set out to develop a wide-ranging counter-culture in opposition to the one being imposed by their 'masters' by means of Presbyterian sermons, the didactic novel, lectures on political economy and newspapers. An appreciation of the context in which both sides fought an ideological war for the mind of the 'lower ranks' is indispensable to an understanding of the cultural activities of the working-class radicals. For in opposition to the employers' poor wages and social and political values, the cultural, economic and political strands of the working-class radicals' critique of *Scottish* capitalism were indivisible.

While the Scottish universities suffered from a decline of scholarship and learning as a result of the witch-hunting of the Whig intellectuals down to 1820; and, though John Wilson, a dull and unimaginative Tory, was given the chair of moral philosophy in Edinburgh university in 1820 in preference to the much more distinguished Whig scholar, Sir William Hamilton, the Tory and Whig intellectuals henceforth closed ranks against the challenge posed by the working-class radicals.[21] As the Scottish Whigs were now given a stake in the Parliamentary game of ins-and-outs, with appropriate prizes for judges, sheriffs and scholars depending upon which group was in office in London at a particular time, there was much less tension between the Whigs and the Tories than had been the case before 1820. In one sense the Whigs of 1789-1820, who had been witch-hunted by a provincial Tory dictatorship in Edinburgh for wanting to spread enlightenment to keep the 'lower orders' in their place instead of depending on brute military force, had been vindicated; for the struggle between 'capital' and 'labour' was now seen by the possessing classes as a whole as an essentially ideological one.

But if the Scottish possessing classes, and particularly the Whig and Tory intellectuals, were now united in the common cause of imposing the social and ideological hegemony of 'capital' on the working classes, an influential minority of working-class radicals were fashioning their own counter-culture. Just as John Younger, the working-class radical, knew that novelists like Sir Walter Scott were ignorant of the day-to-day lives of 'souters, tailors, weavers, shop-keepers and labourers about St Boswells and other villages' and took notes of 'the rural pleasures and beauties of the fine harvest fields' from their 'open coaches', so did the working-class radicals discourage working people from reading the novels of Walter Scott, the Rev. Henry Duncan, Elizabeth Hamilton and the other spokesmen and spokeswomen for 'capital'.[22] In the *Chartist Circular,* too, there was a sustained criticism of Scott's writings and particularly his biography of Napoleon.[23]

A constant feature of the writings and utterances of the provincial elite of novelists, sheriffs, lord advocates, members of Parliament and journalists was their schizophrenic attitude towards all things Scottish. By placing a high value on peculiarly Scottish features of social life at the same time as they accepted and approved of the 'inevitability' of their demise, the provincial elite contributed to the nostalgia and authoritarianism that begot and sustained the didactic novel ranging from Mary Brunton's novel, *Discipline,* to Elizabeth Hamilton's novel, *The Cottagers of Kilbirnie,* and the Rev. Henry Duncan's novel, *The Young South Country Weaver or A Journey to Glasgow.* For if Henry Cockburn could equate the demise of the Scots' dialect with a process in which we lost ourselves by becoming 'a poor part of England',[24] he could nevertheless approve of the imposition of the English legal system − the Ellenborough Act − to eradicate the combination of Scottish working men.[25]

It is, moreover, very important to emphasise that the Whig and Tory intellectuals and Whig and Tory sheriffs and law officers shared a largely common outlook; and, if they inherited the philosophy of the Scottish Enlightenment with its stress on the innate peculiarities of their own commonalty, they were agreed on the need to repress any radical, democratic movement of the working classes or even trade unionism. Aware of the 'underground', if inchoate, nationalism of the 'lower orders', the schizophrenic 'nationalism' of the provincial elite, that is, their own complex sense of provincial identity and inferi-ority, led them, in the absence of a Scottish Parliament, to emphasise the importance of the independence of 'the Bar' as 'the next best preservation of public spirit'.[26]

In practice the determined radicalism and militancy of considerable sections of the working class forced the Scottish law officers, whether Whig or Tory, to use the courts in a partisan way as instruments of repression. As they were only too conscious of the lack of liberal institutions and liberal traditions in Scottish society, anyway, and obsessed by their own complex sense of provincial inferiority, they had no hesitation in abandoning any pretence of operating the rule of law in circumstances where they felt social stability to be in danger. Besides, it was the Scottish legal authorities, who had previously complained about the imposition of English law, who were panicked into requesting 'the legislature to extend the Act of Lord Ellenborough to Scotland to deter the lower orders and repress such an evil spirit of combination'.[27]

In 1812 over 100,000 workers in Glasgow and the west of Scotland were actively involved in 'secret combinations';[28] and as illegally organised workers were driven further underground after the failure of the Radical War of 1820 mills belonging to rapacious employers in Glasgow were set on fire.[29] In a series of anonymous letters to employers throughout Glasgow the leaders of the illegal trade unions signed themselves 'Captain Blood', 'Arthur Thistlewood', 'Captain of the Vitriol Forces' and 'Com. of the Royal Colliers';[30] and in conditions where trade unionism was held to be illegal under common law,[31] the journeymen tailors in Dundee, who combined to get an increase in wages, were described as 'deluded individuals' who were inviting 'the vengeance of the law'.[32]

From 1820 to 1838 many Scottish workers — and particularly those in Glasgow and the west of Scotland — were organised in illegal trade unions; and in Paisley in 1821 two cotton spinners who had discharged loaded pistols at a cotton master were whipped through the streets before being transported. A great deal of sympathy existed for these unfortunate men, and as the men were flogged by the public hangman troops were needed to keep back the protesting crowds.[33] In 1824 the Glasgow cotton spinners took the lead in organising a Committee of Trades' Delegates from over twenty different trades; and, when the presence of two reporters from the employers' press was discovered, a majority of the delegates voted for a resolution asking them to leave the meeting.[34] On most other occasions the activities of the trade unionists and working-class radicals were not reported in the Scottish press except when law officers intervened to crush combinations of illegally organised working men.

As the Orange lodges first came to the surface of the Scottish scene in 1822-3 when they were engaged in riotous activity against Roman Catholic workers, it was clear that an extra-Parliamentary force had arisen to split the working-class movement and assist the authorities in their task of bolstering the status quo.[35] In spite of legal repression and an unsympathetic press strikes of paper-makers in Edinburgh, weavers and cotton spinners in Glasgow and colliers in Ayr broke out in 1824;[36] and in 1825 there was a prolonged strike of cotton spinners in Glasgow.[37] As nine delegates from different collieries in Stirlingshire attempted to organise the miners at the Duke of Hamilton's colliery at Redding, Falkirk, they were arrested by Sheriff MacDonald who made it crystal-clear that combinations would not be tolerated in Stirlingshire.[38]

In 1825 a strike of Glasgow cotton spinners led to a 'mob' of over five hundred men, women and children demonstrating against blacklegs who had taken 'the place of those transported for throwing vitriol';[39] and a few weeks later a 'mob' paraded through Camlachie 'with an effigy to which was affixed a label: "A warning to all traitors to the cause" '.[40] Moreover, trade union or 'combination songs' — songs used as Crown evidence in the trial of the men and women who were found guilty of 'mobbing and rioting' outside the Dunlop works — were sung in the streets by workers who wanted to justify their attempts to shoot 'nobs' or 'blacklegs';[41] and other illegally organised workers who had combined to secure higher wages and better conditions sent the following letter to Mr MacPhail, a powerloom manufacturer in Hutchinsontown, Glasgow:

> I answer by all that is sacred, that I will lay the whole matter before the public, if there are printing types within fifty miles of Glasgow. I advise you therefore to keep a sharp lookout, and you will have every chance of procuring a copy of it from 'Blue Thumbs' who swears he will lay it off with his best attitudes and emphasis; you will then be placed in your proper sphere in the estimation of the public. But the ends of public justice and morality require that something more should be done to a person already dead to every principle of honour and virtue. Infamy is no punishment; something really personal and substantial is required — something that will make a lasting impression, not only on the mind, but also on the body.[42]

So even before Chartism arose in Scotland, the working-class radicals were engaged in a struggle for the mind of the unorganised workers and the 'middle ranks'.

By abandoning any pretence of operating the rule of law and using the machinery of 'justice' as an instrument for repressing trade union-ism, the provincial elite made trade unionism more political and class conscious than it might otherwise have been. In Glasgow in 1826, for example, a shoemaker was sent to jail for six months simply because he was a member of a trade union;[43] and the combination of shoemakers in Perth was similarly stamped out.[44] In 'sleepy' Dumfries the 'mob' mounted their first meal riot for ten years;[45] in Dundee the shipwrights came out on strike;[46] and in Edinburgh the shoemakers formed themselves into 'the most overbearing and audacious' trade union that had been seen till then.[47] Besides, the savagery of the courts in sentencing rebellious workers who took direct action against 'nobs' to transportation overseas did nothing to still their rebellion; and in March 1828, the Sheriff of Stirlingshire was again compelled to break-up the 'combinations' of colliers at the Duke of Hamilton's colliery at Redding, Falkirk.[48]

A decisive turning-point in Scottish working-class radical history was provoked by the Parliamentary reform crisis in 1830-32. In 1830 'the real battle' was, as Francis Jeffrey put it, 'not between Whigs and Tories, Liberals and Illiberals and such gentleman-like denominations but between property and no property — Swing and the law'.[49] However, as a battle soon developed between 'democracy' and 'aristocracy', the Scottish possessing classes were, like their English counterparts, thrown into a serious dilemma where the slightest mistake might threaten the established social order.

The great divide between the radical working classes on the one hand and the possessing classes, whether Whig or Tory, on the other was seen in the public utterances of the working-class radicals and the activity of the 'mob'. At a time when Francis Jeffrey was the Lord Advocate of Scotland the radical trade union newspaper, *The Herald to Trades' Advocate*, criticised him for failing to defend 'popular rights';[50] and the second reading of the Reform Act inspired a 'mob' including sailors and weavers to attack the local police, liberate prisoners and burn 'the records of the Dundee Police Court'.[51] The working-class press also attacked the authorities for sending police spies into the cotton spinners' trade union in Elderslie, Thorn, Johnstone and elsewhere;[52] and sections of the landed aristocracy began to use the Orange lodges as a divisive political force to dish the working-class radicals.[53]

In 1831 a meeting of 100,000 working people in Glasgow for Parliamentary reform gave the Scottish possessing classes a terrible fright;[54] and far from particular occupational groups identifying with 'their natural friends and supporters', the 'weavers of Hamilton and Airdrie, Perth, Dundee, Hawick and Galashiels' were uniting with 'the noble families of Hamilton, Breadalbane and Minto'.[55] In this situation, where private property and the whole social fabric of society seemed to be threatened by the 'mob', some of the landed aristocrats decided to use the Orange order as a last bulwark against Parliamentary reform.

The Orange lodges in Scotland were under the patronage of the Duke of Gordon; and in a riot in Girvan in 1831, where the Orangemen fired shots at working men and women who were demonstrating for Parliamentary reform, a constable was killed and many women and children were wounded. Even so, the sheriff officer in Ayrshire refused to use force to put them down or even interfere with their unlawful activity.[56] As at least two-thirds of the men and women who worked in the local cotton mills were Irish immigrants who were sympathetic to the agitation for Parliamentary reform, the groups of Orangemen who came into the town to break up the Reform procession carried out their task with vigour, panache and violence. As the Orangemen were preceded by a cart load of whisky, they not surprisingly used violence before the Reform demonstration got underway. Elsewhere in Ayrshire and the south-west of Scotland drunken Orangemen, whether 'hired or not', broke up many other working-class demonstrations for Parliamentary reform.[57]

Just as sections of the Tory landed aristocracy used 'hired' or volunteer members of the Orange lodges to break-up demonstrations for Parliamentary reform, so did the middle-class Whigs like Henry Cockburn approve of the actions of the working-class radicals in agitating for Parliamentary reform. As the working-class radicals were not disturbing the public peace and were providing the rising bourgeoisie with the muscle of an extra-Parliamentary force, they were seen to be serving a very useful purpose. But if the usefulness of Parliamentary reform in giving Scotland 'a political constitution for the first time' was a necessary part of the 'liberalisation' dictated by the events of 1820, so were the members of the most progressive section of the provincial elite haunted by the potential political power of the 'masses'.[58] Just before the 'mob' began to take things into their own hands, this danger was summed up by Henry Cockburn: 'As yet, however, the unions are avoided by the prudent, and are chiefly composed of the poorer classes or wilder spirits. They are useful at present, because wherever they have been established the peace has been preserved; but they are most dangerous engines. If their force be once experienced, they may easily be applied to all other questions'.[59]

The interaction of a literate and educated, if inarticulate, working class committed to radicalism, together with the problems of ethnic conflict and alcoholism, rendered them volatile, unstable and dangerous to the established social order.[60] For if there was no doubt about the superior education of the Scottish 'labouring classes',[61] the provincial elite were now wondering whether this 'superior education' was 'a blessing or a curse'.[62] Furthermore, it is possible that migration weakened the stability of the working-class organisations outside of Glasgow; and an already volatile political situation was accentuated by the spectre of Scottish nationalism.

Far from the peaceful, law-abiding, docile working class portrayed by most historians, the Scottish working class was already the most militant, class conscious and politically aware working class in Europe. This militancy was seen when a 'mob' in Maybole, Ayrshire, in 1831, engaged in the breaking up of machines for grinding potatoes. As they saw machinery as the cause of high food prices, it seemed to them only sensible to destroy the machines.[63] Then in Dundee it took troops to prevent a 'mob' of over five hundred men and women from destroying the property and driving all the Irish out of the city;[64] and shortly afterwards another 'mob', who were determined to get Parliamentary reform, demanded the release of all prisoners in the Dundee police station before they set about burning the houses of the members of the local police force.[65] But if ethnic conflict sometimes vitiated a united struggle against the status quo, the Reform crisis itself kindled the flames of Scottish nationalism among the 'lower orders'.

As the Whigs and Tories argued about the efficacy of Parliamentary reform for the 'government of Scotland', a fierce debate raged around the relationship between Scottish economic 'prosperity' and 'the infusion of English freedom and the influence of English legislation'.[66] A Parliamentary reform demonstration consisting of over 200,000 people was organised by the trade unions; and, when a majority of Scottish members of Parliament voted against the Reform Act, the antagonism between 'labour' and 'capital' was also infused with Scottish nationalist sentiments.[67] For inchoate and subterranean as working-class nationalism was, it did provoke the editor of the Scottish trade union newspaper, *The Herald to Trades' Advocate,* to comment thus:

> To the middle and lower ranks, the genius of Scotland must turn for the recovery of her lost fame. Among these it may be presumed her ancient spirit still lingers unimpaired, and only wants an opportunity of bursting forth in all its wonted energy.[68]

As the Scottish working classes were aroused by the agitation for

Parliamentary reform, riots — or the fear of riots — were reported in places as far apart as Ayr,[69] Lanarkshire,[70] Dumfries[71] and Edinburgh.[72] In 1832 'a certain class of people' who were very hostile to the military went to the army barracks in Dundee where they tried to provoke 'the troops to commit themselves by some act of violence' against the 'mob'.[73] Moreover, in Edinburgh a vast Reform demonstration articulated the hitherto inchoate and subterranean fusion of radicalism and nationalism when a gigantic crowd sang 'Scots wha hae wi' Wallace bled'. As Henry Cockburn put it: 'This part of the ceremony was sublime and effective; the last song particularly which was joined in by thousands all over the field, with the earnestness and devotion of a sacrament'.[74]

In some of the demonstrations of the Scottish working-class radicals against the police and the military, spies and sheriffs repeatedly informed the Lord Advocate of the drunkenness of some of the protesters; and the drink problem presented the leaders of the trade unions and radical groups with unique problems unknown to their counterparts elsewhere in the United Kingdom. In Edinburgh the annual average of men arrested for drunkenness amounted to 8,630;[75] in the most populous districts of Glasgow 'every second shop [was] a spirit dealer's or a pawnbroker's';[76] and in Scotland as a whole 'the proportion of whisky' consumed was 'twice or thrice as much as in any similar population upon the face of the globe'.[77] In a society where hard-drinking was common to all social classes, the working classes were already evolving their own culture in which 'etiquettes [were] much more binding on the lower classes than among their superiors'.[78]

This distinctive working-class culture was strong enough to ostracise those workers who were committed to the temperance movement. At a time when an increasing number of employers were trying to impose temperance on their employees, this workers' culture succeeded in pressurising individual workers to desert temperance societies rather than suffer the experience of being ostracised in their own communities.[79] A worker who signed himself 'A.L.' sent a letter to *The Herald to Trades' Advocate* entitled 'Temperance Persecution' in which he complained of the temperance persecution being practised by particular employers in the Duntocher mills; but the editor said he had not published most of the 'communications on the subject' as he had no desire to alienate the 'friends of temperance' who were 'warm and constant supporters' of his journal.[80]

As this was a time of unprecedented crisis, turmoil and social upheaval, it is necessary to sketch in the background to the contradictory reality of a seemingly docile and moderate radical movement depicted by one Tory historian, J.T. Ward, as the quintessence of 'sleepy Scotland' and the existence of an unruly, rumbustious and unstable working class.[81] By failing to examine the social situation of Scottish society, F.C. Mather could inspire the imagery of a pacific and 'sleepy' country rendering Scottish Chartism a 'predominantly moral force' and therefore ineffective.[82] In a total social situation of near-dictatorship, where the escalation of crime and drunkenness, the on-going Highland clearances, conflict within the Presbyterian church and the legal repression of trade unionism and radicalism were well-known to contemporaries, Scottish society was certainly not sleepy.

If Glasgow was the stronghold of radicalism and 'lawlessness', a series of diffuse and disparate working-class protest 'movements' and moods of discontent existed in the Highlands as well as in the Lowlands. In circumstances where the rule of law was ignored by the authorities, Highland peasants sometimes resisted evictions and industrial workers engaged in acts of incendiarism. In 1836 cotton mills in Glasgow, Dundee and Perth were set on fire;[83] and, if the strikes of workers were infused with the inseparable elements of radicalism and economic discontent, the authorities did not hesitate to use illegal methods to break them up.[84]

Not only was there a much bigger and more determined radical working-class movement than Scottish historians have realised; but it had to operate in a context where both sides were struggling to impose what the Italian socialist thinker, Antonio Gramsci, described as 'cultural and ideological hegemony'. In contrast to the period 1789-1820 when Tories and Whigs were divided about whether to use either brute force or ideology to keep the 'lower orders' in their place, they were now united in using both methods to preserve the status quo. As the Whigs now had full freedom to indoctrinate the working classes with their ideas about the relationship between 'labour' and 'capital',[85] the Scottish Chartists lamented the absence of 'a bold, decided Radical press'.[86]

Just as new Liberal newspapers and journals were engaging in what the Liberals described as a 'great struggle between aristocracy and democracy', so was the Glasgow Chartist newspaper, *The Liberator*, able to profit from the reduction of the stamp-duty on newspapers by coming out twice instead of once weekly.[87] Moreover, the *Liberator* sold more copies than any other newspaper in the west of Scotland except the *Glasgow Herald*.[88] As the working-class radicals were using what press they had to fight for their own cultural and ideological hegemony, so were they aware of what the possessing classes were doing. As one trade union newspaper, *The Weavers' Journal,* put it:

> Nor is the public or newspaper press the only instrument that the wealthy classes use for the advancement of their cause; they have also under their control numberless Reviews, Magazines and other periodicals, all of which, in their several ways, support their patrons' interests; and whose learned and dignified editors appear to be more like owls perched in the seats of wisdom and criticism, walking with their wings to cuff down plebeian merit and opinions, as they rise, than like the impartial, liberal and enlightened philosophers which they profess to be.
>
> Besides, these two powerful engines, which would be sufficient to promote their views and interests to the utmost, they generally keep in pay a motley train of churches and divines, patientless doctors, briefless barristers, together with a number of poets, novelists, and pamphleteers, who are always ready to act on the offensive or defensive, as their own 'honourable' and munificent patrons give the hint.[89]

In a situation where economic discontent and radical aspirations in Glasgow and the west of Scotland were intertwined inextricably, Archibald Gemmell, the lawyer for the Scottish trade unions, had occasion again and again to complain about 'the maladministration of the law'. But if Gemmel used legal language to describe the abuse of the law against radicals and trade unionists, a number of witnesses before the Select Committee on Combinations of Workmen told the Committee that ordinary working folk spoke of 'the partial justice of the masters'.[90] Not surprisingly, distinctions between 'political' and 'economic' protest and activity became purely academic.

A blatant case of the law being abused in a strike of Chartist workers employed by Kirkman Findlay and Buchanan at the Catrine works was discussed in the Select Committee on the Combination of Workmen. In a sleekit reference to this strike in the official history of *James Findlay and Company, 1750-1950,* a professional but anonymous historian told part of the story when he asserted that: 'In 1835 there was further trouble with a strike which was a result of the Chartist agitation. Then the strike was broken after a long resistance and much misery'.[91] What he did not mention was the mechanism used to break the strike — the maladministration of the law.

As this happened before the subsequent trial of the cotton spinners in 1838, it is worth quoting the evidence before the Select Committee. 'Do you recollect the committal of five persons in the village of Catrine to Ayr goal *also* upon illegal warrants? Yes. Mr Buchanan sent for two of his brother justices to his counting-house, got hold of the five individuals, carried them before the justices, and a sort of trial was gone through before the relations of the parties were aware and the justices sentenced them to imprisonment without the benefit of consulting their relations, or having a legal adviser; and they were escorted to Ayr goal by a party of cavalry, and there imprisoned. I petitioned the Court of Justiciary and they were liberated.'[92] By then the strike was broken; and working-class radicalism was again driven underground.

II

The Cotton Spinners' Association was the most militant, wealthy, well-organised and politically conscious section of the Scottish working-class movement. For they not only contributed large sums of money to the Chartist newspaper, *The Liberator,* but they also struggled to oppose the view of the masters' journalists, lawyers and novelists. This was why Archibald Alison, the sheriff of Lanarkshire, described their trade union as 'an example of democratic ambition on a large scale';[93] and since it was impossible for ordinary workers to get employment in the mills without first joining the trade union, anyway, it is not difficult to see why the authorities were so worried by the challenge to their authority.[94]

In 1837 cotton spinners, colliers 'and other trades in and around Glasgow' persisted in coming out on strike for higher wages;[95] and in October 1837, Captain Millar of the Glasgow police acted on Alison's instructions to arrest the members of the executive committee of the Cotton Spinners' Association who were sitting in a tavern in one of their weekly sessions.[96] One member of the executive committee, Angus Campbell, was 'confined to jail for five weeks without being brought to trial or having known the charge on which he was committed'; and the five men who were 'as yet only suspected of crime' were 'subjected to severe privations during their incarceration' and their 'legs were heavily fettered' before they were taken to court for trial.[97]

Before the five members of the Cotton Spinners' Association were brought to trial on charges of sending threatening letters to the masters of certain cotton mills, assaulting certain of their operative brethren, murder and setting fire to the house of a cotton manufacturer, Glasgow was on the verge of civil war.[98] In his evidence before the Select Committee on Combinations of Workmen, Alison justified his violations of the rule of law and his offer to the twelve leaders of the Cotton Spinners' Association to frame the charges against them on the basis of their degree of co-operation with him because of the enormous strength of radical trade unionism in Glasgow and the west of Scotland.[99]

It is not just that an 'undisciplined' and unruly working class was so alienated from official society that they wrecked mills in Glasgow and imposed a 'reign of terror';[100] but also that trade unionists were being murdered by 'mobs'.[101] Thus when the Rev. J.R. Stephens, the English revolutionary preacher, spoke at a meeting organised by working men in Glasgow during the trial of the cotton spinners of 'a raging civil war', he was unwittingly convincing the Scottish legal authorities of the need to take further action against the working-class insurgents.[102]

Though five of the twelve members of the executive committee of the Cotton Spinners' Association were sentenced to seven years' transportation, a recent historian of their strike in 1837 suggests that a verdict of 'not proven' would have been much more appropriate.[103] But what Sheriff Alison described as 'the stroke against the cotton spinners' committee' did not deter the radical activity of the colliers until 'two companies of the 42nd' were brought into Lanarkshire.[104] Even after the cotton spinners' union had been broken up and the *Liberator* had collapsed, the *Scotsman* newspaper was infuriated by 'the oratory of certain itinerant spouters' who had been active among working people 'in various parts of Scotland'.[105]

The most important outcome of the trial of the cotton spinners in the High Court, Edinburgh, in 1838, was Alison's subsequent defence of his conscious decision to abandon the rule of law altogether. Far from denying that he had abused the rule of law, Sheriff Alison told a hostile questioner at a meeting of the Select Committee on Combinations of Workmen that they did not understand the peculiarities of the Scottish situation which compelled him to use force to uphold the status quo. As he put it:

> I should not think there is less intelligence; perhaps in some cases there is superior intelligence; although I am satisfied that the common opinion in reference to the extent of moral and religious feeling among the working class is unhappily exaggerated, at least in the great towns. But I think the great circumstances of difference

is that *the Scotch have not been habituated to the enjoyment of
wealth, and to the long enjoyment of liberal institutions* which
the English have. I think that in fifty or a hundred years, when
wealth is more generally diffused, and the enjoyments and artificial
wants of society consequent upon wealth have taken roots in the
lower classes of society, we may then be prepared for liberal
institutions, such as those connected with combinations, which
possibly may be perfectly innocuous in London; but I am clear
that we are not arrived at that state yet.[106]

Archibald Alison was thus giving voice to the provincial elite's *Enlightenment vision* of Scottish society and their sense of provincial identity,
inferiority and fear of the 'masses'.

For if 'all the combinations and strikes of workmen in the manufacturing districts of Scotland' were, in the words of Henry Cockburn,
'interwoven with all the manufacturing turbulence of England', the
Scottish working classes were aware of their own peculiar problems.[107]
Like the Scottish possessing classes, the working classes were entering
increasingly into relations of exchange in the cultural and political
life of England without abandoning their awareness of the peculiar
problems they faced within an internal colony of the British Empire.
Moreover, Archibald Alison's indifference to the rule of law was
defended by the House of Commons and all the Scottish law officers
whether Tory or Whig.

By organising petitions and mass meetings the Scottish working-class radicals 'abused the law of Scotland and its administration' in
relation to the trial of the leaders of the cotton spinners; but the
working-class protesters 'got no decent support' in either the House
of Commons or the House of Lords and Henry Cockburn had never
known the proceedings of a Scottish court to be 'so triumphantly
defended in Parliament before'.[108] United at last, the Scottish Whigs
and Tories were agreed about how to deal with those working-class
trouble-makers who wanted to interfere with the rule and rights of
'capital' and 'property'.

But if the Whigs and Tories were united in rallying round the common cause of suppressing working-class radicalism, they sometimes
disagreed about their respective analyses of the Scottish predicament.
In an internal colony, where even the Whigs saw the endeavours of the
Scottish members of Parliament as a 'humbling one of insignificancy
and inefficiency',[109] and where Michael Hechter's characteristics of
internal colonialism expressed themselves in high levels of drunkenness

and crime, an indigenous Chartist newspaper described Scottish prisons as 'worse' and 'more corrupting' than English ones.[110]

As Scottish society lost its former 'virtue and simplicity of character' as a result of industrialisation, a fragmented society arose to haunt the provincial elite.[111] For as English crime increased by seven hundred per cent, Irish crime by eight hundred per cent and Scottish crime by three thousand six hundred per cent between 1805 and 1844,[112] Sheriff Alison, a Tory, attributed this development to the 'astonishing high migration of the human species in so short a time' into the Lowlands, while the Lord Advocate, a Whig, attributed it to 'stricter police in Scotland from 1810 and the greater number of convictions of small offences in consequence'.[113] In any event the peculiarly Scottish sense of provincial identity and inferiority which had crystallised with the Enlightenment thinkers in the eighteenth century was still influencing the responses of the possessing classes to the challenge of working-class radicalism in an industrial society.

As the underlying assumption of most historians who have written about Scottish Chartism is that the Scots were not 'ardent Chartists', anyway, it is necessary to look at some of the wider societal problems which inhibited mass support for Chartism at the level of local organisation except in 1837, 1842 and 1847-8.[114] Ethnic conflict between Gaels, Lowlanders and Irish immigrants, together with the language problem, presented the Scottish Chartists with unique opportunities. The leaders of the Chartist movement in Scotland were certainly aware of the language problem they faced;[115] and, when a 1,200 strong 'mob' of Highlanders attacked Irish immigrants working on the railway lines at Bothwick in 1846, the sheriff had to caution them in Gaelic.[116] Moreover, when Highland peasants who had resisted eviction from their farms in Inveraray were arrested in 1847, they were 'examined and interrogated in the Gaelic language'.[117]

The language difficulty made it impossible for foreigners to understand the dialect spoken by Scottish artisans;[118] but, though few Highlanders could speak Gaelic *and* English fluently, they were anxious to get 'the necessary funds' for the acquisition of English.[119] Not only were the authorities in the Highlands forced to abandon their previous efforts to teach everything in the English language only;[120] but in 1830 the Gaelic Society asked the King for financial assistance to teach the Highlanders the English and Gaelic languages.[121]

Out of a total Highland population of 500,000 in 1835 more than 80,000 of them were 'totally unable to read or write';[122] and the Highlanders were generally regarded as 'a primitive race'. But if the Highlanders' commitment to their native language survived the process of English cultural imperialism,[123] they still spoke of travellers who were dressed in tartan as fools or Englishmen.[124] Moreover, in contrast to the situation in Wales, where the difference of language was 'the cause of unpleasantness and unsettlement' towards England and the English people,[125] English cultural imperialism made many Scots inarticulate rather than hostile to the destruction of their languages. For if the Gaels and Lowlanders clung to their 'mother tongue', they recognised that 'oral or fireside education' could not withstand the onslaught of 'the aggressive system of the public instructor'.[126]

In contrast to the Welsh political situation, where the metropolitan elite in London blamed the Welsh language for perpetuating the 'ignorance' which was responsible for the Chartist riots in the 'disturbed' manufacturing districts,[127] the peculiar linguistic problems in Scotland made it difficult for the Chartists to attract overwhelming mass support in the Highlands.[128] As the Scottish landed aristocracy and the rising industrial bourgeoisie continued to argue about whether there was — or was not — 'any surplus population' in the Highlands,[129] the spokesmen for industrial 'capital' thought the Highland lairds' discovery that 'the peasantry on their estates [were] a nuisance' placed in 'the same category with blind puppies, rats and mice fit only to be drowned' was a 'remarkable thing'.[130] Moreover, just as 'crowds of [English] travellers' were pouring into the Highlands in search of holiday homes,[131] so did the Chartists expose the hypocrisy of the possessing classes who were simultaneously encouraging orations about 'the preservation of the dress and language of the Gael' and ignoring the brutal actions of those who were clearing parts of Sutherlandshire by *burning* peasants out of their cottages.[132]

This was the context in which the Disruption of the Church of Scotland took place; for, far from the 'nine years' conflict' absorbing popular energy in the sense of diverting working-class support away from Chartism, as is often suggested, the peasants and working classes used the Disruption to get at their enemies. If the 'lower orders' in the Highlands and Lowlands were sympathetic to 'the doctrine of non-intrusion' in the affairs of the allegedly democratic Presbyterian church, this did not necessarily have anything to do with their religious commitment. A patroness who expressed surprise to a farmer in East Lothian because the congregation rejected a popular minister was told: 'Yes, Ma'am! but your appointing him was the very reason we wad na' tak' him'.[133]

What 'the nine years' conflict' did was to provide Highland peasants and Lowland industrial workers with an opportunity to get at their *class* enemies whether they were Highland lairds, Lowland aristocrats or just coal owners who insisted on imposing their own nominees on congregations. In 1841 the 'lower orders' in Marnock, Banffshire, were organised by 'the non-intrusion party' before their 'rioting and mobbing' to prevent the induction of a new minister brought them into conflict with the law;[134] in Culsamond a 'mob' consisting of several hundred rioters prevented Sir John Forbes from imposing a new minister on the congregation; and the leaders of the 'mob' — a tailor, a miller and a surgeon — occupied the pulpit and gave out 'psalms in imitation or mockery of public worship, singing or calling out for profane and indecent songs'.[135] Far from being peaceful, constitutional reformers, the 'lower orders' used every opportunity to participate in 'direct action' against the status quo.

Moreover, if the predominantly moral force school of Scottish Chartists were 'moderates', they nevertheless appealed to working people to break 'ecclesiastical tyranny' by rendering themselves independent of both the Established and Dissenting clergy.[136] As they wanted to challenge the cultural and ideological hegemony of the possessing classes by developing their own counter-culture, they urged working people to destroy the tyranny of the Established and Dissenting clergy by getting married in Chartist churches in the presence of witnesses so that Chartist marriages could be 'recognised by the law of the land'.[137]

In a society suffused with sexual repression and an authoritarian Calvinist spirit of conformity and vindictiveness, the Scottish Chartists of the moral and physical force schools set out to change 'the thinking habits' of working people. The Chartist churches and schools they envisaged were to undertake no less a task than teaching 'the rising generation their duties';[138] and they asked the Chartist school masters to pay attention to the education of females at a time when the possessing classes frowned upon such silly notions.[139] Moreover, they organised mass meetings to protest against what they called 'the Coronation Humbug';[140] and they encouraged working people not to take the holiday their employers had offered them on the day of Queen Victoria's coronation.[141] At the same time they also insisted that the people had a right to carry arms, to resist oppression and resist 'an abrogation of any part of the constitution'.[142]

III

In the cities of Aberdeen, Inverness and Dundee, Julian Harney, the

English Chartist missionary, soon discovered that the 'cleavage' between the Establishment and the 'lower orders' was much more fundamental than the one in Glasgow and the west of Scotland; and, when he addressed small gatherings of farm labourers and weavers in the Highlands, he was forced into using 'the simplest type of exposition'. The peculiar problems of cultural alienation and language with which he was confronted in the Highlands led his biographer, A.R. Schoyen, to sum up as follows: 'In a report to the *Northern Star* which summarised his findings, he suggested that in the same way the English Chartists sent their used radical papers to Ireland, so should the southern Scots to the Highlands. The implied comparison is an illuminating one'.

Just as the Presbyterian clergymen 'denounced active Chartists from their pulpits',[143] so did a Roman Catholic clergyman expel a Chartist from his chapel in Dundee.[144] But if the simple social structure of the Highlands made it difficult for Chartists like Harney to develop a sophisticated radical critique, local Chartists were nevertheless jailed for storming 'non-intrusion' meetings.[145] In contrast to the surrounding countryside, the trade union movement in Dundee was highly sophisticated and highly political. A grasp of this complex background of a highly political trade union movement in Dundee and of alienation and disaffection in the surrounding Highland countryside is indispensable to an understanding of the events of 1842.

As the Chartists in Dundee were influential enough to create the climate of opinion in which the trade union movement set up delegate meetings from all the factories and weaving sheds to discuss whether they should strike for higher wages or the People's Charter, the authorities were preparing to deal with the local Chartist leaders once and for all. Moreover, such local leaders as John Duncan were aware of the problems they faced; and in a prophetic warning to a mass meeting of workers who voted to 'strike for the Charter', Duncan 'endeavoured to impress his hearers with the belief that the magistrates and the police would wish to *pick a quarrel with them* for the purpose of getting them in their *grasp and they would destroy them*'.[146]

As this particular meeting was attended by over 10,000 people, the authorities clearly had cause for concern. But if Duncan and other local Chartist leaders advised the unemployed to help themselves by going to 'the turnip and potato fields', they were also aware of the grip of the Presbyterian clergymen on the minds of working people. In challenging the cultural and ideological hegemony of the Establishment head-on, they appealed to the working classes to support the Chartist churches instead of paying seat rents and stipends to the 'irreverant infidels', that is, the Presbyterian clergymen.

As working men in Dundee demonstrated their determination to launch a general strike for the People's Charter by leaving 'the various manufactories, mills, foundries and workshops', the authorities were making their own plans to crush working-class radicalism altogether. A Queen's proclamation to read the Riot Act in Dundee was already drawn up at Windsor castle on 13 August; and on 23 August a riot was provoked by the authorities, Lord Duncan read the Riot Act and twelve of the local Chartist leaders were arrested on charges of 'mobbing and rioting'.[147] The Chartist movement in Dundee was broken and demoralised; and John Duncan died in a lunatic asylum in 1845, a victim, in the words of James Myles, of 'the constant terror of the law'.[148]

In Glasgow and the west of Scotland, too, there was widespread disaffection; and in 1841 there was a serious riot at the infantry barracks involving a crowd numbering between 10,000 and 15,000.[149] In places as far apart as Aberdeen and Bannockburn the Chartists came into physical conflict with the middle-class Anti-Corn Law League;[150] and in Airdrie and other towns in the west of Scotland vast crowds engaged in the effigy-burning of such unpopular figures as William Baird, M.P., and Sir Robert Peel.[151] But in conditions where Chartism at the institutional level was often alienated from the 'masses' by its advocacy of temperance, some of the middle-class Chartist leaders in Lowland Scotland alienated themselves still further by their association with the Establishment.

For in Dunfermline during the colliers' strike for the People's Charter, Provost Henderson, who was a Chartist leader, the Sheriff and the magistrates issued proclamations prohibiting Chartist meetings.[152] As the Chartist movement in Dundee was in the process of being smashed down by an insecure provincial elite, the colliers in Airdrie and Clackmannan announced that they had been inspired by the lead given by the Chartists in Dundee and England.[153] Far from the initiative for a strike for the granting of the People's Charter coming from Chartist activists among the colliers, they in fact used the mass meetings of the colliers throughout Lanarkshire to move amendments opposing strikes for either political or economic purposes. However, it was only in the Lothians that mass meetings of colliers voted down demands for a general strike for the People's Charter; and in the west of Scotland, where the Irish immigrants were active in the collier's trade unions, the situation got out of hand.[154]

In Dunfermline an illegal meeting of the colliers and other trades consisting of 20,000 people demanded the granting of the People's Charter;[155] in Airdrie and Alloa riots occurred with raids on the farmers' fields; and Irish troops were brought over from Belfast to restore public order.[156] A number of working men and women were charged with 'riotous assault' and imprisoned;[157] and all meetings of over six persons were made illegal.[158] In Aberdeen the trade unions voted to come out on strike until the People's Charter was granted;[159] and in Dumfries a rumour of a conspiracy of grain-dealers to enter into a combination to raise the price of grain led to a meal riot.[160]

A meeting of all the trades in support of the People's Charter was held in Dunfermline in September 1842; and when the Sheriff declared the meeting attended by 12,000 people illegal, the supporters of Chartism simply 'walked across the boundary into Perthshire where his authority did not extend'.[161] In circumstances where the machinery of the law was used quite openly as a bludgeon to beat down radicalism, and where distinctions between 'economic' and 'political' discontent were academic, it is only possible to grasp the important dimension of the colliers' strike in 1842 if we remember that they sustained it for over three months. Besides, the colliers were again supported by the cotton spinners in Glasgow and the west of Scotland.

Far from the Scottish courts being more 'lenient' than the English ones in their treatment of Chartists,[162] they sentenced three Chartist colliers who used intimidation against blacklegs in the colliers' strike in Ayrshire, in 1842, to ten years' transportation overseas.[163] Besides, if the Scottish courts were not as crowded as the English ones were with 'political prisoners', Henry Cockburn was less than honest when he asserted that the Scots did not resort to 'the terrors of the law' (a phrase the Chartist author, James Myles used to prove the opposite) in dealing with Chartist agitators.[164] Moreover, if 'the spirit of Lord Braxfield lived on on the Scottish bench',[165] historians have underestimated the threat to the status quo that existed in Scotland in 1837-8, 1842 and in 1847-8.[166]

This was the background against which the disaffection of the weavers, farm labourers, small lotters and fishermen in the Highlands became interwoven with the agitations leading to the Disruption and the extensive food riots in 1846-7. For if the appeal of Chartism in the Highlands was, as Julian Harney discovered in 1840, a simple one, the 'lower orders' were certainly alienated and disaffected long before the food riots of 1846-7. As the Highlanders have been depicted by Kailyard historians like John Prebble as passive victims of history, it is worth recalling what Robert Somers wrote in 1847 about the 'bitter animosity' between the sheep-farmers and the lotters:

> The parish church was a common centre where all classes met; and though the minister was frequently a nominee and a partisan of the laird, he could not but regard the victims of the clearances as a portion of his flock, and extend to them the amenities of his office. But even religion, 'the source of comfort', was converted at the Disruption into a new fountain of bitterness. The social wrongs of the lower classes inclined their minds to the doctrine of non-intrusion, and when the crisis came the instantaneous unanimity with which this class turned their backs upon the Establishment, showed with what ease they could rend the last badge which recommended them to the smile and sympathy of their superiors.[167]

What was happening in the Highlands can only be characterised as genocide; for when 'the warehouses of Liverpool and Glasgow [were] literally bursting with the prodigious mass of grain stored in them',[168] countless numbers of Highlanders were being driven from their native heath or dying from starvation.[169] But if sections of the possessing classes rejoiced because the barriers to a 'free intercourse' between the Saxon and Celtic districts (including the Gaelic language) were being broken down under 'the pressure of necessity', it was sheer hypocrisy to pretend that 'strong men [were] lying down to die in the Isles' when there was 'a want of labourers in the Lowlands'.[170]

For if some of the dispossessed Highlanders ended up in the factories and coalmines of Glasgow and the West of Scotland, many of them died in and around Glasgow as well as in the Highlands. Since there was widespread distress and destitution throughout the Highlands,[171] and when 'many of the poorer classes' could not afford 'supplies sufficient for the support of their families',[172] it is appropriate to quote Somers' description of what happened to those of them who were forced into the Lowlands in 1846-7:

> Anyone who witnessed the groups of wretched creatures who crowded into the large cities last summer and autumn who knows the want and privation which awaits them — who saw hundreds of families lying night after night on the damp grass of Glasgow Green, or amid the still more pestilental vapours of the wynds and lanes, and who listened to the barking coughs of the infants, as if their

bosums were about to rend, can require no statistics to satisfy
them of the fearful destruction of human life occasioned by the
ejectment of the peasantry from the parishes in which they were
born and lived, and the property which should have been made
responsible for their sustenance in the day of famine.[173]

However, the most important point to emphasise is that the Highlanders were not just passive victims of fate; for even in far-away
Ross-shire troops had to be sent in to allow the farm managers to ship
grain out of Scotland.[174]

As food riots occurred all over the Highlands in a context where
the Disruption had already raised disconcerting questions about the
application of the Clerical Tests in the Scottish universities and the
Union of 1707, the Lord Advocate requested a full report of the
number and location of all troops and artillery 'in North Britain'.[175]
Moreover, if the food riots were a mixture of old and new forms of
political protest and the older 'moral economy', the famine in the
Highlands heightened the schizophrenia of the provincial elite in
Edinburgh and forced them to articulate a perverted sort of Scottish
'nationalism' when they asserted:

> England has replied to the senseless clamour, the disgraceful
> ingratitude, by voting ten millions sterling in a single tax year
> to relieve the distress which the heedlessness and indolence of
> the Irish had brought upon themselves. For mark-worthy
> circumstance! the destruction of the potato crop has been just
> as complete, and the food of the people has been just as entirely
> swept away in the West Highlands of Scotland, as in Ireland, but
> there has been no *grant of public money to Scotland*. The cruel
> Anglo-Saxon have given it all to the discontented, untaxed Gael
> in the Emerald isle.[176]

Moreover, a large number of peasants were expelled from the Highlands at a time when there were an estimated 100,000 persons out of
work in Glasgow and its neighbourhood;[177] and as Scottish society
no longer constituted 'a safe and docile arena for popular movements',
a new crisis was imminent.[178] Far from being either docile or passive,
the 'lower orders' had 'come forward in a manner unexampled' in
the Scottish experience to demand poor relief through the courts
of law.[179]

As early as 1839 the provincial elite had threatened to use the

Clerical Tests imposed under the Revolutionary Settlement Act of 1690 to oust the Presbyterian dissenters from the Scottish universities, and the latter retaliated by threatening to secede and set up their own seminary.[180] By the 1840s learning in the Scottish universities was 'at a very low ebb';[181] and the Clerical Tests were seen as providing 'a bridge of easy passage to the bold and unprincipled'.[182] But if the Clerical Tests sharpened the tensions in Scottish society, they also led the *Edinburgh Review* to question the assumption that 'the articles of the Union of 1707 were unalterable'.[183] Nationalist feelings were inflamed when English members of Parliament voted against a Bill brought in by the Lord Advocate and supported by a majority of Scottish members of Parliament to abolish the Clerical Tests.

Nationalist and Radical working-class sentiments were therefore fed by many diverse sources; and the widespread and nation-wide food riots in the Highlands (and in the Lowlands on a lesser scale) demonstrate that the commonalty were not passive victims of history. In Inverness, for example, rioters who raided a ship carrying a cargo of grain were assisted by factory workers who returned to their factories once the task of removing all the grain from the ship had been completed.[184] Besides, some of the Inverness factory workers who helped the 'mob' to take grain from this ship were in sympathy with Chartist ideas.[185] This is not, however, to deny that a variety of factors alienated the 'masses' from organised Chartism at the institutional level; and though Highland peasants and Lowland industrial workers were sometimes quite passive, Scottish Chartism occasionally touched off mass discontent. When the mass discontent of Highland peasants and Lowland industrial workers reached new peaks of high social tension, the provincial elite did not hesitate to put them down.

In an article on 'the Secession from the Church of Scotland' in *Blackwood's Edinburgh Magazine,* an anonymous contributor argued that industrialisation had radicalised the 'lower ranks'. This anonymous writer already warned the provincial elite of the problems facing them when he argued that: 'And at this moment, so fearfully increased is the overbalance of democratic impulses in Scotland, that perhaps in no European nation – hardly excepting France – has it become more important to hang weights and retarding forces upon popular movements amongst the labouring classes'.[186] But if there was any doubt in 1844, after the Chartist revolt of 1842 had been put down by using 'the terrors of the law', about what was meant by the phrase 'weights and retarding forces', the Chartist upsurge of 1848 was soon met by the widespread use of police spies in the trade unions and

Chartist organisations.

By the beginning of 1848 Scottish society was again caught up in political turmoil, and on 5 March a letter from Whitehall informed the Scottish law officers that the National Charter Association was 'an unlawful combination'.[187] As touchy and insecure as ever before in the face of mass discontent in conditions of fearful unemployment, the provincial elite sent spies into the labour movement. Though Henry Cockburn would later argue that he had neven known 'the general population' to be 'so unanimous in favour of our system of things',[188] G.W.T. Omond chose to emphasise the presence of 'disaffection' and 'rumours of arming all over Scotland'.[189]

In their agitational speeches to the unemployed in Glasgow and Edinburgh before the Chartist riots of March 1848, a number of Chartist lecturers told their audiences about how the people of France 'had thrown off the yoke there'. A Dr Darval, who was regarded by the authorities as a particularly dangerous agitator, told the unemployed in Glasgow that when 'labour was wronged, property was in danger'.[190] On 7 March an armed 'mob' took control of the main streets in Glasgow, and as dusk began to fall they were joined by the workers who were leaving the factories. In riots in Glasgow and Edinburgh members of the crowd were heard to shout 'Bread or Revolution' and 'Vive la Republique'.[191] Then the Chartists were blamed for bringing the miners out on strike in Lanarkshire and Ayrshire; and in Kilmarnock a number of policemen were wounded when miners and policemen engaged in a physical conflict over the issue of free speech.[192] A riot in the town of Falkirk was blamed on the Irish, and in an assessment of the political situation created by Chartist unrest John Gair informed John Brodie, the Crown Agent, of the need for military assistance.[193]

One of the leaders of the Chartist riots in Glasgow was accused of 'mobbing and rioting' and given what Lord Medwyn described as a 'lenient' sentence of eighteen years' transportation;[194] and Archibald Alison argued that the Chartists were 'so morally slaughtered they would not recover from it for years to come'.[195] Nevertheless, by August 1848, the discontent of the Lanarkshire colliers was so serious that Alison and the magistrates in Airdrie asked Sir George Gray, the Home Secretary, for permission to give the police and special constables 'firearms and cutlasses'.[196]

This was at a time when the police spies discovered and informed the authorities that the Irish miners in Lanarkshire were drilling and expanding their secret clubs; and by November the Chartists in Glasgow were exerting such moral pressure on men who had helped to crush their revolt in March 1848, that some of those who had acted as special constables were begging the authorities to find alternative jobs for them outside of Scotland.[197] The vanquished had become the victors.

But if it is clear that the Scottish working class was not cowed by a ruthless, dictatorial, provincial elite, Scottish working people certainly took on cultural peculiarities that were unique among the working classes of western Europe. As the intellectual members of the provincial elite were insecure, schizophrenic and authoritarian, they reinforced the inarticulacy, drunkenness, aggressiveness and militancy of the 'lower orders'. For stultifying to the human personality as capitalism usually is everywhere, its cultural impact on the Scottish working class was particularly vicious and de-humanising. This was why Henry Buckle was correct to identify 'the peculiarity of Scotland' down to 1850 as the dominance of superstition and 'the authority of the priesthood'.[198]

Notes

1. Robert Mudie, *A Historical Account of His Majesty's Visit to Scotland* (Edinburgh, 1822), p. 2.

2. Robert Turnbull, *The Genius of Scotland* (New York, 1847), pp. 199-200.

3. Grant Thornburn, *Men and Manners* (Glasgow, 1835), p. 116.

4. Michael Hechter, *Internal Colonialism* (London, 1975), pp. 32-3.

5. 'The average quantity of distilled spirits annually consumed by an adult is, in England above two gallons; in Ireland, 3½ gallons; and in Scotland no less than 11 gallons.' *Edinburgh Review,* vol. C, no. 203, 1854, p. 60.

6. G.W.T. Omond, *The Lord Advocates of Scotland* (London, 1914), p. 334.

7. 'In 1840 the cost of poor relief in England stood at £4,570,000 and in Scotland it was only £115,121.' L.J. Saunders, *Scottish Democracy* (Edinburgh, 1950), p. 198.

8. See below.

9. William L. Mathieson, *Church and Reform in Scotland* (Glasgow, 1916), p. 168.

10. By a Modern Greek (Robert Mudie), *The Modern Athens* (London, 1825), p. 279.

11. 'Celtic Tenures and Highland Clearings', *Tait's Edinburgh Magazine*, December 1846, p. 780.

12. *Edinburgh Annual Register for 1822* (Edinburgh, 1924), p. 237.

13. Mudie, *Historical Account*, p. 256.

14. Ibid., p. 90 and p. 311.

15. John Galt, *Literary Life* (Edinburgh, 1834), vol. 1, p. 241.

16. John Galt, *The Gathering of the West* (Edinburgh, 1823), p. 48.

17. Ibid., p. 27.

18. J.G. Lockhart, *Memoirs of the Life of Sir Walter Scott* (Edinburgh, 1842), vol. 2, p. 191.

19. 'Advertising in Scotland', *Tait's Edinburgh Magazine,* vol. III, 1836, p. 192.

20. Preface to the Rev. Henry Duncan's novel, *The Young South Country Weaver or A Journey to Glasgow* (Edinburgh, 1821), p. iii.

21. Mudie, *Modern Athens*, pp. 212-15 and Turnbull, *Genius of Scotland*, p. 74.

22. John Younger, *Autobiography* (Kelso, 1881), p. xxii and *passim*.

23. *The Chartist Circular*, 13 February 1841.

24. Henry Cockburn, *Journal* (Edinburgh, 1874), vol. 2, p. 89.

25. Ibid., vol. 1, p. 156.

26. *Edinburgh Review*, vol. 39, 1823, p. 377.

27. *Caledonian Mercury*, 2 May 1825.

28. Second Report from the Select Committee on Artisans and Machinery, *Parliamentary Papers*, vol. V, 1824, p. 70.

29. Ibid., First Report, p. 529.

30. Ibid., pp. 530-2.

31. Ibid., Fifth Report, p. 529.

32. *Dundee Advertiser*, 30 June 1820.

33. *Glasgow Chronicle*, 7 April 1821.

34. *Caledonian Mercury*, 21 October 1824.

35. *Scotsman*, 3 May 1823.

36. *Caledonian Mercury*, 15 March 1824 and 29 November 1824.

37. *Scotsman*, 2 February 1825.

38. *Caledonian Mercury*, 9 April 1825 and 23 April 1825.

39. Criminal processes, AD 14 25/127, Scottish Record Office, Edinburgh.

40. *Caledonian Mercury*, 5 May 1825.

41. 'Combination Songs', AD 14 25/192.

42. AD 14 25/127.

43. *Caledonian Mercury*, 2 January 1826.

44. Ibid., 21 January 1826.

45. Ibid., 20 July 1826.

46. Ibid., 29 July 1826.

47. Ibid., 5 August 1826.

48. RH 2 4/155, Scottish Record Office.

49. Quoted in Alan Rogers, 'American Democracy: the View from Scotland, 1776-1832', Albion, vol. 6, no. 1, 1974, p. 68.

50. *The Herald to Trades' Advocate*, 12 February 1831.

51. AD 14 31/378.

52. *The Herald to Trades' Advocate*, no. 1, 1830.

53. See below.

54. Cockburn, *Journal*, vol. 1, p. 29.

55. 'State of Public Feeling in Scotland', *Blackwood's Edinburgh Magazine*, vol. 31, no. 136, 1832, p. 67.

56. *Report from the Select Committee on Orange Institutions in Great Britain and the Colonies*, Parliamentary Papers, vol. XVII, 1835, p. 23 and p. 2942.

57. RH 2 4/76.

58. Cockburn, *Journal*, vol. 1, p. 13.

59. Ibid., p. 25.

60. For an account of this problem, see James D. Young, 'The Making of the Inarticulate Scot', *Scotsman*, 12 February 1977.

61. Mudie, *Modern Athens*, p. 279.

62. Duncan, *Country Weaver*, pp. 61-2.

63. AD 14 32/48.

64. AD 14 30/51.

65. RH 2 4/18.

66. 'The Rejection of the Bill – the Scotch Reform', *Blackwood's Edinburgh Magazine*, vol. 30, 1831, p. 775.

67. *The Herald to Trades' Advocate*, 7 May 1831.

68. Ibid., 2 April 1831.
69. RH 2 4/30.
70. RH 2 4/33.
71. RH 2 4/24.
72. RH 2 4/23.
73. AD 12 32/29.
74. Cockburn, *Journal*, vol. 1, p. 35.
75. R.K. Greville, *Facts Illustrative of the Drunkenness of Scotland* (Edinburgh, 1834), p. 6.
76. 'Social and Moral Conditions of the Manufacturing Districts of Scotland', *Blackwood's Edinburgh Magazine*, November 1841, p. 67.
77. *First Report of the Select Committee on Combinations of Workmen*, Parliamentary Papers, 1838, vol. VIII, p. 113.
78. *Report of the Select Committee Inquiry into Drunkenness*, Parliamentary Papers, vol. VIII, 1834, p. 4646.
79. Ibid., p. 4637.
80. *The Herald to Trades' Advocate*, 14 May 1831.
81. J.R. Ward, *Chartism* (London, 1973), *passim.*
82. F.C. Mather, *Chartism* (London, 1965), p. 17.
83. *Caledonian Mercury*, 11 February 1836, 29 February 1836 and 7 March 1836.
84. See below.
85. H. Tyrell, 'Political Economy, Whiggism, and the Education of Working-Class Adults in Scotland', *Scottish Historical Review*, 1969.
86. 'In Scotland we have no bold decided Radical press. Few papers give us any assistance. In spite of all this, Radicalism lives and thrives'. *The Edinburgh Monthly Democrat and Total Abstinence Advocate*, 1 October 1838.
87. 'The Liberal Newspapers − Effects of the Reduction of the Stamp Duty', *Tait's Edinburgh Magazine*, November 1836, p. 635.
88. 'Advertising in Scotland', *Tait's Edinburgh Magazine*, p. 194.
89. This editorial concluded with the following words: 'Let the "Village Hampdens", and the "mute inglorious Miltons", be called forth to speak, and to act in their proper sphere, as well as those who possess the republicanism of Buchanan, or the patriotism of Wallace'. *The Weavers' Journal*, 1 August 1836.
90. *Select Committee on Combinations of Workmen, passim.*
91. *James Findlay and Company, 1750-1950* (Glasgow, 1951), p. 64.
92. *Select Committee on Combinations of Workmen*, p. 199.
93. A. Alison, *Some Account of My Life and Writings. An Autobiography*, Lady Alison (ed.) (Edinburgh, 1883), p. 373.
94. *Select Committee on Combinations of Workmen*, p. 16.
95. 'Social and Moral Conditions of the Manufacturing Districts', *Blackwood's*, p. 663.
96. W.H. Fraser, 'The Glasgow Cotton Spinners, 1837', *Scottish Themes*, John Butt and John T. Ward (ed.) (Edinburgh, 1976), p. 91.
97. A.H. Millar, *The Black Kalendar of Scotland* (Dundee, 1884), p. 108.
98. *Scotsman*, 11 November 1837.
99. *Select Committee on Combinations of Workmen, passim.*
100. George MacGregor, *The History of Glasgow* (Glasgow, 1881), p. 429.
101. *Select Committee on Combinations of Workmen*, p. 200.
102. *Aberdeen Journal*, 17 January 1838.
103. Fraser, *Glasgow Cotton Spinners*, p. 96.
104. Alison, *Some Account*, pp. 389-90.
105. 'The New Scotch Radicals', *Scotsman*, 29 August 1838.
106. *Select Committee on Combinations of Workmen*, pp. 179-80.

107. Cockburn, *Journal*, vol. 1, p. 155.

108. Ibid., p. 157.

109. *Tait's Edinburgh Magazine*, vol. IV, no. 131, 1834, p. 226.

110. *The Scottish Patriot*, 14 September 1839.

111. *Blackwood's Edinburgh Magazine*, vol. LX, 1844, p. 537.

112. 'Causes of the Increase of Crime', ibid., vol. LXI, 1844, p. 11.

113. *Select Committee on Combinations of Workmen*, p. 165.

114. Alexander Wilson, *The Chartist Movement in Scotland* (Manchester, 1970), p. ix.

115. 'Languages of the United Kingdom', *The Scottish Patriot*, 3 August 1839.

116. AD 14 44/81.

117. AD 14 48/319.

118. Robert Hunter, *A Brief Account of a Tour through some Parts of Scotland* (London, 1839), p. 38.

119. Catherine Sinclair, *Scotland and the Scotch*, (Edinburgh, 1840), p. 115.

120. *Scotsman*, 2 February 1825.

121. RH 2 4/477.

122. 'Political State of the North of Scotland', *Tait's Edinburgh Magazine*, September 1835, p. 621.

123. Turnbull, *Genius of Scotland*, p. 22.

124. Sinclair, *Scotland and the Scotch*, p. 137.

125. 'Moral and Social Condition of Wales', *Blackwood's Edinburgh Magazine*, September 1849, p. 339.

126. James Paterson, *Origins of the Scots and the Scottish Language* (Edinburgh, 1855), p. 165.

127. Joseph Downes, 'Notes on a Tour of the Disturbed Districts in Wales', *Blackwood's Edinburgh Magazine*, vol. LIV, no. 338, 1843, p. 776.

128. See below.

129. *Tait's Edinburgh Magazine*, vol. V, 1838, p. 200.

130. 'The Corn Laws', ibid., April 1836, p. 200.

131. Rev. Francis Trench, *Scotland: Its Faith and Features* (London, 1846), vol. 2, p. 21.

132. *The Chartist Circular*, 30 May 1840.

133. Sinclair, *Scotland and the Scotch*, p. 112.

134. AD 58/80.

135. AD 2/13.

136. *The Chartist Circular*, 2 May 1840.

137. Ibid., 28 March 1840.

138. Ibid., 18 September 1841.

139. Ibid., 14 March 1840.

140. *The Edinburgh Monthly Democrat and Total Abstinence Advocate*, 7 July 1838.

141. Ibid., 7 July 1838.

142. 'The Right of Having Arms', *The Chartist Circular*, 25 January 1840.

143. A.R. Schoyen, *The Chartist Challenge. A Portrait of George Julian Harney* (London, 1958), p. 103.

144. I owe this information to Dr James Treble.

145. Schoyen, *Chartist Challenge*, p. 104.

146. Precognition of Thomas Keith, reporter with the Dundee Advertiser, AD 14 44/81, AD 14 42/354 and AD 2/14.

147. AD 14 44/81 and AD 14 42/354.

148. James Myles, *Rambles in Forfarshire* (Edinburgh, 1850), p. 79, and the *Northern Star*, 22 February 1845.

149. *Scotsman*, 19 June 1841.

150. Ibid., 16 May 1841 and 19 February 1842.
151. Ibid., 9 March 1842.
152. Ibid., 3 September 1842.
153. Ibid., 24 August 1842.
154. Ibid., 17 August 1842.
155. *Caledonian Mercury,* 28 August 1842.
156. Ibid., 19 August 1842.
157. Ibid., 26 December 1842.
158. *Scotsman,* 6 August 1842.
159. *Aberdeen Journal,* 31 August 1842.
160. *Scotsman,* 6 July 1842.
161. *Aberdeen Journal,* 7 September 1842.
162. R.H. Campbell, *Scotland Since 1707* (Oxford, 1965), p. 221.
163. AD 2/13.
164. Lord Cockburn, *An Examination of the Trials for Sedition which have Hitherto Occurred in Scotland* (Edinburgh, 1888), p. 227.
165. Fraser, *Glasgow Cotton Spinners,* p. 96.
166. See below.
167. Robert Somers, *Letters from the Highlands or the Famine of 1847* (Edinburgh, 1847), pp. 65-6.
168. 'Lessons from the Famine', *Blackwood's Edinburgh Magazine,* vol. XLI, 1847, p. 517.
169. Somers, *Letters, passim.*
170. 'Highland Destitution', *Blackwood's Edinburgh Magazine,* vol. LXII, 1847, p. 632.
171. *Scotsman,* 30 January 1847 and 14 April 1847.
172. Ibid., 16 January 1847.
173. Somers, *Letters,* pp. 159-60.
174. AD 14 47/136.
175. Lord Advocate's Papers, Box 116, Scottish Record Office.
176. 'Lessons of the Famine', *Blackwood's,* p. 524. Emphasis in the original.
177. 'How to Disarm the Chartists', *Blackwood's Edinburgh Magazine,* vol. LV, 1844, p. 655.
178. 'Secession from the Church of Scotland', ibid., vol. LV, 1844, p. 232.
179. Trench, *Scotland,* vol. 2, p. 195.
180. Hunter, *A Brief Account,* p. 45.
181. 'The Scottish Universities', *Tait's Edinburgh Magazine,* vol. XII, 1845, p. 377.
182. 'The Scottish Universities and the Established Church', ibid., vol. X, 1843, p. 580.
183. *Edinburgh Review,* vol. 81, 1845, p. 494.
184. AD 14 46/31.
185. Lord Advocate's Papers, Box 116.
186. 'Secession from the Church of Scotland', *Blackwood's,* p. 232.
187. AD 58/71.
188. Cockburn, *Journal,* vol. 2, p. 212.
189. Omond, *Lord Advocates,* pp. 154-5.
190. AD 58/79.
191. *The Scotsman,* 8 March 1848.
192. *Edinburgh Advertiser,* 14 March 1848.
193. 'But we have within the district a very considerable population of colliers and miners, who are at all times discontented and unsettled, and of whom I am more afraid than of the population in and immediately around the town', AD 58/74.

194. Wilson, *Chartist Movement*, p. 581.
195. Alison, *Some Account*, p. 581.
196. AD 58/68.
197. RH 2 4/296.
198. Henry T. Buckle, *History of Civilisation in England* (London, 1904), vol. 3, p. 182.

4 COLONIALISM AND THE SCOTTISH LABOUR MOVEMENT, 1865-1879

> Scottish wage rates remained on the whole much below the English level throughout the nineteenth century. The mid-Victorian growth industries had a tradition of harshness and compulsion (until 1799 Scots miners were actually serfs), and recruited their labour from the unorganised and helpless, and especially from the Irish and Highland immigrants used neither to a decent income nor to urban and industrial life. Scots housing was and remains not only scandalously bad, but notably worse than English housing . . . But in the years from the 1830s to the 1880s there was little to fill the lives of Scotsmen except work and drink. Even labour organisations remained feebler and less stable than in England. If the mid-Victorian years were a gloomy age in the social life of the English poor, they were a black one in Scotland.[1]

As the unique features of Scottish capitalism in the mid-Victorian period consisted of extreme poverty, poor wages, extreme authoritarianism, scandalous housing, weak, unstable labour organisations and mass drunkenness, it is necessary to ask the question why. Faced with the evidence of higher levels of crime, disease, ill-health, consumption of alcohol, illegitimacy, migration, immigration and inarticulacy than existed elsewhere in the United Kingdom, it is clear that poverty alone did not deepen and intensify these problems.[2] For if extreme poverty and oppression breeds crime and drunkenness more in some societies than in others, it ought to be part of the historian's job to explain what was specific in the Scottish experience.

As the concrete problems of extreme poverty, migration and immigration were a consequence of what Michael Hechter identifies as the peripheral relationship of the Scottish economy to 'the core' of British metropolitan capitalism, it could be argued that there was a certain 'inevitability' about the peculiarities and peculiar identity evolved by the Scottish working class. But if the Scottish working class often seemed to be even more unruly and rumbustious than the English, Irish or Welsh working class, this was partly due to the social behaviour of the insecure, provincial bourgeois elite who ruled Scottish society with heavy-handed authoritarian methods. For the peculiarities of the Scots — a working class already well-known for its inarticulacy and high levels of illegitimacy, migration, immigration, consumption of alcohol, ill-health, disease and crime — were shaped by the social behaviour of the provincial elite just as much as by the responses of the working class to exploitation within a particular capitalist society.[3]

The peculiarities of Scottish society in the mid-Victorian period were shaped by what happened during the Enlightenment in the eighteenth century; for, if the Scottish elite surrendered so completely to English culture in the eighteenth century, they were still articulating their complex sense of provincial identity. From the eighteenth century onwards the Scottish provincial elite could not confront the 'superior' metropolitan culture of the South without articulating their own complex sense of inferiority which was the key to their conception of their own provincial identity. Moreover, as the social behaviour of the provincial bourgeois elite was still motivated by their Enlightenment vision of the peculiarities of the Scottish working class and the relationship of Scottish society to her 'superior' neighbour in the South, the relationship between the Scottish and English bourgeoisie was influenced by the Scots sense of psychological inferiority.

As Scottish society was very poor and economically backward, the provincial elite, who inherited the social and ideological legacy of the Scottish Enlightenment, attributed the country's backwardness to the particular characteristics or peculiarities of its people. The Scottish working class that they perceived all around them seemed to be much more unruly and rumbustious than its English, Irish or Welsh counterparts; and, if they sustained the schizophrenic vision of the eighteenth century Scottish Enlightenment thinkers about the social peculiarities of the commonalty, they also practised the authoritarian methods of their predecessors by sending more men and women to jail for drunkenness and petty crime than any other country in the United Kingdom. What was specific in the Scottish experience in relation to the high level of crime was the extreme authoritarianism — and repression — being practised by the provincial bourgeois elite.

The authoritarianism of the provincial elite was accompanied by chronic social insensitivity towards the labouring poor. As the provincial elite, and the intellectual who tried to impose bourgeois social values on the 'lower orders', were utterly insensitive towards the extreme poverty and suffering of the working class, they also had few inhibitions about attacking the culture of the commonalty. This was seen in the atrocious housing provided by most of the employers of coal miners and farm labourers, in the harshness of the Scottish system of poor relief and in the continuing assault on the Scots dialect and Gaelic.

In contrast to the English experience, where the process of industrialisation was complete by 1850, industrialisation in the west of
Scotland did not reach its culmination until 1885.[4] This important
sociological factor was of crucial importance in sustaining the assault
on the language of the Gaels as well as the genocide and systematic
de-population of the Highlands. With a vast pool of potential labour
in the Highlands at a time of heavy migration from the Lowlands,
British capitalism needed, in Victor Kiernan's phrase, 'a homogeneous
population and a single language for its markets'.[5] The incompatibility
of the Gaelic language with the needs of a still evolving capitalist
economy were spelt out by W. Pitt Dundas, the Registrar General of
Scotland, in 1871:

> But a formidable barrier to the emigration of females to our towns
> exists in the fact that over a great proportion of the north and west
> of Scotland, and all the Western Isles, the Gaelic tongue is still
> encouraged, and the population are cut off from emigrating to the
> towns from a want of knowledge of the English language. The Gaelic
> language may be what it likes both as to antiquity and beauty, but
> it decidedly stands in the way of the civilisation of *the natives*
> making use of it, and shuts them out from the paths open to their
> fellow-countrymen who speak the English tongue. It ought,
> therefore, to cease to be taught in all our national schools; and
> as we are one people, we should have but *one* language.[6]

As the notion of the Scottish Enlightenment thinkers that Scottish
backwardness could be sought in the particular characteristics of a
'rude', 'simple' and 'primitive' people was carried over into the mid-
Victorian period, the provincial elite could give this cultural and ideological legacy a new contemporary relevance by blaming the Irish immigrants in Scotland for lowering 'the moral tone of the lower classes'.
For if the provincial elite could, in a particular context, argue that
the Scots were 'one people', they now saw the Irish immigrants rather
than industrial capitalism as the real source of the crime, drunkenness
and deteriorating environment that dictated the need for 'extra sanitary
and police precautions'.[7]

The demise of Chartism in 1848 meant that the Scottish labour
movement was fragmented and driven underground. Moreover, in the
coalfields of the west of Scotland, where the Orange lodges were
extending their activities, the employers began to exploit ethnic and
religious prejudice to 'drive the Scots and Irish into antagonism';[8] and

the Scottish miners — and other workers — were often egged on by the Presbyterian clergy who blamed the social problems thrown up by industrial capitalism on the Irish immigrants.[9]

Being prisoners of the social thought that crystallised during their own Enlightenment, the provincial elite took advantage of the presence of the large number of Irish immigrants in Scottish society to emphasise the contrast between the generally well-behaved, docile and uniquely democratic outlook of the Scottish workers and the unruly, rumbustious behaviour of the Irish immigrants. In newspapers, Parliamentary reports and books the myths about the docility and unique democratic outlook of the Scottish workers were cultivated so assiduously and systematically that even English observers of the Scottish scene came to believe — and repeat — them. In a study of the British colliers published in 1856 an anonymous English observer argued that most of the organised miners in the Scottish coalfields were Irishmen, not Scots. As these convenient notions became increasingly popular among the English as well as Scottish students of the social question, it is worth quoting him at length:

> In taking as examples of the best educated classes of colliers, the Scotch and the English, you are surprised to find so perceptible a difference in favour of the Scotch. When you enter some of the Scotch colliers' houses, you are not prepared for the choice of books you find there. Many of them read such books as Adam Smith's *Wealth of Nations,* and are fond of discussing the subjects he treats of . . . Such men will have nothing to do with the Union. They scorn to read the penny and twopenny publications current in other places.[10]

Just as the Scottish possessing classes cultivated the myth of the docility and democratic outlook of the 'lower orders', so they also took advantage of any outbursts of class conflict in England to popularise the notion of the 'superior' behaviour of the Scottish working class.[11] This commitment to the eighteenth century Enlightenment vision of the unique docility of the Scottish working class explained why they sometimes tried to explain away the higher levels of crime and drunkenness in Scotland by engaging in what can only be described as special pleading. For example, as soon as the Royal Commission on Trade Unions had reported on the 'Sheffield outrages', a number of Scottish newspaper editors claimed that 'rattening' (or industrial sabotage) did not exist in Scotland. But they had no sooner made their claims for the unique docility of the Scottish workers than there were outbreaks of 'rattening' in Greenock, Alloa and Glasgow in 1868.[12] Nevertheless, the Enlightenment visions of the provincial elite did impinge on the social consciousness of the working classes and helped to reinforce the image of a seemingly homogeneous society.

A system of 'democracy' inherited from the Calvinist revolution of 1559, social mobility and the comparatively superior educational opportunities of working class children were, in the considered opinion of a large number of journalists, clergymen and members of Parliament, the dominant characteristics of Scottish democracy.[13] In practice, the educational opportunities and social mobility open to the working classes were severely circumscribed by the conditions industrial capitalism had engendered; and in the mid-1860s the labour movement, though influenced by the traditions — and the mythology — of Scottish 'democracy', looked to America for their model of a democratic society.[14]

I

In 1865 the labouring poor were socially, culturally and politically fragmented, and the Scottish working class now had 'many subdivisions and gradations including occupations as various as those of the dexterous artisan and the rude miner, the intelligent factory hand and the casual dock labourer'.[15] The artisans possessed the characteristics of 'industry, skill, independence and self-respect',[16] and labourers were labourers because they were 'lazy and profligate'.[17] Such characteristics as industry, skill, independence and self-respect were allegedly restricted to the artisans and skilled workers, and a Scottish educationalist argued that: 'There are in every school boys who are fit only to be hewers of wood and drawers of water'.[18]

The superior education and the 'democratic instincts' of indigenous working people occupy a major niche in the mythology of Scottish history,[19] and 'the popularity of the democratic (Presbyterian) church with the middle and lower classes'[20] was proverbial among journalists, clergymen, educationalists and members of Parliament. The reality was somewhat different, and the provincial elite recognised and encouraged class differences, status differentiation and social stratification.[21] In social, economic and political life there were, as the *Edinburgh Review* put it, 'orders and degrees' which did not 'jar with liberty'.[22] Nevertheless, alongside the 'educational destitution' discovered by the Royal Commission on Schools in Scotland known as the Argyll Commission, Scotland had the highest number of students in proportion to population in Europe[23] and 16.2 per cent of them were said to be working-class.[24]

The social misery, gloom, brutality and insensitivity of Scottish society were reflected in the socially stratified and authoritarian educational system. Moreover, the poverty and brutality of social life were manifested in the statistics of drunkenness, overcrowding and illegitimacy; and the possessing classes had little sympathy for the plight of the labouring poor. Besides, every town and city contained a 'floating mass of shivering, shirtless and shoeless humanity',[25] and in towns and cities such as Falkirk, Dunfermline, Glasgow, Edinburgh and Dundee, a large, shiftless population was commonplace. As boom and slump alternated during the second half of the nineteenth century mass unemployment was often widespread,[26] and in 1867 the *North British Daily Mail* estimated that, in Glasgow, thirty thousand working men had been unemployed for nine months.[27] In Edinburgh the convener of the relief committee was appalled by 'the abstract political economy' of the provincial elite which, he claimed, looked 'with a cold eye' upon the exertions being made to mitigate 'the existing destitution'.[28]

By 1865 self-help and thrift were the hallmarks of the ideology embraced by the urban labour movement, and in towns and cities working class leaders, together with middle class Liberals, were uncompromisingly opposed to legislative interference with the hours of labour of adult workers. At the same time the provincial elite was no longer opposed to trade unions *per se,* and in schools and in school textbooks there was a general tolerance of trade unionism provided it kept itself within proper limits.[29]

This subtle accommodation of trade unionism within a still evolving internal colony enabled the possessing classes to promote their *images* of Scotland as a seemingly homogeneous society. By contrast the textbooks used in the Church of England schools were notorious for their hostility to trade unions; and this allowed the Scottish Presbyterian trade unionists to tell the delegates to the British Trade Union Congress of their superior, democratic way of life.[30] For at the same time as the provincial elite depicted Scottish society as a homogeneous one, they also perfected a system of national education through the church schools and the universities which aimed at silencing an unruly and rumbustious working class.

But if the Scottish educational system was narrow, practical, utilitarian and authoritarian, it also provided education up to university level for a minority of working-class children.[31] Alongside the widespread educational 'destitution' a significant number of working-class children were indoctrinated in church — and later state — schools; and in 1862 a Presbyterian inspector of education reported that the Revised Code was designed to 'produce a growth of peace-loving citizens instead of political firebrands'.[32]

Since Scottish society was inherently 'democratic', it was 'quite within the scope of school instruction that correct views (on strikes and combinations) should be formed by the pupils in their schools'.[33] Trade unionism could therefore be tolerated as the price of one kind of self-help; and by the time the First Education Act was passed in 1872, the pattern of Scottish education was already set in a narrow, utilitarian and authoritarian mould.[34]

This was the backcloth — a backcloth of mounting discontent, poverty and unemployment — against which the Scottish National Reform League was formed at a public meeting in Bells' Temperance Hotel on 17 September 1866. The radical reformers in Glasgow adopted several resolutions identifying themselves with the National Reform League in London, the principle of manhood suffrage protected by the ballot, and announced a great Scottish demonstration for Parliamentary reform.[35]

But if the leading radicals in the Scottish National Reform League had been stung by critical comments about the apathy and ignorance of the working classes made in the House of Commons, they were nevertheless moderate reformers. However, if the British possessing classes were to be pressurised into granting a limited franchise, the moderate reformers still had to create a mass working-class movement. But a mass working-class movement is, in a period of crisis and social tension, easier to create than control. One sign of the dominant role to be played by the labour movement was indicated by the invitation to 'all trade, provident and other temperance societies' to attend the proposed Reform demonstration in Glasgow.[36]

Whether a revolutionary spectre threatened the established social order or not, the great majority of Scottish Liberal MPs supported the enfranchisement of the artisans.[37] In late 1866 the artisans had been so angered by derogatory remarks about the working classes that their aroused class-consciousness had now reached a high pitch of intensity, and they were therefore prepared to involve the unorganised and the unskilled workers in the mass reform demonstrations. This contemptuous Parliamentary criticism of working-class apathy had the unsought result of unleashing popular energy, a rising wave of mass discontent, and new social and political expectations.

Faced with a situation of acute social tension, independent Liberals like Duncan McLaren, the member of Parliament for Edinburgh, decided to support working-class agitations for Parliamentary reform in a perhaps desperate attempt to keep working-class discontent under the control of local Liberal committees rather than risk radicalising working people still further by their intransigent opposition. As middle-class Liberals were not always willing to do so by supporting the popular agitations for manhood suffrage, they could not be accepted as leaders of a movement for Parliamentary reform. Where moderate Liberals like James Moir became leaders of local branches of the Scottish National Reform League, they had to pay lip-service to the agitation for complete manhood suffrage.

The greatest political demonstration that Scotland had seen till then was witnessed in Glasgow on 16 October 1866. A vast congregation of people stretched along the streets of Glasgow for five miles; and an estimated 200,000 people marched to Glasgow Green to hear speeches by John Bright, Edmund Beales, George Potter, Ernest Jones, George Newton, John Proudfoot and Alexander MacDonald. Resolutions were passed unanimously calling for manhood suffrage and the secret ballot; and Ernest Jones told the demonstrators that 'the voice of the people was the voice of God'. George Newton, secretary of the Glasgow Trades' Council, expressed the sentiments of thousands of working people when he declared the question of Parliamentary reform had been too long ignored. 'They had been mere puppets in the hands of the parties ever since the last Reform Bill', he continued, 'and it was time now that they should take the matter into their own hands. They did not need to despair. Gigantic monopolies had fallen before the trumpet blast of the people's breath, and it would be the case again'.[38]

What worried the possessing classes was that the working-class leaders were linking the demand for manhood suffrage to new expectations of social reform, and their hopes were encouraged by some of 'the old Chartist orators'.[39] The artisans' interest in Parliamentary reform as a means of getting social reform was seen when the operative masons carried a banner in the great Reform demonstration: 'Nine hours – a new era in the history of labour'.[40] However, as soon as a separate Scottish Reform Bill was passed in the House of Commons in 1868, the mass workers' movement disintegrated. For the 'masses' apathy was to become the norm once again; and the Scottish labour movement was to remain small and isolated.

In a society where concerted efforts were made by the possessing classes to create a comparatively homogeneous milieu, it is not surprising to find a strong workers' antipathy towards true unionism. The miners in the west of Scotland frequently failed to form branches of the miners' union as a result of the men's commitment to the Orange lodges;[41] and the shipbuilding industry was established on the Clyde in the 1860s to escape the high wages and strong craft unions of the south of England.[42] By comparison with the English the Scottish trade union movement was very weak in the mid-Victorian period. This relative weakness of Scottish trade unionism isolated activists from most working people, and this isolation was one of the factors which helped to push the Scottish to the *left* of the English labour movement. It was, however, only one factor. Another important factor was the electoral predominance of the Scottish Liberal Party.

The Scottish National Reform League was created by middle-class advanced (or left-wing) Liberals who were initially to the right of the Reform League in England. Since the Scottish middle-class advanced Liberals were dependent on the support of the activists in the labour movement if they were to win support for the programme of advanced Liberalism and capture control of local Liberal Associations in constituencies where branches of the Reform League also existed, they soon had to move to the left of the English Division of the League.

In contrast to England, where some of the labour leaders felt compelled to abandon the programme of advanced Liberalism under pressure from wealthy Liberals who were supplying them with funds in 1868 in case the Tories should gain an advantage in marginal seats where the Liberals could not afford to fight each other over policy issues, the Tories in Scotland were so numerically weak that Whigs, independent and advanced Liberals could fight each other without being threatened by the possibility of the Tories gaining Parliamentary seats. It was significant that in the constituencies in those Scottish cities where advanced Liberalism was influential, the middle-class advanced Liberals depended on labour organisations such as Trades Councils for their dominance over the Whigs or independent Liberals. Except for the miners, the Scottish labour movement supported the Liberal Party.

If a relatively smaller proportion of Scottish than English artisans were organised in the 1860s, then the differences between the Scottish and English miners, whether organised or not, were significant; and, while there were many English miners who owned their own houses and thus qualified for the franchise in 1874, most Scottish miners lived in hovels which the coalowners let to them on a basis of day-to-day tenure. Moreover, there were very few miners who enrolled in the Scottish Division of the Reform League, and of those who did, John Muir, a veteran miners' leader, broke solidarity with the miners by backing Bouverie, the Whig, in the general election of 1868. For the organised miners as a whole, however, the Tories were preferable to the Liberals, whether the latter were Whigs, independent or advanced Liberals.[43] Sooner or later the latent tensions between the artisans and the miners were destined to 'explode'.

By July 1867 the National Reform League had 488 provincial branches, and only 64 of these branches were Scottish ones. Moreover, in sixteen of the thirty-two Scottish counties there were no branches of the League,[44] and trade unionists formed a small minority of the Scottish membership except in a few branches.[45] Most of the branches of the Scottish National Reform League were dominated by middle-class advanced Liberals, and on 13 October 1867, George Howell, the secretary of the British League, wrote to George Jackson, the secretary in Glasgow, as follows:

> It was reported at our Council last night that your resolutions
> were to be of the old Milk and Water sort, instead of manhood
> suffrage and the Ballot. Now Mr Beales will support no resolution
> unless it goes for manhood suffrage, and he wishes me to tell you
> this. Moreover, our Council will not allow any of its advocates to
> go for less.[46]

This Scottish Reform League was accurately described by the press as an association of 'advanced Liberals' with their headquarters in Glasgow; yet they had to be persuaded by their English associates to campaign for manhood suffrage and the ballot.[47] From then on they would be to the left of the National Reform League.

The Scottish Reform League was from the beginning autonomous; it issued its own membership cards; and it did not pay a percentage of its membership dues to the Central Association in London.[48] Not only were the day-to-day affairs of the Scottish Reform League controlled by such middle-class Liberals as George Jackson, James Moir and John Burt; but the League's Honorary Presidents included three Liberal members of Parliament, Robert Dalglish (Glasgow), A.M. Dunlop (Greenock) and James Merry (Falkirk). They were all advanced Liberals who supported the labour movement's agitations for the ballot and a considerable extension of the franchise.[49] But in time they would incur the active hostility of Alexander MacDonald and the miners' agents in the west of Scotland.

There were already evident differences between the National and the Scottish Reform League. By 1867 the English trade unionists had effective majorities on the Councils of the Reform League in London and the English provinces;[50] but the Scottish trade unionists were outnumbered by middle-class Liberal elements who were concerned about the outcome of the ensuing general election. While English trade union leaders within the National Reform League had forfeited their opportunity to foster working-class candidates independent of the two major parties by accepting money from wealthy Liberals during the Reform campaign,[51] Scottish trade unionists, already at odds with each other,[52] were not in a position to influence the Scottish Reform League. The English labour leaders, who were in a position to push for independent labour politics, opted for a secret pact with the Liberal whips; and it has been argued that 'the existence of some pact or arrangement could not be inferred from the election results by any intelligent political observer'.[53]

In contrast to the Reform League in England, the numerical weakness of the Scottish trade unionists was revealed when the annual meeting of the Scottish League took place in September 1867. Of the three hundred delegates who attended the conference on 17 September, only sixty-one delegates represented trade unions. Their financial contribution was not, therefore, very important; and only £253 of the Scottish Division's annual income came from subscriptions under £5. Moreover, Liberal MPs such as Dalglish and Corbet had given donations of £25 and £20 respectively, and there had been an anonymous donation of £50.[54]

For the sake of efficiency and effectiveness the leaders of the Reform League in London were willing to sacrifice individuality for authority, and the Central Association did not hesitate to impose its authority on recalcitrant branches in the English provinces.[55] When the annual meeting of the Bradford branch of the League met in October 1867, the Rev. Sharman had no difficulty in persuading the meeting to accept a third clause to the future programme on which the League would fight the general election:

> Justice to labour in its struggle with capital, by the protection of
> the funds of trade societies and by the revision of the Acts relating
> to conspiracy and intimidation.

A further resolution, urging 'the early assembly of a people's convention to determine upon the action to be taken by the League on the election of 1868', was also adopted.

The proposals being canvassed by those members of the English provincial branches like Sharman, who were to the left of George Howell, were incompatible with the plans being shaped in London,[56] particularly during the months before the general election when they were engaged in delicate — and secret — negotiations with the Liberal whips.[57] Then in mid-January 1868, the Reform League in Bradford, where the advanced Liberals had been fairly strong, abandoned their previous commitment to campaign for justice for Ireland and a system of national education.[58]

In the English provinces, and particularly in Leeds, the programme of advanced Liberalism had been characterised from the mid-1850s by such tenets as justice for Ireland, a national system of education, reform of the land laws, a Ballot Act, disestablishment of the Irish church and a modification of the laws affecting trade unions. Nonetheless, the tests, deciding whether Liberal candidates were advanced or otherwise, were very loose, and the basic opposition to trade unionism by Liberal employers such as Robert Kell, a Liberal notorious for his anti-trade union attitudes, did not mean that they could not be described as advanced Liberals.[59] Whether potential Parliamentary candidates were defined as advanced, independent or Whig really depended on local Liberal Associations, and they were usually dominated by middle-class elements who were more interested in other tenets of the programme of advanced Liberalism than reform of the laws affecting trade unions.

In England the programme of advanced Liberalism lacked — or was assumed to lack — a wide, popular appeal,[60] and this, together with the League's financial dependence on wealthy Liberals, was an important factor in pushing the London leaders into accepting a more moderate programme. By contrast Scotland was, in electoral terms, to the left of England in so far as the programme of advanced Liberalism had a wider, popular appeal. A crucial factor in allowing the Scottish Reform League to campaign for the agitational demands of the advanced Liberals — a programme almost identical with the English one — was the relative absence of a Tory Party which constituted a serious electoral force. Nevertheless, Scottish *society* was characterised by a right-wing, authoritarian ethos; and it was — except in electoral terms — far to the right of England.

The Liberals had won a large majority of the Scottish seats from 1832 onwards, and whatever electoral strength the Tories had was mainly restricted to the rural areas. Indeed, it had been fairly common-place for the Tories not to contest many urban seats during the two decades before 1868, and many electoral fights had been between Liberal candidates belonging to different factions of the Liberal Party. In Scotland the three major political tendencies within the Liberal Party were advanced, independent and Whig, or, in modern parlance, the left, the centre and the right.

The Scottish National Reform League was dominated by middle-class advanced Liberals — most of whom were ex-Chartists — and they campaigned to strengthen the advanced elements within the Liberal Associations. Yet they made no attempt to impose a uniform electoral programme on the other Scottish branches of the League, and programmes of some branches were to the left as well as to the right of the one approved by the leaders in Glasgow. By the middle of 1868, by which time the general election was underway, the leaders of the Reform League in Glasgow — James Moir, George Jackson and Robert Cochrane — were prepared to promote the candidatures of advanced Liberals even in constituencies where there were good prospects of pushing the claims of independent working-class candidates.

Alexander MacDonald and some of the leaders of the Glasgow Trades Council had long associations with Lord Elcho, the Tory MP who had opposed Parliamentary reform, and they were attached to him because of his prolonged efforts to amend the Master and Servant Act. Elcho had, moreover, frequently promised to secure legislation beneficial to the miners. But by the time the general election campaign was underway the Glasgow Trades Council members who assisted MacDonald's promotion of Tory candidates at the expense of the Liberals did so as individuals rather than as representatives of their trade unions.

The Scottish miners entered the general election with their own strategy and programme. The miners' organisations in the west of Scotland — in Fife the miners supported Henry Campbell, the advanced Liberal[61] — were the only Scottish working-class organisation which initiated and sustained a systematic campaign against Liberal Parliamentary candidates. In contrast to the Scottish workers' political programme,[62] the miners' programme attracted considerably less attention from the Liberal and working-class press.[63] The latter programme, in the form of a series of test questions to be put to all Parliamentary candidates, was published in the *Glasgow Sentinel*, a working-class newspaper, in July. A little later the Edinburgh branch of the Scottish Reform League and the Edinburgh Trades Council drafted a series of test questions which formed the basis of the Scottish workers' programme.[64] This programme again enabled the provincial bourgeois elite to boast about the unique democratic outlook of the Scottish artisans.

In June the miners' leaders launched their first attacks against Liberals in general and James Merry, the member of Parliament for the Falkirk burghs and and Honorary President of the Scottish National Reform League, in particular. The *Glasgow Sentinel* put the miners' argument very sharply: 'Instead of being returned to his present consti-tuency, Mr Merry may be thankful if he is not hooted from every meeting in which he may appear in the mining constituencies'.[65] The miners' leaders hated Merry as a coalowner, and his terrible record as an employer of miners was of much greater concern to Alexander MacDonald and the miners' leaders in the west of Scotland than his genuine support of the programme of advanced Liberalism. Before this general election was over, large numbers of miners and artisans engaged in physical fights and some miners' agents were sent to jail for attempting to bribe electors to vote Tory.

II

The Scottish working classes had played a major part in the struggle for the second Reform Bill, and the general election had seemingly provided the Scottish working-class movement with an opportunity to evolve an independent political posture.[66] In fact the general election exposed and accentuated splits and divisions in the working-class movement. A heterogeneous working class, existing in a capitalist internal colony dominated by *laissez-faire* ideology, lacked the liberal traditions and liberal institutions of the English. The miners represented an implicit threat to social and political stability; but, since most of them had not been enfranchised by the second Reform Act of 1868, their almost innate militancy and opposition-mindedness were not sufficient to transform the political situation.

Emigration had been a prominent feature of Scottish life since the early nineteenth century, and the psychological acceptance of emigra-tion had a major influence on culture and imaginative literature.[67] Trade union leaders, in marked contrast to their English counterparts,[68] *were* enthusiastic about the emigration of unemployed members. Scottish trade union leaders, depending on whether they were miners or artisans, quarrelled about the methods by which the emigration of unemployed working people should be promoted. The leaders of the carpenters, iron moulders and engineers, with their secure funds for assisting unemployed members to emigrate, were not in sympathy with the agitation for state-aided emigration. During the general election of 1868 the miners in the west of Scotland opposed George Anderson, the advanced Liberal Parliamentary candidate for Glasgow, because of his refusal to support their demand for state-aided emigration.[69] Much later *Blackwood's Edinburgh Magazine,* the Scottish Tory journal, criticised the agitation for state-aided emigration as detrimental to 'the impulses of self-help'.[70] In 1868 James Dawson Burn, who had been a leading member of the Glasgow Committee of Trades' Delegates in the 1830s and 1840s, expounded his view that unemployment and poverty could only be effectively solved by emigration:

> This could be done by enabling the surplus hands in the various trades to emigrate either to the United States or some of the other colonies. The money spent on strikes in the last seventy years, if it had been applied to the purpose of emigration, would have been sufficient to have relieved the country of at least thirty thousand people who are a dead weight on the labour market.[71]

Side-by-side with the Scottish trade union leaders' acceptance of emigration as an aspect of self-help, they also propagated and practised a more positive philosophy of collective self-help. What Scottish working-class leaders envisaged by collective self-help was explained by Robert Cranston, the ex-Chartist leader, when he addressed the Edinburgh Working Men's Club:

> If you take my advice, do what you have been doing for the last twenty years — do what the Convention of London recommended you to do — stick to your trade unions, co-operative and investment companies and mechanics institutes. Depend upon it, none will attend to your interests but yourselves.[72]

However, the miners were the most oppressed group of industrial workers in the whole of Scotland, and the formidable difficulties confronting the miners — and the near impossibility of forming stable and effective trade union organisation in the coalfields — meant that collective self-help was denied to a very large number of the mining population. Moreover, the miners who did emigrate to America were usually the relatively well-off elite of skilled workers; and in conditions of appalling poverty and oppression — the coalowners, for example, imposed compulsory deductions from the men's wages for housing, schooling, medical attention, lamp oil, blasting powder and pick-sharpening — there were not many miners who could afford to pay the trade union dues or imitate the thrifty artisans. Nevertheless, the miners' leaders constantly urged the miners to 'lift themselves out of servitude' by practising self-help.[73] Alexander MacDonald frequently blamed the miners for 'much of their poverty',[74] and he criticised them for gambling, dog-fighting and drinking.[75]

A distinguished historian of British working-class politics has described the Scottish workers' programme of 1868 — a programme formulated by Presbyterian artisans but not miners — as an attempt by some working men to strike out in the direction of independent political action.[76] An important plank in the Scottish workers' programme was the demand for a national compulsory system of education, and the *Spectator* observed that the agitation for free and unsectarian education had been influenced by the example of the American system. American ideas and reports of American experience were publicised and popularised by British radicals; and Scottish trade unionists occasionally visited America, lived there for brief periods,[77] or were in touch with activists in the American labour movement. But the workers who formulated or wholeheartedly welcomed the Scottish workers' programme, also sabotaged the formidable efforts of the miners' leaders to put forward independent working-class candidates.[78]

The attempts of the miners' leaders to promote independent working-class candidates had been at least partially inspired by what American labour was doing; and, ironically, they had been opposed by working-class leaders who were enchanted with American democracy. The urban labour movement — most miners lived in relatively isolated rural communities and their trade unions were not affiliated to the Trades Councils — had been very impressed by American educational institutions, opportunities of social mobility and the creation of enormous wealth which they largely attributed to the existence and functioning of democratic institutions.[79] This was the background against which James Dawson Burn bitterly attacked the decision the American Federation of Labour had taken in 1867 to send delegates to Europe to persuade foreign workers not to emigrate to the United States of America.[80]

But if Alexander MacDonald and the miners' leaders envisaged tremendous social opportunities for miners who could afford to emigrate to America, they were nonetheless vaguely aware of the existence of a class struggle within America. Thus MacDonald, who was on one of his visits to America, described what he regarded as the emergence of American labour as an independent political force:

> The working class of this country are slowly awakening to a sense of their power at the polling booths of the country. In several instances of this they have shown that they will no longer be duped by the Reps or Dems, as the politicians are called . . . The working men have adopted a platform, and on that they have acted with some show of strength. At Cincinnati, Ohio, they concentrated their energy on the return of a working man candidate to Congress, and they carried their point most triumphantly in the return of General Carey.[81]

And later on he welcomed the publication of two American labour newspapers — the *Working Man's Advocate* and the *Monitor* — and expressed the hope that they would be sufficiently powerful to 'smite the oppressors and to defend the oppressed'.[82]

But if the Scottish labour movement could sometimes be outward-looking in the 1860s, it was basically preoccupied with aspects of the national question. Moreover, the most important political question in Scottish politics was the land question; and the questions of land ownership and the on-going Clearances in the Highlands were drama-tised by Alexander Robertson who was better-known as the Chief of Dundonnachie. In the 1850s Robertson contented himself with writing books and pamphlets on the Highland Clearances. However, in 1868 this quiet, studious intellectual was leading Highlanders in Dunkeld into 'direct action' against the landed aristocracy, that is, Highlander against Highlander or, more precisely, Highland-Scots against the Anglo-Scottish exploiters. For already in 1868 the Scottish labour movement was obsessed with the land question; and some of the descendants of the dispossessed Clans who were employed in the mines, mills and factories, alongside the Lowland Presbyterians and the Irish immigrants, engaged in sustained agitations against the landed aristocracy.[83]

In 1868 the Chief of Dundonnachie decided to challenge the Duke of Atholl for taking toll money from Free Church members who used his bridge in Dunkeld on Sundays; and he was supported by the whole of the Scottish labour movement. The *Glasgow Sentinel*, the main working-class newspaper, supported Robertson's direct action methods of struggle in an editorial entitled 'How Highlanders Abolish Tolls: the Revolt of a Clan'.[84] Though troops were called in after he organised several physical attacks on the Duke's bridge and heckled Parliamentary candidates, the Clan's agitation was successful. Indeed, Robertson considered standing as 'a Working Man's Candidate' in the city of Perth in 1878;[85] and in the same year the Roads and Bridges Act abolishing tolls was pushed through Parliament before the labour movement could fight a general election on the land and labour issue. But the vicious, insecure provincial elite had old scores to settle with the Chief of Dundonnachie; and the winners who usually write history portrayed him as an eccentric and threw him into a lunatic asylum. Just as they previously depicted John Duncan, the Dundee Chartist, as a 'lunatic', and just as they subsequently dubbed John MacLean, the famous Clydeside socialist, as a 'lunatic', so they resolved the dilemma of integrating Alexander Robertson into Scottish history by declaring him 'mentally unsettled'.

A price was paid for the legislative achievement of the Roads and Bridges Act of 1878; for Robertson was soon imprisoned for 'slandering' Sheriff Barclay, and, when he was released from prison, he sought legal redress for his grievances. Then he suffered a further spell of imprisonment for assaulting the Lord Justice Clerk. The insecure, witch-hunting provincial elite were not in any doubt about his insanity; but a large number of people supported him and doctors in Perthshire testified to his sanity and secured his release from the lunatic asylum. But the important point to keep in mind is that he was the spokesman for a mass movement.

In contrast to the period down to 1820, when the labour movement was struggling to establish a Scottish people's republic, the nationalist sentiments of the working people were now somewhat inchoate and subterranean. Nevertheless, the political crisis of the mid-1860s provoked the working-class radicals to evoke the name of Sir William Wallace and images of Scotland's lost nationhood. And just as the general election of 1868 was dominated by the land question, so were the agitations over the land question infused with strong Scottish nationalist sentiments.

But if the Scottish nationalism of the labour movement was often inchoate and subterranean, it only took a serious political crisis to bring it out into the open. This was why the printers in the Glasgow Trades Council were opposed to a proposal to send delegates to a trade union conference in London in 1867. James Nicholson told the Glasgow delegates that they ought to organise a conference of the United Trades in Scotland instead of 'sending delegates to London'.[86] Thus the demand for a separate Scottish Trade Union Congress was already articulated before the British TUC was founded in 1868.

Moreover, there was a strong feeling among activists in the Scottish National Reform League that Scottish interests were neglected in the House of Commons; and in 1869 the editor of *The Reformer* argued that the members of Parliament, who were in the process of amending the Trade Union Bill in relation to English trade union objections, had ignored some of the peculiarly *national* problems of the Scottish labour movement.[87] This was why the first conference of the Scottish Confederation of the United Trades was held in Edinburgh in 1870. As the first, if hesitant, attempt to form a Scottish TUC without contemplating breaking away from the rest of the United Kingdom, the foundation of the Scottish TUC in the late nineteenth century was already foreshadowed.

Yet if the nationalist sentiments were still somewhat inchoate, the editor of *The Reformer* described this first meeting of the Confederation of the United Trades as 'our Scottish Labour Parliament'. Moreover, when he singled out what was distinctive in the Scottish labour movement, he made it clear that the ideology of the Scottish Enlightenment was not dead among the spokesmen for organised labour. As he put it: '*Democratic opinion* and *the instinct for self-government* are better grounded in Scotland than in other parts of the country. We owe that partly to the democratic form of Church government which has long prevailed in our northern part of Britain'.[88] However, by the time the Scottish Confederation of the United Trades met again in 1872 in the midst of an outbreak of strikes all over Scotland, the numerical and financial weaknesses of Scottish trade unionism could no longer be concealed.[89] Then the onslaught of the economic recession between 1875-85 caused 'so thorough a setback to Scottish trade unionism that its revival in the later eighteen eighties may be regarded as opening a new phase'.[90]

Small as it was, the Scottish labour movement clung to its distinctive features. For if there was a concrete sense in which the Scottish workers (as distinct from the Irish immigrants) displayed a real capacity for self-government in their trade unions, the real significance of the provincial elite's oft-repeated boast about the unique democratic outlook of the Scots was the separation of the Presbyterian-dominated labour movement from the 'masses'. By constantly emphasising the 'superiority' of indigenous working-class women in contrast to the Irish women who did all the heavier and inferior jobs, the anti-nationalist provincial elite were sharpening the native Scots sense of nationality without dulling their awareness of class oppression.[91]

In the hands of the labour leaders the inherited ideology of the Scottish Enlightenment could sometimes encourage the indigenous workers to vitiate solidarity with the Irish immigrants and to engage in a radicalism of the mouth. Nevertheless, there was a very concrete sense in which Scottish society was more 'democratic' and more 'open' than other capitalist societies; and, though indigenous Presbyterian women frequently refuted some of the mythology about Scottish 'democracy' by doing very menial jobs for a mere pittance, they sometimes found jobs denied to their counterparts elsewhere. This was particularly true of the Scottish nursing profession. As Lavinia L. Dock explained in admittedly bourgeois language: 'The "lady probationer" was never a feature of Scottish hospital life, and the schools are genuinely democratic, candidates, provided they are well educated and have natural refinement, being accepted from all ranks of society'.[92]

Puzzled as English labour historians are by the Scottish working women's evident capacity to 'do more' and to strike more frequently than their English counterparts, the key to this enigma resided in the dual, contradictory use to which the Scottish working classes could put their 'Presbyterianism' and legacy of the Enlightenment.[93] For if the provincial elite often encouraged the notion of the 'superiority' of the indigenous women of the labouring poor and a radicalism of the mouth, this could occasionally be turned to advantage by the proletariat.

At a time when strikes of English working women caused amazement even more than consternation, Scottish working women mounted a whole series of spontaneous strikes. In the Wallace factory, Perth, in 1871, the women workers struck for a ten per cent increase in their wages; and they only called their strike off after they had forced their employers to offer them at least half of what they originally asked for.[94] Then a strike of power-loom weavers in Nithsdale, in 1873, provoked their employers to use the partisan machinery of the law against the six hundred women workers who had struck work for higher wages. Eleven of their leaders were charged in the Sheriff court with breach of contract (the workers in this factory required to give eleven days' notice before they could leave their employment); and Sheriff Hope told them he would not 'exact penalties' if they persuaded the other women to go back to work. However, in spite of the appeals of the leaders the women had thrown up in the course of their struggle, only sixty of the three hundred women were intimidated by the Sheriff's threats.[95]

As the myths about Scottish democracy enabled the provincial elite to undermine the solidarity of labour by using the Irish immigrants as scapegoats for the problems thrown up by a particular capitalist society, it is easy to see why working-class radicalism did not really threaten the status quo. Even the militancy of working-class women could be incorporated into the myth of Scottish democracy; and the temperance commitment of the labour movement seemed to provide further proof of the unique behaviour of the Scottish working class. However, underneath the apparent good behaviour of the artisan-oriented labour movement, an unruly and rumbustious proletariat struggled to articulate the inchoate feelings of the 'voiceless'.

Already isolated from the mass of the workers, whether they were Irish immigrants or natives, by its commitment to what the American labour historian, Peter Sterns, calls the middle-class values of thrift and self-help, the Scottish labour movement deepened this isolation still further by practising Sabbatarianism (that is, by campaigning to keep museums, public houses, galleries and public parks closed on Sundays) and temperance.[96] For if the English labour movement only adhered, in the language of John Saville, 'to the petty-bourgeois values of betterment, thrift and self-help' after the demise of Chartism,[97] the Scottish labour movement had been committed to self-help and temperance from the 1840s. However, the Scottish labour movement's advocacy and practice of temperance now began to create serious problems.

The drink problem was responsible for the demise of the Glasgow Committee of Trades' Delegates in the 1830s;[98] and this sort of experience led labour organisations (except the miners) to impose temperance beliefs on working-class activists in a most rigid and monolithic fashion. For if the English and Irish trade unions met in public houses,[99] a considerable number of their public houses and taverns were owned by former militants who had been victimised for their trade union activity.[100] In contrast to the practice of most of the English and Irish trade unions, the Scottish ones met in temperance coffee houses.[101]

As there was already ample evidence of the disruptive effects of whisky drinking in Scottish social life, anyway, and as the Presbyterian social philosophy had an unshakable grip on the labour movement in the form of Sabbatarianism, self-help and temperance, the consequences were of considerable importance. For if the Scottish labour movement was more radical and class conscious than the English one, it was also more distant from the majority of working people. Furthermore, as Scottish pubs were just drinking dens with no facilities for meetings or social activity, the labour leaders were forced to face a serious problem.

In Lanarkshire and the west of Scotland coalfields generally, where the Irish immigrants were significant numerically and politically, there was no real drink problem *within* the labour movement. As trade union organisation among the miners was weak, anyway, and since the infrequent mass meetings of the miners took place in the open-air, whisky drinking was not so disruptive as it could be in committee meetings elsewhere. But in Fife, where the miners were organised from 1870, whisky drinking did disrupt business meetings. The Association of the United Miners of Fife and Clackmannan were, in 1874, compelled to insert the following new rule into their constitution: 'Any officer, or member, attending a meeting while in a state of intoxication, and disturbing the business, shall be fined sixpence and required to leave the meeting place, if he refuses to leave the meeting place he may be fined an additional sixpence and forcibly removed therefrom'.[102] Yet not even the indigenous Fife miners were, in spite of the provincial elite's propaganda to the contrary, so well-behaved as the artisans.

For if historians of Scottish labour have often seen the Fife miners as 'superior' to the miners in Lanarkshire, the former did not really behave like the artisans in the Trades Councils. In contrast to the organised artisans, who were usually 'respectable', highly literate and 'active churchmen of temperate and puritanical habits',[103] the miners were described by the artisans as 'a lot of serfs'.[104] Nevertheless, the comparative stability of trade unionism among the Fife miners owed a great deal to the fact that the coalfields in the east of Scotland were producing for markets in Germany.

The differences between the social conditions in the Lanarkshire and Fife coalfields inspired observers of the social question – and later on, Kailyard novelists, too – to ignore Lanarkshire and portray Fife as an idyllic, rural community where class conflict was inconceivable. In contrast to Lanarkshire, the Fife coal companies let their houses to their workers on a fourteen days' contract, and this made it more difficult to evict strikers from their homes. But in the west of Scotland striking miners were evicted from their homes after a day's notice; and as the striking miners could pitch tents in the summer months, it is not surprising to find little evidence of strikes in the winter. Nevertheless, sheriff officers in the east of Scotland attributed these social differences to the indigenous Presbyterian culture of the native Fifers rather than a complex interaction of cultural economic factors.

There were certainly very few strikes in the Fife or Clackmannan coalfields in the mid-Victorian period; and contrary to the assertion of R. Page Arnot, the Fife Miners' Association was smashed by the employers in the bitter strike of 1877.[105] By the time the miners' leaders put the Fife and Clackmannan Miners' Association together again in 1879, they could not muster more than a thousand members. Moreover, the Irish immigrants in Lanarkshire were frequently more militant than the indigenous miners; and under the leadership of Alexander MacDonald and Andrew McCowie, the Roman Catholic Scoto-Irishman, repeated attempts were made to unite all the miners. Also it was in the west rather than the east of Scotland that the miners evolved the 'darg' system of restricting output to protect the older and slower workers. However, in the Scottish coalfields as a whole the miners refuted the provincial elite's images of their well-behaved docility by engaging in widespread poaching.

But in spite of the considerable differences between the Fife and Lanarkshire miners, the Presbyterian churches had much less influence on the Scottish miners than on the artisans. One sign of this was seen in the disruption of trade union meetings by drunken delegates in contrast to the more solidly 'respectable' and well-behaved artisans in the Trades Councils. Though the sameness of the miners in Fife and Lanarkshire was more obvious than any differences, the provincial elite still attempted to claim exceptionalism for the social behaviour, self-help and democratic outlook of the indigenous miners of Fife.

However, if religious influences were much less marked among the Scottish miners than the artisans, the three Presbyterian churches — and especially the Free Church — made concerted efforts by means of revivalist meetings to persuade the miners as well as the agricultural labourers to practise self-help, thrift, temperance and sexual restraint by keeping down the rate of illegitimate births. By its imposition of Sabbatarianism and reinforcement of what the left-wing Scottish nationalist literary critic, William Power, described as 'the inhibitions of Gradgrind Calvinism' in the working-class mentality, they contributed to the special misery of capitalism in Scotland relative to elsewhere.[106]

This special misery was the outcome of extreme poverty, extreme authoritarianism and linguistic insecurity. In the form of terrible housing and other social conditions, together with the very gloomy aspects of social life, the special misery of Scottish capitalism was concrete and specific. For just as the legacy of material poverty contributed to this situation, so did the intellectual heritage of the Enlightenment. Besides, if every capitalist society is unique, it is important to identify the specific features of the condition of Scotland question in the mid-Victorian years.

III

The key factor in deepening the special misery of Scottish capitalism was the social behaviour of the provincial elite. As they were Calvinistic, insecure, schizophrenic and aggressive about their 'Scottishness', anyway, they lived in constant fear of the 'masses'. In contrast to the rest of the United Kingdom, where adaptation to an industrial society was accompanied by open social struggles and a vast growth of human awareness through the Condition of England novel, the provincial elite in Scotland promoted silence, conformity and obedience. In a perceptive comment on this overall social situation William Power observed that 'the effect of Calvinistic commercialism and crude industrialism upon the popular imagination was devastating to an extent hardly paralleled elsewhere'.[107]

But if men and women are active agents in the making of history as well as victims, it is clear that the provincial bourgeois elite was just as much responsible for the gloominess of social life as the extreme poverty of the country. Certainly, Karl Marx already recognised the distinctiveness of what he called the 'bourgeois brain' of the philistine entrepreneurs in the west of Scotland in the 1840s and 1850s; and he contrasted the impartial scientific investigations of the English factory inspectors with '*the capitalistic method of thinking*' of their Scottish counterparts. And in contrast to the Scottish factory inspectors who were willing tools and accomplices of a ruthless bourgeoisie, the English ones upheld the rule of law.[108]

Moreover, Karl Marx also observed that trade union organisation among the Scottish farm labourers was very weak; and he described a meeting to organise farm labourers at Lasswade, near Edinburgh, in 1865, as 'an historic event'.[109] But if few of the Scottish contemporaries of Joseph Arch, the leader of the English agricultural labourers, belonged to trade unions in the mid-Victorian period, this was due to specific circumstances. In contrast to some of the English constituencies, where the middle-class Liberals organised the farm labourers into trade unions to provide them with additional electoral support in marginally held Tory seats, the Scots had no ulterior motives for organising the farm labourers.[110] Furthermore, Scottish Liberalism was monolithic and largely unopposed on the electoral plane.

What prevented Scottish society from being a 'totalitarian' one was the cultural resistance of the commonalty. Gradgrind Calvinism certainly had a much greater impact on the Scottish working classes than it did elsewhere; and many working men and women were taught to participate in their own repression. For even below the level of the labour movement — in a situation where most of the activists in the Trades Councils were involved in one or other of the Presbyterian churches — the social behaviour of some of the unorganised men and women bears testimony to their religious commitment and sensibility. Within the context of a repressive, authoritarian society, where 'totalitarian' controls were evident, artisans, farm labourers and miners who wanted to join — or sometimes re-join — one of the Presbyterian churches — did not even require to be prompted before they confessed to 'the sin' of antenuptial fornication.[111]

But in the dialectical interplay of the conflict between traditional pre-industrial and bourgeois ideas, it needs to be emphasised that traditional ideas and attitudes about sex and social life were not always conservative ones. In opposition to the Scottish Enlightenment notion that sexual intercourse should be restricted to the function of pro-creation, many farm labourers and miners clung to the much healthier sexual practices of the pre-industrial peasantry. The survival of traditional ideas about sexual practice found expression in some of the newer folk songs of the miners, farm labourers and industrial workers; but they were practised, too, by working people who defied bourgeois convention by adhering to the traditions of 'hand-fasting' and other forms of 'irregular' marriage.[112] In keeping alive a counter-culture of the 'lower orders' and a tradition of dissent, this form of cultural resistance was just as important as militant trade unionism.

Nevertheless, trade union opposition to the established social order extended beyond 'bread-and-butter' issues: and the Trades Councils campaigned against the land laws, the game-laws and the Criminal Law Amendment Act. They also discussed the possibility of putting forward working-class candidates in Parliamentary elections; but they were thwarted by the lack of finance and the weakness of the trade union movement. In 1873, when the Glasgow Trades Council discussed plans to put up a working-class candidate at the next general election, a quarrel developed about the religious opinions of such a candidate.[113] Moreover, the secularism and Republican sentiments of some trade unionists split the labour movement and inhibited independent political action. As the printers in Edinburgh put it:

A local election instantly transforms the Council into a democratic election committee; the marriage of a member of the reigning family reveals the real tendencies of the men; the visit of a free-thinking Republican lecturer is hailed with delight, and his sage utterances passed from lip to lip as morsels of unsurpassing sweetness; Communist insurgents are sympathised within their most objectionable transactions; and the doctrine enunciated, that 'until there is a universal Republic the world can never enjoy the blessings of peace'.[114]

Clearly, a militant labour movement existed in the 1870s, and militancy and class consciousness were not sudden or abrupt eruptions in the 1880s. The cultural attitudes and the consciousness of class among the vast majority of working people have been hitherto ignored by most Scottish historians, but two distinct, though ascending levels of class consciousness — the elementary and the intermediate — have been defined as 'a fairly accurate perception of class membership on the part of a particular individual' and 'a certain perception of the immediate interests of the class of which one is conscious of being a member'.[115] In both senses the Scottish labour movement was class conscious, and the anti-capitalism of the activists in the labour movement found expression in the manifesto published by the Edinburgh Workmen's Electoral Council immediately after the general election of 1873. A part of it read thus:

> Bitter experience has taught us that common justice for working people is not yet a tenet of Middle-Class interests, we are abandoned the moment we begin to attend to our own. We are still despised as a servile class, and it is for us to wipe out the stain of class-inferiority by incessantly demanding from the legislature equality before the law.[116]

Class consciousness was also expressed in the decision of the Glasgow Trades Council, in 1876, to create 'a consolidation fund to furnish some little assistance to those who, in their struggle with capital, were worsted from the lack of the sinews of war'.[117]

The Scottish labour movement was, therefore, articulating a class consciousness and an inchoate nationalism shared by many unorganised men and women; and it was already searching for new ways forward in a situation of internal colonialism where the provincial bourgeois elite sought to impose conformity and cultural uniformity. Moreover, as working-class militancy and national sentiments were seen as anachronistic and troublesome, the labour movement could not restrict itself to simple 'bread-and-butter' agitations. From 1880 onwards money wage-militancy and nationalist feelings began to coalesce, and the role of working-class nationalism in the fight for a socialist Scotland would become a crucial one.

Notes

1. E.J. Hobsbawm, *Industry and Empire* (London, 1968), p. 264.

2. For statistics on Scottish drunkenness in the 1860s, see the *North British Daily Mail,* 9 January 1867.

3. 'Immorality in Scotland' and 'The Clergy and Immorality', *Glasgow Sentinel,* 23 April 1870, 4 June 1870 and 1 June 1872.

4. Henry Hamilton, *The Industrial Revolution in Scotland* (London, 1966), p. 11.

5. 'An important feature of Scottish labour was its mobility. There is ample evidence of international, geographical and occupational mobility.' T.G. Byers, *The Scottish Economy during the 'Great Depression', 1873-1896,* B.Litt. thesis, University of Glasgow, p. 673.

6. *Eighth Decennial Census of the Population of Scotland, 1871,* Parliamentary Papers, vol. II, 1874, p. xx. Emphasis in original.

7. Ibid., p. xxxiv.

8. Thomas Johnston, *The History of the Working Classes in Scotland* (Glasgow, 1920), p. 335.

9. J. Handley, *The Irish in Modern Scotland* (Cork, 1947), *passim.*

10. A Traveller Underground, *Our Coal and Coal-Pits, the People in Them and the Scenes Around Them* (London, 1856), p. 224.

11. Lord Elcho asserted that the Scottish workers were 'more intelligent' and 'superior' to English working men. *The Times,* 7 July 1867.

12. *The (Edinburgh) Reformer,* 19 December 1868.

13. For a useful critique of the concept of Scottish democracy, see Father Anthony Ross, 'Resurrection', *Whither Scotland,* Duncan Glen (ed.) (London, 1971), pp. 112-27.

14. 'The workmen, and it may be remembered they are Scotch Presbyterians, are clearly in favour of the American system — free and secular education for all.' *Dundee Advertiser,* 30 October 1868.

15. *Edinburgh Review,* vol. CXXVIII, 1868, p. 489.

16. Ibid., p. 490.

17. *The (Edinburgh) Reformer,* 25 March 1871.

18. *Report on Scottish Education for 1871.* Parliamentary Papers, vol. X, 1872. I owe this reference to Mrs Madeleine Monies.

19. 'Scottish democracy was the ideological basis of the Liberal Party in Scotland, but it could not apply to the Irish. Roman Catholic, uneducated, and not too concerned with the dignities of man in the face of a struggle for survival, the Irish working class (and there were not many in any other class) seemed a threat to the Scottish way-of-life.' James Kellas, *The Development of the Liberal Party in Scotland, 1868-1895,* PhD thesis, University of London, 1966, p. 22.

20. 'Secondary Education in Scotland', *North British Daily Mail,* 18 March 1868.

21. S. Mechie, *The Church and Scottish Social Development, 1780-1870* (London, 1960), p. 60.

22. *Edinburgh Review,* vol. CXXVII, 1867, p. 452.

23. *Elementary Schools. Second Report.* Parliamentary Papers, vol XXIX,

1867-8, p. viii.

24. Ibid., p. 156.

25. *Edinburgh Evening Courant,* 19 January 1867.

26. Byers, *Scottish Economy,* p. 693.

27. *North British Daily Mail,* 28 September 1867.

28. *Edinburgh Evening Courant,* 19 January 1867.

29. A.D. Wilson, *Trade Unions and Self-Help* (Edinburgh, 1873), p. 11.

30. 'If articles of that nature were found in a book in Scotland, the school in which it was used would be closed tomorrow.' *Report of the British TUC,* 1879, pp. 34-5.

31. James Scotland, *The History of Scottish Education* (London, 1969), vol. 1, pp. 333-4.

32. Report of Dr Middleton, Church of Scotland, HMI, Parliamentary Papers, vol. XXII, 1871, p. 305.

33. William Ellis, *Combinations and Strikes from the Teacher's Point of View* (London, 1865), p. 1.

34. James D. Young, 'Belt, Book and Blackboard: the Roots of Authoritarianism in Scottish Education', *Scottish International,* September 1972.

35. See the pamphlet, *The Great Reform Demonstration at Glasgow,* 16 October 1866.

36. *North British Daily Mail,* 18 September 1866.

37. On related problems in England, see 'Revolution in Relation to Reform' in Royden Harrison, *Before the Socialists* (London, 1965), pp. 78-136.

38. *North British Daily Mail,* 17 October 1866.

39. Johnston, *Working Classes,* p. 260.

40. F.E. Gillespie, *Labour and Politics in England, 1850-1867* (Durham, 1927), p. 282.

41. See, for example, *Glasgow Sentinel,* 21 July 1877.

42. Sidney Pollard, 'The Economic History of British Shipbuilding, 1870-1914', PhD thesis, University of London, 1951, pp. 207-8.

43. For documentation for the above statements, see James D. Young, 'Working Class and Radical Movements in Scotland and the Revolt from Liberalism, 1866-1900', PhD thesis, University of Stirling, 1974, *passim.*

44. *Glasgow Sentinel,* 2 February 1867.

45. A.D. Bell, 'The Reform League From Its Origins to the Reform Act of 1867', D.Phil. thesis, Oxford, 1961, p. 292.

46. *League Letter Books,* Howell Collection, Bishopsgate Institute, London.

47. *Dunfermline Press,* 5 September 1868.

48. Bell *Reform League,* p. 130.

49. Ibid., p. 336.

50. Ibid., p. 385.

51. Harrison, *Before the Socialists, passim.*

52. W.H. Fraser, 'Trade unions, reform and the general election of 1868 in Scotland', *Scottish Historical Review,* vol. 50, 1971.

53. R. Harrison, 'The British Working Class and the General Election of 1868', *International Review of Social History,* vol. V, 1960, p. 425.

54. Bell, *Reform League,* pp. 292-3.

55. Michael R. Dunsmore, 'The Working Classes, the Reform League and the Reform Movement in Lancashire and Yorkshire', M.A. thesis, University of Sheffield, 1961, p. 22.

56. Ibid., p. 221.

57. Ibid., p. 24.

58. Ibid., p. 222.

59. Ibid., p. 63.

60. Ibid., p. 221.

61. *Dunfermline Press*, 5 September 1868.

62. 'The Scottish Programme for Workmen', *Reynolds Newspaper*, 8 November 1868; *Spectator*, 24 October 1868; *Dundee Advertiser*, 30 October 1868; *Kilmarnock Advertiser*, 30 October 1868; *Edinburgh Reformer*, 26 December 1868.

63. *Glasgow Sentinel*, 11 July 1868.

64. *Scotsman*, 16 July 1868 and the *Minutes of the Edinburgh Trades Council*, 11 August 1868.

65. *Glasgow Sentinel*, 6 June 1868.

66. Harrison, *Before the Socialists*, p. 206.

67. 'In the mid-nineteenth century the Scottish literary tradition – the writing by Scotsmen of fiction and poetry of more than parochial interest – paused; from 1825 to 1880 there is next to nothing worth attention. This was also a period of very heavy emigration – a landslide of people away from the soil. It seems, *prima facie,* likely that the literary break was connected somehow with the social force which was then bursting in upon thousands of Scottish lives.' David Craig, *Scottish Literature and the Scottish People, 1680-1830* (London, 1961), p. 273.

68. 'Emigration, as a cure for unemployment, was a panacea in which the (English) trade union oligarchy itself had little faith.' Royden Harrison, 'The Land and Labour League', *Bulletin of the International Institute of Social History*, vol. VIII, 1953, p. 185.

69. *Glasgow Sentinel*, 12 September 1868.

70. *Blackwood's Edinburgh Magazine*, vol. CXLVI, no. 885, 1889, p. 48.

71. James D. Burn, *A Social Glimpse of the Conditions of the Working Classes during the First Half of the Nineteenth Century* (London, 1868), p. 148.

72. *Glasgow Sentinel*, 20 June 1867.

73. Ibid., 26 January 1867.

74. Ibid., 18 April 1868.

75. *North British Daily Mail*, 16 October 1873.

76. Harrison, *Before the Socialists*, p. 206.

77. Robert Brown, the leader of the Mid and East Lothian miners, worked in the American coalfields during the years 1869-71. *Monthly Circular of the Northumberland Miners' Mutual Confident Association*, February 1918. I wish to thank my friend, Provost David Smith, Dalkeith, for this reference.

78. *Glasgow Sentinel*, 11 July 1868.

79. See the *Address to the People of Scotland,* Scottish National Reform League, Glasgow, 1867.

80. Burn, *A Social Glimpse*, p. 152.

81. *Glasgow Sentinel*, 11 January 1868.

82. Ibid., 30 March 1872.

83. Sources for Alexander Robertson's biography are: Henry Dryerre, *Blairgowrie, Stormont and Strathmore Worthies* (Blairgowrie, 1903); *Glasgow Weekly Herald*, 11 July 1868; *Scotsman*, 13 October 1892.

84. *Glasgow Sentinel*, 18 July 1868.

85. Alexander Robertson's letter indicating his intention to stand as 'a Working Man's Candidate' is pasted into the *Minute Book of the Labour Representation League.* Library of the London School of Economics and Political Science.

86. *Glasgow Sentinel*, 2 March 1867.

87. *The Edinburgh Reformer*, 19 June 1869.

88. Ibid., 12 February 1870.

89. *North British Daily Mail*, 12 June 1872.

90. W.H. Marwick, *A Short History of Labour in Scotland* (Edinburgh, 1967), p. 47.

91. 'Calico Printing and Turkey-Red Dying', *North British Daily Mail*, 18 January 1868.

92. Lavinia L. Dock, *A History of Nursing* (London, 1912), vol. 3, p. 76.

93. Sheila Lewenhak, 'The Lesser Trade Union Organisation of Women than Men', *Bulletin of the Society for the Study of Labour History*, no. 26, 1973, pp. 19-21.

94. *The Times*, 20 November 1871.

95. *North British Daily Mail*, 4 July 1873.

96. Young, *Working Class and Radical Movement in Scotland*, pp. 286-9.

97. John Saville quoted in *Bulletin of the Society for the Study of Labour History*, no. 16, 1968, p. 9.

98. J.D. Burn, *Autobiography of a Beggar Boy* (London, 1855), p. 125.

99. F. and R. Harrison, *Bulletin of the Society for the Study of Labour History*, no. 23, 1971, pp. 81-84.

100. Henry Broadhurst, *The Story of His Life* (London, 1901), p. 92 and A.W. Humphrey, *Robert Applegarth* (Manchester, 1913), p. 125.

101. Young, *Working Class and Radical Movements in Scotland, passim.*

102. Rules and Regulations of the Association of the United Miners of Fife and Clackmannan, Dunfermline, 1874.

103. Marwick, *A Short History*, p. 46.

104. *North British Daily Mail*, 14 November 1868.

105. R. Page Arnot, *A History of the Scottish Miners* (London, 1955), p. 59.

106. William Power, *Literature and Oatmeal* (London, 1935), p. 177.

107. Ibid., p. 83.

108. Karl Marx, *Capital* (London, 1949), p. 275 and p. 298.

109. Ibid., p. 237.

110. W.H. Fraser, *Trade Unions and Society* (London, 1974), *passim.*

111. *Session Minutes of the Kirkintilloch Free Church*, 16 December 1869, 23 April 1878 and *Session Minutes of New Monkland Kirk*, 2 June 1867, 7 July 1872. Scottish Record Office.

112. D. Lennox, 'Working Class Life in Dundee, 1878-1905', unpublished typescript, (n.d., probably 1905), St Andrews University Library, MS DA 890, p. 54.

113. *Glasgow Sentinel*, 6 December 1873.

114. *Scottish Typographical Circular*, vol. III, 1 July 1877.

115. Ralph Miliband, 'Barrave: A Case of Bourgeois Class Consciousness', *Aspects of History and Class Consciousness*, I. Meszaros (ed.) (London, 1971), p. 22.

116. This manifesto was only published in the middle-class press in 1880. See the *Edinburgh Evening Courant*, 19 March 1880.

117. *Glasgow Weekly Herald*, 20 May 1876.

5 THE RISE OF SCOTTISH SOCIALISM AND NATIONAL IDENTITY, 1880-1900

> One feature which stands out prominently in Glasgow is the temporary nature of its citizens' habits. There is no expression of permanency in their social, ethical, industrial, or economic movements. The house will do for a 'whup of dearth'; we sin today and repent tomorrow; the job will last till we get a better; the clothes will pass muster; the food will do for a 'shove past'; and when in debt we borrow another loan. Thousands of citizens live in lodgings like birds of passage, and there is practically no limit to the method of exploitation. Home is almost an unknown quantity, so intense is the feverish rush, and so insecure are the industrial conditions — so fierce is the ever-accelerating competition.[1]

A new and dramatic aspect of Scottish society during the last two decades of the nineteenth century was the renaissance in political and cultural life. As the political and cultural aspects of this renaissance were interwoven with the rise of international socialism, it was absolutely impossible for *bourgeois* nationalism to get a foothold in Scottish society. In a society still stuck in the eighteenth century, where a philistine provincial elite ruled with the authoritarian methods and vision they had inherited from the Scottish Enlightenment, a bourgeois nationalist movement was doomed to isolation from the mainstream of Scottish life. Moreover, as the Scottish renaissance and the emergence of a Scottish identity in the 1880s and 1890s were accomplished by the agitations of the labour movement, nationalist and internationalist sentiments developed hand-in-hand.

When the decade of the 1880s opened, the Scottish labour movement was still small, with a predominantly Presbyterian artisan-oriented outlook, and caught — however unwittingly — in a sometimes self-imposed isolation from the majority of working men and women. Besides, the now perennial problems of inarticulacy, women's oppression, the high levels of crime, drunkenness, illegitimacy and cultural imperialism formed the backcloth against which the labour movement tried to break out of its isolation and ineffectiveness. But if this background was both inhibiting and generally favourable, and if the colossal achievements of the labour movement are to be kept in proper perspective it ought to be appreciated that the Scots had two big advantages working for them. In the first place they tried to break out of their isolation just as a renaissance of international socialism was developing; and secondly the very backwardness of the Scottish labour movement forced it to challenge the Establishment head-on.

It is, moreover, impossible to understand the coalescence of Scottish socialism and nationalism and the social forces that pushed the Scots into the vanguard of international labour unless the problems of cultural imperialism and the authoritarian ethos of late nineteenth century society are kept in the forefront of any analysis of nationalism and the labour movement. For if the Scottish nationalist sentiments of militant men and women had been inchoate and subterranean in previous decades, the very backwardness of the labour movement now forced it to transcend the primary concern with the economic issues that dominated the labour movement in countries where trade unions were much better organised and more influential amongst the 'masses'. Indeed, the struggle for democracy and a Scottish Parliament became, if we may borrow a phrase from Eugene D. Genovese, 'indissolubly linked to the economic struggle'.[2]

The economic problems facing working people, though not new, were nevertheless real enough; and in conditions of savage poverty and authoritarianism, where Scottish working people of diverse ethnic origins began to develop an authentic sense of national identity in the process of class struggle and solidarity on the picket lines, working people also took up a positive stance against the provincial elite who were trying to finish off their distinctive culture. But if an important ingredient in the culture of Scots men and women was their inarticulacy, their inarticulacy did not prevent them from deepening their cultural nationalism. A mixture of the social values and attitudes of the pre-industrial labour force and their responses to living in appalling poverty within an industrial society, this distinctive workers' culture allowed a small number of socialists to transform the labour movement into an agency of social change. Far from being totally conservative or backward-looking, this cultural inheritance inspired the discontent and rebellion of Highland crofters, miners, agricultural labourers and urban industrial workers.

Meanwhile, the Presbyterian, artisan orientation of the Scottish labour movement reinforced the *backwardness* which had been a prominent feature of its existence in the mid-Victorian years; and as it was essentially a very small movement of urban artisans and semi-skilled workers, it is not difficult to see how and why its left-wing Liberal-Labour activists and leaders were destined to play a more conservative role in the new social conditions of the late nineteenth century. Imprisoned in the mythology of the Scottish Enlightenment and proud of the native Presbyterian cultural 'nationalism' which cut them off from the Irish immigrants and the Highland peasants, they were actually inhibiting the emergence of a sense of nationality – of 'identity' – among working men and women of diverse ethnic origins.

On the negative side, the Presbyterian-orientated urban labour movement contributed to deepening the gloom and special misery of social life by campaigning for Sabbatarianism and temperance instead of trying to re-shape the drinking habits and customs of working people. At the annual conferences of the British Trade Union Congress in 1884 and in 1886 *all* the Scottish delegates voted against and thus helped to defeat resolutions from the secularists in the London Trades Council asking for the Sunday opening of national museums and picture galleries;[3] but by then the power of 'the Scottish Sabbatarians' in the trade union branches and Trades Councils was very tenuous and fragile.[4] By 1894 the Aberdeen Trades Council was campaigning for the opening of museums and picture galleries on Sundays;[5] and in Glasgow in 1896 the Jewish tailors were mounting a sustained agitation against temperance and Sabbatarianism.[6] By 1899 they were being supported by the Trades Council, the Secular Society, the Irish National League and the local socialist organisations.[7]

But if a sense of nationality and identity emerged among working men and women, this should not blind the historian to the *class* reality of this national identity. A proper recognition of the class content of this sense of national identity which emerged among working people of diverse ethnic origins – that is, of Lowland Scots, Irish immigrants and Highland peasants – should not be allowed to obscure the legacy of the Scottish Enlightenment as a divisive influence directed at perpetuating ethnic and class divisions amongst working people. Furthermore, as Irish immigrants and Highland migrants constituted a large and important segment of the Scottish working class, the provincial bourgeois elite persisted in attributing the social ills of a class society to the presence and rumbustious and unruly behaviour of the Irish immigrants and their alien ways.

Moreover, in the wider British context of the 1880s, when the general socialist challenge led to the rediscovery of poverty, socialists contributed to the emergence of a Scottish identity – an identity which was at once a class and a national one – by challenging the myths perpetuated by those who had inherited the Scottish Enlightenment. For if the traditions of the past often press down, as Karl Marx suggested after the defeat of the Left in 1848, like a mountain on the brain of the living,[8] the divisive forces unleashed by the provincial elite were ever present.

In contrast to what happened in the mid-Victorian years, however, the provincial elite were no longer allowed to blame the special misery of capitalism in Scotland on the Irish immigrants without being challenged to produce evidence. This is why the members of the Glasgow Presbytery's Commission on the Housing of the Poor in relation to their Social Condition were very annoyed when Bruce Glasier, a leading Scottish socialist, refused to acquiesce in their self-comforting myth that appalling housing conditions were produced by the particular characteristics and habits of the poor. But if they tried to dismiss Glasier's evidence that poverty rather than the ethnic composition of the labour force in Glasgow was the cause of appalling housing conditions, they now — for the first time since the beginning of industrialisation — had to record his analysis of the reasons for a *social question* within the land of social equality and the democratic intellect:

> You are of the opinion that poverty is the chief, if not the only, cause of the crowded and insanitary dwellings of the poor? Exactly. The overcrowding which exists in such districts as at the foot of the Crown, Rose, and Thistle streets, and in the congested parts of Bridgeton, Tradeston, Anderston, and Townhead, is, in your opinion, in most cases, due to poverty; and you know from personal observation that amongst that class of persons there are many families whose position is not due in any measure to drunkenness, or sloth, or any other form of personal misbehaviour? That is so. Some of the saddest cases you know are persons whose condition is due to their poverty and not to their crime? Yes. The persons you refer to are generally labourers, foundry labourers, porters in warehouses, cobblers, old and debilitated workmen, widows with little children, and women and girls, without any male support? Yes, that is the class of persons I refer to. Then a large proportion of the poor in such houses are Irish? Yes. And that is due to the fact that the bulk of them are not craftsmen, and that their fathers had no trade before them? That is so. They get very uncertain work, and their children follow very much on the same lines? Yes.[9]

As the rediscovery of poverty was part of a bigger British response to the socialist challenge that emerged in the decade that began in

1880, the provincial bourgeois elite had no wish to blur the universalistic elements of the culture their predecessors evolved during the Enlightenment in the eighteenth century. However, the universalistic elements of the Scottish Enlightenment had not only been much less developed than they were in, say, France, but they had also sprung from − and had continued to reinforce − a repressive, authoritarian ethos, anyway. Moreover, the perpetuation of the eighteenth century vision − a vision usually at odds with the objective reality − of the 'primitive' nature, 'rudeness' and 'docility' of the 'lower orders' led them to accommodate an obvious dichotomy between their own mythology and the disruptive behaviour of an unruly, rumbustious working class by blaming the Irish elements. This is not very surprising when we remember that their notion of the almost innate democratic intellect of the Scot (including the nineteenth century proletarian) rested on the myth about the greater 'intelligence' and 'superiority' of the Lowland Scots (as distinct from Irish immigrants or Highland migrants).

I

For if it was known from the early nineteenth century that there were already much higher levels of illegitimacy, drunkenness, consumption of alcohol, crime and imprisonment in proportion to population than existed elsewhere in the United Kingdom, it was not until the late nineteenth century that detailed comparative crime statistics were prepared by British governments. These comparative statistics presented the provincial elite with formidable problems in terms of sustaining the myth of the docility and uninflammability of a Scottish working class committed to Presbyterian social values. Perhaps the best way to begin examining the dichotomy between the myths about the so-called exemplary behaviour of working people from the standpoint of bourgeois social values and the objective historical reality is by looking at the problems of drunkenness and illegitimacy.[10]

The problem of illegitimacy had *plagued* the 'Scottish' provincial elite since at least the mid-Victorian years. In the context of the new socialist challenge to the cultural and ideological hegemony of the possessing classes, the socialist critique was implicitly questioning the whole legacy of the Scottish Enlightenment. In response to the socialists' intellectual challenge to their hegemony and within the wider British context of the rediscovery of poverty, the provincial elite took up the challenge by developing social analyses of the problems and peculiarities of Scottish crime, drunkenness, inarticulacy and illegitimacy.

The paradox of the formidable problem of the higher levels of

Scottish illegitimacy than existed elsewhere was admirably summed up by Alfred Leffingwell, an English student of social problems, when he wrote thus:

> The subject of illegitimacy in Scotland deserves a special study, occurring as it does in a country distinguished above every other in Europe by its zeal for orthodox belief.

However, a closer examination of the hard evidence related to this social problem suggested that the high level of Scottish illegitimacy — higher in certain counties than in any part of France except Paris — existed quite independently of ignorance, literacy or poverty.[11] But if the provincial elite — and particularly the Free Church clergymen[12] — could only engage in moralistic attitudinising, they nevertheless attempted to provide some sort of explanation in terms of social causation. For though there had been a diminution of illegitimacy from the mid-Victorian years, and though the decrease of illegitimacy had been significantly greater in the towns than in the country districts, the provincial elite could only explain the exceptionally high Scottish illegitimacy statistics by reference to the Teutonic origins of many working-class Scots.[13]

By being forced to look for the causes of such social problems as drunkenness, inarticulacy, crime and illegitimacy, the provincial elite unwittingly assisted the socialists to undermine the whole mythology of the Scottish Enlightenment — an Enlightenment which had from the eighteenth century onwards vitiated the attempts of radical Scots to provide social explanations of authoritarianism, poverty and oppression and simultaneously stifled the emergence of a permanent and meaningful sense of national identity among all working-class Scots. For while the provincial elite as a whole persisted in trying to sustain the mythology of the Enlightenment, the socialist challenge which forced them to engage in sociological investigations of social problems weakened some of their own myths about the Irish immigrants being responsible for the problems that were really thrown up by capitalist society.

As the provincial elite were forced to recognise the *results* of a much more pervasive and tangible authoritarianism than existed elsewhere in Britain, they created new problems for themselves when they analysed the Scottish social scene from their own class standpoint. In a total social situation where 12.3 per 1,000 persons were imprisoned every year in Scotland against 5.6 per thousand persons in England,[14] it became increasingly difficult to blame everything that was distasteful and obnoxious on the Irish. For in spite of their efforts to explain away the higher levels of crime and imprisonment in Scotland than elsewhere in the United Kingdom by arguing that only 52 per cent of their convicted prisoners were Scots, 4 per cent English and 43 per cent Irish, they had to admit that the number of offenders who paid fines was much smaller in Scotland than in England. Moreover, and since they were still imprisoned by their Enlightenment ideology which led them to argue that the Scottish offenders who ended up in jail were not unwilling to pay fines, the student of the social question can only conclude that Scottish society was either much more authoritarian or that a greater proportion of the Scots were too poor to pay the fines imposed on them.[15]

Besides, if the thinking elements in the provincial elite were too imprisoned in the myths of the so-called Scottish Enlightenment to see that the nature of capitalist society rather than Irish immigrants or the ancient racial origins of Scottish working people was responsible for the high levels of crime, drunkenness, inarticulacy and illegitimacy, outside observers like Alfred Leffingwell could be much more objective. Leffingwell's investigations made it clear that Irish peasant women were 'more solicitous for the chastity of [their] daughters than [their] sisterhood [in] Scotland and England';[16] and in other countries, too, the daughters of the Irish immigrants did little to push up the illegitimacy rates.

Though the daughters of the Irish immigrants did not push up the high levels of illegitimacy in Scotland and thus implicitly challenged the myth of Scottish democracy repeated again and again by such historians as James Kellas that the Irish were responsible for such social problems as bad housing, crime, drunkenness and illegitimacy,[17] the social behaviour of Irish immigrant women (as distinct from men)[18] raises the question of the survival of peasant attitudes and social values among non-industrialised groups who came into an industrial society. For if the provincial bourgeois elite still attempted to foster the elite nativism that came out of the Scottish Enlightenment, the agitations of the labour movement for solidarity on the picket lines produced a new sense of class and national identity in the consciousness of Scottish working people. As the towns and cities were melting pots, where a more unified proletariat emerged from the crucible of industrialisation, a key factor in workers' culture was the survival of their pre-industrial traditions.

As the various non-industrialised groups such as Irish immigrants and

Highland migrants who came into the cities and towns of Lowland Scotland brought different cultures with them, it is not really surprising to discover that they had different attitudes towards sexual behaviour, drink, women, private property and strikes than those being fostered and imposed on them by the provincial elite. Just as the daughters of Irish immigrants in Scotland were generally chaste, so were those of them who took up residence in the United States of America.[19] The common factor was the particular peasant attitudes of the older Irish women towards chastity; and if the chastity of Irish immigrant women ought to have pleased the Scottish elite, they would have been forced to destroy their own myths by offering any sign of recognition of this social reality.

Moreover, as the intellectual critique of Scottish capitalism developed by the socialist minority forced the provincial elite to recognise the social causes of prostitution,[20] the latter counter-attacked by arguing that the diminution of prostitution in the towns and cities had not led to a decline in 'sexual immorality' there.[21] They were, indeed, just as worried by sexual immorality, whether it resulted in illegitimacy or not, as by illegitimacy itself; but they could not bear to admit that the illegitimacy rates, though still the highest in the United Kingdom, had probably come down in the towns and cities as a result of the growing practice of abortion.

But if there had been an occasional awareness in the mid-Victorian years that the illegitimacy rates connected with the feeing markets were sometimes the outcome of rape,[22] the new militancy of working women led the authorities to come face-to-face with the problem of factory women and mill girls who were being raped by foremen and overlookers. This problem came to light in Dundee in the early 1880s when a mill girl ended up in the Sheriff Court after stabbing a foreman who attempted to rape her;[23] but in contrast to the experience of factory women in the north of England, who took action against foremen who were in the habit of raping working women by mounting strikes for their dismissal,[24] Scottish working women seemed to have opted for a more individualistic form of protest.

Nevertheless, if Scottish working women opted for a more personalised and individualistic form of opposition to rape, they were also contributing to the socialists' struggle to re-organise the whole of Scottish society by linking social, economic and cultural agitations against the possessing classes and the social values being fostered by the provincial elite. The older sexual attitudes in the countryside — and to a smaller extent in the towns — and particularly the survival of 'handfasting' and ballads extolling the bawdy and rumbustious sexuality of the peasantry and rural workers gave the authorities cause for concern since their world view was being challenged and defied. It was, moreover, the survival of the traditional attitudes, social values and language of the Scots which gave the minority of socialists in the labour movement so much edge and influence.

Throughout the nineteenth century the United States of America was, as Floyd Dell put it, 'culturally an English colony';[25] and the process of Americanisation was designed to eradicate minority languages, the folk ways and folk memories of immigrants from foreign countries and cultures. Yet just as the Americans were less successful in imposing their brand of English cultural imperialism on national minorities and immigrants, so the native elite in Edinburgh were still striving in the late nineteenth century to destroy Gaelic and the Scots' dialect. Like the native elite in America who failed to destroy the folk memories of immigrant groups from non-industrialised countries,[26] the provincial elite in Scotland faced a similar failure. However, in the Scottish experience the native elite was itself even less culturally authentic than its American counterpart; and the three major ethnic groups which made up the Scottish working class did not simply cling to the old ways in a mood of nostalgic, backward-looking social conservatism but started to fight back — both politically and culturally — through the labour movement.

The context in which the Scottish working class began to fight back to preserve their culture was a political one; a political context shaped by socialists who often had a Gaelic connection. In a very profound sense much of the social and psychological damage — the hidden injuries of class — inflicted on the Scottish working class by a provincial elite committed to their Enlightenment view of the need for an inarticulate proletariat had left its mark, for the Scottish worker was not 'aimlessly talkative'.[27] Moreover, Patrick Geddes was very critical of the functioning of the educational system in the Highlands as it destroyed the children's Gaelic without allowing them to learn English.[28] So in the Highlands as well as in the Lowlands and southern Uplands a whole host of factors were still operating to produce the proliferation of the 'inarticulate Scot'.

A number of perceptive Scots like Patrick Geddes were now aware of the presence of the 'inarticulate Scot', and they were determined to challenge those responsible and seek remedies for this deplorable situation. As the rise of the Crofters' Party in the Highlands in the 1880s gave the Highlanders a voice in the House of Commons for the first time, together with an increasingly socialist dominated labour movement in the Lowlands where the miners' trade unions were now affiliated to the urban Trades Councils in the cities and towns, the economic, political and cultural agitations of the dissident Scots could no longer be ignored by either the provincial elite or their superiors in London.[29]

More than ever before, the distinctive economic, political and cultural agitations of diverse and disparate 'working class' groups in Scottish society were unified in struggle against English cultural imperialism, the dispossession of Highland crofters, exploitation in the mines, fields and factories and even the domination of English socialists. Within this new situation, where John Murdoch, the veteran Highland land agitator and champion of the Gaelic language, was working with Michael Davitt and Irishmen in the coalfields of the west of Scotland to win support for the agitations for Home Rule for Scotland and Ireland,[30] the provincial elite and the Establishment in Westminster found it much more difficult to resist the demand of the Gaelic Society of Inverness for a census of the number of Scots who still spoke Gaelic.[31]

This conflict about the cultural value of Gaelic was fought out within the context of a political renaissance engendered by the labour movement. As the provincial elite and the labour movement were really fighting over the realisation of conflicting versions of a homogeneous society, the Gaelic Society of Inverness achieved a great moral victory when they forced the Registrar General to admit that 71.08 per cent of the population in the north-western division of the Highlands spoke Gaelic with proficiency.[32] It is also interesting that the women in the Fife mining districts only spoke in the older Scots' dialect when they discussed women's problems;[33] and one historian claimed that the appeal of the Kailyard novelists rested on their sympathetic handling of the Scots' dialect in their dialogue.[34]

Moreover, the Scots' dialect was bound up with the political conflict between the provincial elite and the peasantry.[35] For if the authorities claimed that only 4.53 per cent of all Scots spoke Gaelic and English in 1900,[36] the Gaelic Society of Inverness were able to demonstrate that at least 50,000 people in Glasgow alone still spoke the Gaelic language.[37] This linguistic diversity contributed to the same feelings that allowed the socialists to challenge the cultural and ideological hegemony of the possessing classes. As Hugh MacDiarmid put it: 'This class antagonism has been strong in me from the very start: when I was a boy to speak English was to "speak fine", i.e. to ape the gentry, and the very thought of anything of the sort was intolerable'.[38] Besides, the presence of Gaelic-speaking socialists like Duncan MacPherson in the labour movement served the practical purpose of gaining access to workers who did not speak much English.

The crofters in Skye and elsewhere in the Highlands had actually taken and held possession of their lands since 1881;[39] and the labour movement in the Lowlands, where there had long been strong feelings over the land issue, immediately expressed its solidarity with the Skye crofters who opposed the might of British imperialism at the Battle of the Braes. In 1886 the Trades Councils, in common with the bulk of Scottish public opinion, campaigned against the sentences imposed on the Skye crofters;[40] and throughout the late nineteenth century the crofters' leaders, who were often schoolmasters, were followed by Highland policemen and police spies on their frequent trips to meetings organised by the labour movement in Glasgow and Edinburgh.[41]

It was, moreover, claimed that the Skye crofters had been treated very harshly inside prison;[42] and the authorities were worried because the disturbances in the Highlands had radicalised the Free Church and the labour movement.[43] Under the impact of the agitations in the Highlands the socialist elements in the trade union branches and Trades Councils persuaded the labour movement to move from its previous position of demanding reform of the land laws to agitation for land nationalisation. In this new situation of militancy and armed resistance to the Highland lairds, the Highlanders' traditional attachment to the land became a catalyst of social change.

It is impossible to convey the strength of the social forces that pushed Scottish labour into the vanguard of the international socialists movement unless the dimension of the crofters' struggle is kept in mind. William Stewart, the socialist pioneer, noted and stressed the importance of the fact that the Scottish Labour Party was represented at the Second International in 1889 before a Labour Party had been formed in England.[44] In a country where miners and agricultural labourers justified their poaching in terms of 'primitive' socialist or egalitarian social values, and where Highland crofters and Lowland industrial workers shared a common hatred of lairds and landowners, some of the pre-industrial traditions and social attitudes of labouring men and women pushed the labour movement into a new stance of militancy. The radical content of the traditions of the crofters was described by Patrick Geddes: 'Hence then that ineradicable feeling of Highland peasant and Irish crofter of the superiority of "right" over "ownership" in pasture, for him mere might, let Duke of Argyll or

Saxon Parliament say what they may. For where immemorial tradition is the title, what can there be but utter disdain of new-made parchments fetched from town?'.[45] Besides, the members of the Gaelic Society of Inverness were not just appalled by the treatment meted out to the crofters but alienated by 'a hundred years of Enlightenment' which had resulted in 'an increase of fifty additional policemen in one county alone'.[46]

II

A working-class agitation for Scottish self-government and sympathy for the ideals of international socialism developed side-by-side; and in 1881 John Dunn, a rank-and-file miner, took the lead in helping to form a Scottish Labour Party in the Lanarkshire coalfields.[47] Moreover, a small number of very talented Scottish and Irish socialists such as William J. Nairn, Robert Hutcheson, John Armour, Bruce Glasier, John Leslie, James Connolly and John L. McMahon were in the forefront of the activities of the Social Democratic Federation in most Scottish cities. Formed in 1883, the SDF was the first marxist organisation in Britain. Under the leadership of men like H.M. Hyndman, the SDF was in sympathy with the role of British imperialism in conquering colonial peoples.[48]

As most Scottish socialists were sensitive to their own country's subordinate role as an internal colony and hostile to the arrogant English nationalism of John Bull's SDF, they quickly identified with the much more authentic socialism and anti-imperialism of William Morris when he broke away from the SDF in December 1844 to form the Socialist League. However, as they were already in opposition to the wine-drinking, English chauvinism and anti-semitism of men like Hyndman, the Scots were determined to assert their independence from the domineering leadership of the Socialist League in London.

When the Socialist League was set up in London at the end of 1884 a bitter row broke out between the English and Scottish socialists over the questions of policy and party autonomy. The metropolitan leadership of the League was very annoyed because the Scots had set up their own organisation and issued their own membership cards without having had any previous discussions with their comrades in London. This conflict led James Mavor, the Scottish secretary, to inform his counterpart in London of the stance of the Scots in an internal colony where the problems they faced were both distinctive and a product of Scottish conditions:

> We formed ourselves into a branch of the Scottish Land and Labour
> League (the Scottish section of the Socialist League). In these
> circumstances our executive do not see any necessity for seeking
> any authorisation from your executive.[49]

Moreover, the Scottish socialists objected to some of the formulations
in the Socialist League's Manifesto. A.K. Donald, the secretary of the
Edinburgh branch, complained that the denunciation of religion would
'create unnecessary bitterness against us in religious Scotland'.[50] However, as the Scots were prepared to suffer 'family and social ostracism'
by trying to make socialist propaganda 'popular' by organising Sunday
meetings,[51] they were simply asking for their peculiarly Scottish problems to be recognised rather than opting for soft alternative forms of
socialist propaganda.

As the Scots were much more anti-imperialist and outward-looking
than the English socialists in the late nineteenth century, and as their
agitation for Scottish self-government occurred within a carefully
considered perspective of the struggle for international socialism,
no-one in the Second International questioned their right to self-
autonomy. Indeed, the nationalism and self-assertion of the Scots
occurred at a time when the English socialist movement was forced
onto the defensive for its chauvinism and nationalist arrogance. Daniel
De Leon, for example, did not hesitate to attribute the chauvinism of
the English socialist leaders to the 'hereditary mental infirmity' of an
imperialist culture;[52] and John E. Ellam, an intellectual who lived in
Lincolnshire, wrote to De Leon in 1899 to complain about his 'strictures and criticism of English socialism'.[53] This critical dialogue was,
moreover, conducted within the context of a perspective of internationalism in which James Connolly wrote a fraternal, if very critical,
letter to De Leon which foreshadowed his later appreciation of the
role of nationalism in the struggle for socialism:

> We recognise the enormous importance of being duly represented
> among our countrymen in America, and we also hope you will
> perceive how much it would help you, to assist the socialist
> movement in Ireland. Irishmen are largely influenced by sentiment
> and tradition, and therefore a word from what they affectionately
> call the 'auld sod' will far outweigh any amount of reasoning
> applied to a discussion of American issues only.[54]

Before the systematic murder of the Jews in the Nazi concentration

camps in the twentieth century, socialists who adhered to internationalism could still discuss the problems posed by nationalism in a
rational and critical spirit.

So what gave the Scots the edge in their struggle for Home Rule was
the debates within the Second International about the national question and the insularity of English (as distinct from Scottish) socialism.
For Karl Kautsky, the 'Pope of Marxism', was very critical of the
English labour movement. As he put it: 'Even the latest scourings of
their opponents have not served to rouse the proletariat of England.
They remain dumb, even when their hands are rendered powerless,
dumb when their bread is made more costly. The English labourers
today stand lower as a political factor than the labourers of the most
backward country in Europe – Russia'.[55] One does not require to
accept Kautsky's somewhat unfair evaluation of the English labour
movement to see that the Scots' insistence on the need for self-government in their own labour organisations was sometimes motivated by
the general belief that they were being held back by the more 'economistic' orientation of the English labour movement.

When John Ogilvy and Keir Hardie represented the Scottish Labour
Party at the Paris Conference of the Second International they repeatedly interjected when they were called 'English' delegates;[56] and at the
foundation conference of the Scottish Trade Union Congress in 1896
a delegate articulated a sense of nationalism which was political as
well as cultural when he said:

> They had many trades in Scotland carried on under conditions not
> known in England, and they had many questions coming up which
> would not be of any interest to Englishmen or Irishmen. There
> was no reason why they in Scotland should not strike a line for
> themselves. They had dragged England behind them for a long time,
> and he did not see why they should do so any longer.[57]

The coalescence of this political and cultural nationalism ought to be
kept in the forefront of our analysis of the development of the Scottish labour movement in the late nineteenth century. It overshadowed
and dominated everything that led the minority of politically advanced
working men and women to agitate for the Scots Parliament they
wanted to re-organise the whole of civil society. And at the heart of
their dream of a new Scotland was the restoration of the land to the
people.

An activist in English radical politics recorded his impression that

Henry George, though not a socialist himself, had done more 'than any other single person to stir and deepen in this country an agitation which, if not socialist, at least promises to be the mother of socialism.'[58] In contrast to the English Land and Labour League,[59] the Republicans in the Scottish labour movement in the 1870s had not agitated for land nationalisation, and George's subsequent agitation for the nationalisation of the land had an explosive impact on Scottish politics. There were no Scottish social investigators comparable to Charles Booth or the author of *The Bitter Cry of Outcast London*, and George made an important contribution to the growth of socialist sympathies by rediscovering the poverty of the labouring poor. By dramatically directing attention to the hopelessly inadequate living standards of crofters and industrial workers,[60] he challenged the implicit assumption of the provincial elite that the poverty of working people was an inescapable consequence of thriftlessness and indolence.

By tracing poverty, unemployment and inadequate wages back to structural factors within capitalism, Henry George helped to destroy the Scottish labour movement's enchantment with American democracy. The accusation that poverty was created by capitalism struck at the cultural, psychological and spiritual roots of the hegemony existing in Scottish society, and James Leatham, a leading socialist in Aberdeen, subsequently recalled this forgotten aspect of Georgeite propaganda:

> Like Henry George at a later date and from a different opening,
> Marx taught *la Misère* — the intensification of misery, or as
> George called it, the increase of want side-by-side with the
> increase of wealth.[61]

For once the Scottish Land Restoration League had been formed in 1884, the image of America as 'a land of golden opportunity' for working people was increasingly blurred; the class struggle within America was discovered or in some cases rediscovered; and a discovery of widespread poverty among working people in all capitalist countries led a new generation of working-class leaders to look to American labour organisations for ideas, inspiration and moral support.

In September 1884 Bruce Glasier told a mass meeting of Lanarkshire miners that the extension of the franchise would not touch the problems with which the working class was confronted. As he put it:

In America, France and other countries those measures so loudly called for have already been obtained, and the working classes in those countries were as badly off as were the masses in Great Britain. The reason why people were compelled to waste their lives day by day without sufficient reward for their labour was because labour was day by day systematically robbed.

Then Lawrence Gronlund, the secretary of the Socialist Labour Party of America, addressed meetings of the Lanarkshire and Broxburn miners which had been organised by the Glasgow and Edinburgh branches of the Scottish Land and Labour League. Such lectures on the subject of 'Are the Rich growing Richer and the Poor Poorer?' challenged the egalitarian image that American society had hitherto enjoyed among working people. A number of early socialists were influenced by Gronlund, and James Leatham later recalled the enormous influence that Gronlund's book *The Co-operative Commonwealth* had had on socialists in the north of Scotland, including the Shetlands, in the 1880s.[62]

The Georgeites were important catalysts in the growth of socialist trends in the Scottish labour movement, and in the early 1880s the Georgeites and the socialists worked together in propagating both the nationalisation of the land and 'the nationalisation of society'. In Edinburgh Andreas Scheu, an Austrian *emigré,* concentrated on influencing George's supporters. In a letter to Miss Reeves, a member of the Edinburgh branch of the Scottish Land Restoration League, he argued:

> Not that I believe you to be a socialist; but I am well aware that you are supporting a movement which goes very far in the direction of socialism. Two years ago I heard Mr Henry George admit that himself by saying he knew full well that the nationalisation of the land would not solve the social question; but he was convinced that it was a sure step towards bringing that solution about.[63]

But the Georgeites and the socialists were not so much separated by ideology as they were divided by tactics. The Georgeites worked within the Scottish Liberal Association, where they advocated the nationalisation of the land and the introduction of a legal eight hour day, while many of the members of the Scottish Land and Labour League shared William Morris's antipathy for 'the shams' of bourgeois Parliamentary democracy.

The third Reform Act had created a larger working-class electorate, and the local caucus-dominated committees of the Liberal Party had now to confront the challenge of trade unionists and middle-class radicals who were pressing for the acceptance of certain socialist measures and Scottish self-government. *Laissez-faire* Liberalism, with its 'night watchman's' idea of the functions of Government, was henceforth questioned by permeationists who were committed to collectivist solutions to the social problem. The propertied classes had already been frightened by the spectre of German social democracy, and Labour radicals, who belonged to the Scottish Liberal Association, played on these fears in order to persuade the wealthy Liberals to accept a radical programme of social reform.

A profound fear of social revolution was deeply rooted in the consciousness of the provincial elite, and in 1887 a member of the Glasgow branch of the Scottish Land and Labour League described the response of one influential Liberal academic to the new threat to social stability:

I have just come in from the [Glasgow] Philosophical [Society] where I heard Smart deliver a lecture on Factory, Industry and Socialism. Marx almost from beginning to end — vigorous and outspoken — conclusion of the whole matter something like this: 'If we who call ourselves the upper classes do not take Carlyle's advice and become real Captains of Industry and organisers of the people working not for gain but for the good of all, so as to open up to every man the opportunities for a higher life of culture at present the possession of a very few — if we do not do this within a few years, then we shall have to prevent revolution by leading it'.[64]

Nonetheless the Scottish Liberal Association repeatedly rejected the demands of the socialists and the Georgeites for land nationalisation and a legal eight hour day,[65] and the Liberal-Unionists like Lord Melgund, who had just recently left the Liberal Party, criticised the agitations for the disestablishment of the Church of Scotland and Irish Home Rule. In his election address to the people of Selkirk and Peebles, for example, Melgund attacked the 'Irish-American agitators' who were working for 'the creation of a self-independent, disaffected State close to our own shores'.[66]

Moreover, Scottish Liberal-Unionism, in contrast to its English variety, was a conservative rather than a radical social force, and the Scottish Liberal-Unionists were frightened by the land agitators in the

Highlands where the Whigs were being challenged by the Crofters'
Party. And by then John Murdoch, the crofters' leader who had obtained
financial assistance from Dr William Carroll of Philadelphia, owing to
the collapse of his weekly agitational newspaper, *The Highlander,* was
active in the coalfields.[67] Land and labour agitations were increasingly
converging, and what Harry Hanham has perhaps erroneously called
'the porridgy uniformity of the sixties' was being watered down by
the stirrings of discontented socialists and radicals.[68]

Henry George and the land agitations had a catalystic impact on the
miners' leaders in the west of Scotland,[69] and James Keir Hardie subsequently described his own conversion to socialism:

> Some years later, Henry George came to Scotland and I read
> *Progress and Poverty,* which unlocked many of the industrial and
> economic difficulties which beset the mind of the worker trying
> to take an intelligent interest in his own affairs and led me, much
> to George's horror in later life when we met personally, into
> communism.[70]

In the early 1880s George already had connections with Michael
Davitt[71] and John Murdoch, and in 1884 the miners in the west of
Scotland warmly accepted Davitt's advice to agitate for the nationalisation of mineral royalties. Davitt suggested that mineral royalties should
be nationalised and the funds used to provide State insurance for the
miners, and the miners' leaders proceeded to form a Scottish Anti-
Royalty and Labour League.[72] This important development signalised
the beginning of the labour movement's revolt from the values of
laissez-faire Liberalism.

William Small, the influential miners' leader,[73] tried to enlist the
support of other miners' leaders, and John Weir, the secretary of the
Fife and Clackmannan Miners' Association, was in full sympathy with
the agitation for the nationalisation of mineral royalties.[74] Moreover,
Weir and other working-class leaders in Fife were deeply dissatisfied
with orthodox Liberalism, and they proceeded to form branches of
the Fife People's League. The People's League was committed to a
radical labour programme, including the demand for the nationalisation
of the land, Home Rule, the abolition of Royalty and the House of
Lords, and they were financed by Andrew Carnegie. It is difficult to
believe that Carnegie was aware of their agitations for land nationalisation and a legal eight hour day, as he had taken great pains to inform
the members of the Dunfermline Radical Association, in 1887, that

they should not confuse republicanism with socialism.[75]

In any case Carnegie's unwitting contribution to the growth of socialist agitations in Fife was halted by the decision of the executive committee of the Fife and Clackmannan Miners' Association to withhold their support from Small's agitation for the nationalisation of mineral royalties.[76] In the coalfields of the east of Scotland, where there were few Roman Catholic miners of Irish origin, socialism was halted for a few more years. But in the coalfields of the west of Scotland, where a number of Roman Catholic miners were active in the branches of the Irish National League, socialism spread like wildfire. In most Scottish towns, cities and rural areas, a large minority of industrial workers were in sympathy with the agitation for land reform; but in the coalfields of the west of Scotland, where land nationalisation and the nationalisation of mineral royalties were sanctioned and legitimised by the Roman Catholic clergy,[77] socialist ideas transformed the consciousness of the activists in the labour movement.

In October 1887, Michael Davitt addressed a conference of the Knights of Labour in Minneapolis on the Irish question in relation to the American labour movement. In the course of a long speech he told the Knights of Labour that 'the struggle between the classes and the masses in Ireland was but a counterpart of the battles which were being fought in the cause of industrial humanity in every land under the sun'. The Knights then passed a resolution expressing sympathy with the Irish people's struggle for national independence, and they engaged Davitt's services to 'aid in developing their order in Europe'.[78] A few months later John Ferguson,[79] an Irish nationalist, who was working in the Scottish Liberal Association with Labour radicals such as Shaw Maxwell,[80] published a long letter in the *Scottish Leader* entitled 'The Liberal Association and the Organisation of Labour'.

The readers of the *Scottish Leader*, a Liberal newspaper, were informed that the American Knights of Labour had 'again and again' beaten 'railways rings and other capitalistic forces by which Gould and others' had 'exercised despotic control over production'. Then Ferguson made it clear that the leaders of the Irish immigrants in the west of Scotland would organise Scottish branches of the Knights unless the Liberals were prepared to nationalise the land and introduce a legal eight hour day.[81] Andrew Carnegie had already written to Professor J. Stuart Blackie, of Edinburgh, who had been advocating reform of the land laws since the 1860s, recommending the Danish system of land ownership where there was 'a heavily graduated tax on holdings over 25,000 acres'.[82] By 1887 Carnegie was extolling the virtues of Republicanism and land reform before enthusiastic members of the Dunfermline Radical Association and the Glasgow Trades Council, and the Scottish Trades Councils had not yet come out in favour of land nationalisation. And this was the background against which the Knights of Labour developed in the coalfields of the west of Scotland.

Being more susceptible to socialist propaganda than either the Scottish urban workers or the French, German or Russian coal miners,[83] the miners in the west of Scotland were soon attracted by the Knights' radicalism. In August 1888, William Small took the initiative in organising branches of the Sons of Labour 'on the lines of the Knights of Labour'.[84] Secret oaths among agricultural and rural labourers, who were involved in trade union organisation, were perennial, and the miners, who were flocking to the Sons of Labour, decided to conduct their agitations in the coalfields in great secrecy. The Sons of Labour recruited many members during the early months of 1889,[85] but a conflict soon developed between the advocates of secret organisation and those who wanted to organise 'openly in the old fashion'. A decision was then taken to form new organisations on traditional lines.[86]

The Sons of Labour worked alongside the open branches of the County Unions, though the Knights never again enjoyed mass support among the miners. Miners' leaders were still confused about the best tactics to pursue in conditions where the coalowners were quick to suppress strikes by calling on the police and the military, and even committed socialists among the leadership were often caught in a blind impasse. An understanding of socialist theory did not automatically provide a blueprint for trade union tactics, and their inability to provide a miners' programme superior to the one being offered by the Lib-Labs was reflected in the support and inspiration they sought from the American Knights. Small was at the centre of a controversy surrounding secret oaths, and in May 1889, he broke with the Sons of Labour.[87] The new generation of miners' leaders were hectically searching for new ways forward,[88] and in January 1889 Small wrote to Thomas Binning of the Socialist League, in London, asking for the League's 'specific aims' for bringing trade union organisation into 'harmony with the advanced thought of the age'.[89]

As the Sons of Labour lost substantial support in the Lanarkshire coalfields, new branches of the Knights of Labour were formed among the dock labourers and unskilled workers in Glasgow and Ayrshire.[90] American labour organisations still provided the leaders of the advanced thought of the age with inspiration, and in 1890 Shaw Maxwell wrote to Terence V. Powderly as follows:

I am today desired by my friend R.B. Cunninghame Graham, the
president of the Scottish Labour Party and leader of the Eight
Hour Party in the House of Commons to ask of you a special favour.
His motion for an 8 hours Act for the miners of Great Britain is
down for discussion early next month. He is aware of the fact that
8 hours is one of the principal planks of our platform.
His wish is that you should send to him an Autograph letter,
addressed to the House of Commons, and dealing with 8 hours.
A very short letter will do. In it please state the number of Knights
in the States and possibly also Associated bodies, who are all for
the 8 hours movement. A statement from you to him that it is the
general wish of the Workers of America would greatly strengthen
his hands.[91]

However, when the Glasgow Trades Council refused to let the Knights
of Labour affiliate,[92] efforts to popularise land nationalisation and a
legal eight hour day were temporarily halted, though the Knights had
contributed to serious questioning by working-class activists of the
implicit assumptions of *laissez-faire* Liberalism.

A few months before the dramatic Homestead strike Andrew Carnegie,
who was questioned by a reporter representing a Liberal newspaper in
Aberdeen about the importance of the Knights of Labour, replied thus:

Say rather, we had. It was one of these ephemeral organisations
that go up like a rocket and come down like a stick. It was
founded upon false principles, viz., that they should combine
common unskilled labour with skilled.[93]

After the Homestead strike had broken out, the Glasgow Trades Council
denounced Carnegie as 'a new Judas Iscariot', though they thanked
him for 'calling world attention to the plight of labour'.[94] But American
labour was to make a further contribution to the growth of socialist
ideas in the west of Scotland.

The major importance of American labour organisations in the
1890s was that they heightened the class consciousness of some activists in the Scottish labour movement by transforming 'a perception of
class membership' into a commitment to 'advance the interests of the
class' through agitation for the Parliamentary enactment of a legal
eight hour day and the nationalisation of the land. For though working-
class agitations were focused on the need for Parliamentary legislation
rather than an immediate commitment to the revolutionary overthrow

of capitalist society, the propertied classes were not unaware of the implicitly 'revolutionary' threat to the hitherto untouchable rights of private property. In 1867, for example, a trade unionist told a conference of middle-class radicals of the pre-conditions for an alliance: 'If you will support us, if you will labour with us to gain a fair representation in Parliament, we will aid you in seeking private protection for your private property'.[95] By the 1890s a new generation of working-class leaders had little reverence for the rights of private property, and they were increasingly challenging immigration and thrift as solutions to the problems confronting working people.

What American labour did was to heighten Scottish working-class activists' awareness of the problems and tensions created by capitalist society, and in 1896 Jewish workers, who were refugees from the pogroms in Tsarist Russia, formed branches of the International Cigarette Workers' Union[96] and the International Jewish Tailors' Union.[97] Under the leadership of Maurice Hyman they had become revolutionary socialists 'whose class consciousness had arisen to a very high level, and they had won higher wages and shorter hours in struggles with their employers'.[98] They affiliated to the Glasgow Trades Council, and, while they helped to popularise socialists ideas there, they were also convinced of the need for revolutionary socialists to participate in Parliamentary elections. As well as keeping in touch with their parent organisations in America, they continued to work in the labour movement until the twentieth century. By then American labour had had an enormous influence on Scottish working-class activists, and the Scottish Workers' Parliamentary Election Committee, representing all branches of the labour movement, had evolved a socialist programme of social, economic and political demands.[99]

II

The intervention of the Scottish Land Restoration League in the general election of 1885 marked the beginning of 'the pioneer battles for independent labour representation'.[100] Certainly something significant had happened in Scottish politics, and Dr Fred Reid has argued that in the late 1880s, 'the discontent of the working class provided the main basis for divergence between Scottish and English politics'.[101] As the Scottish labour movement under the leadership of men like Keir Hardie, William Small and R.B. Cunninghame Graham was already to the left of the English one, they demanded a Scottish Parliament from a British Government which was refusing to implement their very radical programme of reform.

This agitation for Home Rule permeated the Scottish labour movement from top to bottom; and the Aberdeen Trades Council had been
in the forefront of the agitation for the setting up of a Scots Parliament
before the Scottish Labour Party was formed in 1888.[102] Moreover,
when H.H. Champion stood as a socialist candidate in one of the Aberdeen constituencies in the general election of 1892 before the ardour
for Scottish self-government cooled at the end of the nineteenth century, he kept the agitation for 'Scotch Home Rule' before working-class
electors.[103] In a total social situation where the advanced Liberals under
the leadership of Dr Charles Cameron were at best lukewarm about the
radical demands of the labour movement, it is not surprising to discover
the working-class activists moving further to the left and campaigning
for a Scots Parliament to implement their own programme. Besides,
Dr Charles Cameron's alleged sympathy for the plight and poverty of
working people did not halt this process of radicalisation.

Indeed, if Dr Cameron and the advanced Liberals in Glasgow were
compelled by a militant labour movement to view the labour question
more sympathetically than they had done earlier, the Liberal-Unionists
sometimes chose to champion a radical programme of reform in order
to attract votes. Scottish Liberal-Unionism[104] was shaped by the initial
leadership which included Sir Edward Colebrooke, and, while they
were to the right of their English equivalents, they were capable of
promising a legal eight hour day and other reforms in order to get
the edge on their opponents. R.B. Haldane's Liberal-Unionist opponent
in East Lothian in 1895 promised the working men old age pensions,
poor law reform, a fixed number of holidays for ploughmen, temperance reform and a legal eight hour day for miners.[105] The Liberal-
Unionists did not, however, think of themselves as being to the left
of the Liberals, and in 1900 W. Stroyan, a Liberal-Unionist who was
standing as a Parliamentary candidate in Stirlingshire, told the electors
that 'the Radical remnant which today calls itself the Liberal Party
is not the old Liberal Party'.[106]

The almost impregnable electoral dominance of Scottish Liberalism
— and the provincial elite's insensitivity towards working-class poverty
— had been the key factor in pushing the labour movement to the
left of the English one from 1868 onwards, and this continuity
remained unbroken in circumstances where the labour movement
could only muster a small minority of votes in successive general
elections. Certainly, a large number of Scottish labour leaders were
ambiguous about their attitudes towards the Liberal Party and some of
the social values of this provincial elite, and one historian has used this

fact to prove his argument that the middle-class Liberals were to the left of the labour movement.[107] But the ambiguity of the labour leaders did not prevent them from opposing Liberal candidates in Parliamentary elections, and even when some middle-class Liberals paid lip service to the agitation for the legal eight hour day their hearts were not in it. In 1891 Dr Cameron's *Glasgow Weekly Mail* attributed working-class poverty to drink and improvidence and denied the need for old age pensions by drawing attention to the large amount of money invested by the working classes.[108]

Moreover, there were other signs in the late-Victorian period illuminating just how far the Scottish labour movement was to the left of the English one. The Scottish Trades Union Congress had been under left-wing influence since its foundation in 1896, and it was later to be to the left of the British Trades Union Congress. In 1897 and 1898 the British TUC had failed to persuade a majority of delegates to support resolutions committing the delegates to pay a political levy, and 'even in 1899 the socialists were not strong enough to carry such a scheme'.[109] In 1897 only four of the seventy-four delegates to the Scottish TUC opposed a resolution on collectivism in which it was stated that the workers would not obtain 'the full value of their labour' until 'the land, mines, railways, machinery and industrial capital' were 'owned and controlled by the State';[110] and in 1898 only nineteen of the sixty-nine delegates opposed a resolution urging Scottish trade unionists to 'morally and financially support the working class Socialist Parties already in existence'.[111]

A majority of the delegates to the British TUC in 1899 supported a resolution which gave birth to the Labour Representation Committee. Though this resolution had been drafted in the office of the *Labour Leader*, a number of historians have pointed out that it made no reference to political independence from the Liberals or a socialist basis for the new party.[112] By contrast the Scottish TUC in 1899 accepted unanimously a resolution calling for a new working-class party to fight for the creation of a socialist society.[113] The Scottish Co-operative movement, too, was 'much more socialist and much less averse to political action than the parallel movement in England'.[114] Then in 1900 the Scottish TUC not only adopted a resolution supporting the Scottish Workers' Parliamentary Election Committee, but also accepted their leaders' recommendation that 'trade unionists should contribute at least one penny per quarter per member to the joint committee funds'.[115] A further indication of the labour movement's alienation from middle-class Liberalism was seen in the repeated demand for the second ballot.[116] For in 1900 a delegate explained why the second ballot was important, as well as illustrating the working class electors' attachment to the Liberal Party, when he said: 'If there were a second ballot, electors would have no objection, after the obnoxious candidate was eliminated, in supporting the Labour candidate'.

Clearly then the Scottish labour movement was to the left of the middle-class Liberals as well as to the left of the English labour movement.[117] The fact that Scotland was excluded from the MacDonald-Gladstone entente in 1905 was another sign of the traditional enmity between the Scottish labour movement and the middle-class Liberals; and the two Labour candidates who won seats in Dundee and Glasgow in 1906 did so in the teeth of Liberal opposition. And this Liberal hostility was behind the labour movement's failure to gain Parliamentary representation between 1886 and 1900; for Scottish Liberalism, as G.D.H. Cole put it, 'would have no truck with Labour, even of the old fashioned "Lib-Lab" brand'.[118]

In England the mining constituencies, except in Lancashire, provided the Liberals with their 'firmest' seats;[119] but in Scotland the miners were in the forefront of the struggle for independent labour representation.[120] The miners were also the main force within the Scottish Workers' Parliamentary Representation Committee, and in the general election of 1900 their five candidates polled an aggregate vote of 14,878. But if the Scottish labour movement was to the left of the English one, it was also the left of the majority of working-class electors.

In contrast to the situation in England where at least a third of the working-class electors had always voted Tory since 1868,[121] the Tories in Scotland never made any real impression on the social consciousness of the working class. Throughout the period between 1868 and 1900 the Scottish Tories were to remain a relatively insignificant electoral force, though the Liberals, in 1900, were in a minority for the first time since 1832. An examination of the total votes cast in the general elections of 1865, 1868, 1874, 1880, 1885, 1886, 1892, 1895 and 1900 provides tangible proof of the strength of the Liberal Party since their percentage of the votes in those years adds up to 88.88%, 82.12%, 67.54%, 72.61%, 91.97%, 72.23%, 55.04%, 52.64% and 50.74%. Even after 1885 when the Liberals had to face the challenge of Liberal-Unionism during the general elections of 1886, 1892, 1895 and 1900, the Tory (as distinct from the Liberal-Unionist) percentage of the total votes cast did not exceed 22.82%, 17.06%, 30.98% and 26.11%.[122]

Within an authoritarian society, where Liberalism was a formidable social and political force, Labour candidates were not able to muster very much electoral support. In 1885 five Land and Labour candidates polled a total of 2,462 votes; in 1892 eight Labour candidates polled 5,267 votes; in 1895 eight Labour candidates 4,878 votes; and in 1900 the two defeated Labour candidates, who had official Liberal support, polled 5,902 against the 8,734 votes of their two opponents. In England, where the Liberals usually allowed Labour candidates straight fights against the Tories, the Lib-Labs and independent Labour candidates did much, much better than the Scots. In England eleven Lib-Labs were elected to Parliament in 1885; in 1892 ten Lib-Labs were elected; and in 1900 eight Lib-Labs and two Labour Representation Committee candidates were elected. Furthermore, in England many unsuccessful Labour candidates polled substantial votes.

Now that bourgeois ideas were being subjected to a rigorous scrutiny, if not ideological assault, by new social forces unleashed by a small labour movement, middle-class administrators, intellectuals and medical experts were forced to declare where they stood in relation to socialist agitation. Towards the end of the century a few Presbyterian clergymen came out in favour of socialism; but the Rev. John Clarke, who probably articulated the views of most clergymen, made the implicit ruling-class assumptions about the nature and causes of poverty sharply explicit when he said: 'Much of our poverty and misery is due to our sins and follies. This is overlooked by socialists. Unless the people can be made moral, sober, industrious and thrifty they cannot be improved'.[123] Other representatives of the views of the provincial elite, who nominally opted for what they considered to be socialist remedies to the social problem, recommended what can only be described as fascist notions. Thus Duncan Lennox, a lecturer in social medicine in the University of St Andrews, put forward his own panacea for solving the problems created by poverty when he argued that 'from a socialistic point of view there is still more to be said in favour of State parentage. It must superintend their pre-natal conditions, determine the progenitors, and keep the mothers in ideal hygenic circumstances after delivery'.[124] But history, as Engels observed, is the most cruel of goddesses, and the vast majority of ordinary working people were much slower to take account of the new socialist forces the American labour movement had helped to unleash than the Scottish provincial elite.

Moreover, the growth of a mass labour vote was inhibited by working-class adherence to some of the values of the provincial elite. A majority of working people thought that *they* were responsible for their own poverty, and the ideas of thrift and self-help were deeply rooted in their consciousness. Within the labour movement itself the older Lib-Lab leaders continued to preach the traditional values of thrift and self-help, and even after the miners' unions affiliated to the urban Trades Councils in the late 1880s the Sons of Labour tried to implement the collective self-help the miners had failed to accomplish by raising themselves up to the social level of the artisans.[125] If these ideas lingered on in the labour movement, they still dominated the social consciousness of ordinary working people for the first decade of the twentieth century. As late as 1900 William Nairn, the militant leader of the Social Democratic Federation in Glasgow, was forced to admit that 'the virtue of thrift' was believed in 'by a very large number of the very poor'.[126] Moreover, Scottish workers were more involved in the process of thrift than their English counterparts, and Professor Payne has concluded a careful study of banking in the west of Scotland by arguing that 'in this matter Scottish economic history appears once again to diverge from the so-called "British" pattern'.[127] But when thrift, with the concomitant implications of individualistic self-help, was the antithesis of collectivism, and when working people believed that their poverty was self-created, the Scottish labour movement, under the influence of Henry George, Lawrence Gronlund and the Knights of Labour, had moved far to the left of the vast majority of working-class electors.

Meanwhile Scottish capital and workers continued to move to America; the Americans exported their socialism to Scotland; and Scottish working-class immigrants to America in 1900 sometimes came back to lead militant, rank-and-file, direct action movements in the coalfields.[128]

Notes

1. Murray Kaye, 'The Transformation of Glasgow, III', *Justice*, 26 September 1896.

2. Eugene D. Genovese, *In Red and Black* (New York, 1972), p. 400.

3. *Report of the British TUC*, 1884, p. 47 and the *Minutes of the Glasgow Trades Council*, 18 August 1886.

4. James D. Young, 'Working Class and Radical Movements in Scotland and the Revolt from Liberalism, 1866-1900', PhD thesis, University of Stirling, 1974, p. 288.

5. *Minutes of the Aberdeen Trades Council*, 4 May 1896.

6. *Arbeiter Freind*, 25 July 1896. I owe this reference to my friend Dr Joe Buckman.

7. Young, *Working Class and Radical Movements*, p. 302.

8. Quoted in Ralph Miliband, *Marxism and Politics* (Oxford, 1977), p. 44.

9. *Report of the Commission of the Glasgow Presbytery on the Housing of the*

Poor in relation to their Social Condition (Glasgow, 1891), pp. 22-3.

10. See the frequent debates in Royal Glasgow Philosophical Society in the 1880s and 1890s.

11. Alfred Leffingwell, *Illegitimacy* (London, 1892), pp. 60-4.

12. *Scottish Standard*, 12 March 1892.

13. Dr E. Duncan, 'Some Points on the Social Progress of Scotland in Recent Times', *Proceedings of the Royal Philosophical Society of Glasgow*, vol. XXX, 1898-9, p. 5.

14. *Report of the Departmental Committee on Habitual Offenders, Etc., in Scotland*, Parliamentary Papers, vol. XXXVII, 1895, p. 235.

15. *Report on the Judicial Statistics of Scotland for the Year 1899*, Parliamentary Papers, vol. CIII, 1900, pp. 8-10.

16. Leffingwell, *Illegitimacy*, p. 10.

17. James Kellas, 'The Development of the Liberal Party in Scotland, 1868-1895', PhD thesis, University of London, 1966, p. 26.

18. T.C. Smout, 'Aspects of Sexual Behaviour in Nineteenth Century Scotland', *Social Class in Scotland*, A. Allan MacLaren (ed.) (Edinburgh, 1976), p. 73.

19. Mr and Mrs John Martin, *Feminism* (New York, 1916), p. 213.

20. A.M.B. Meakin, *Women in Transition* (London, 1907), p. 70.

21. Duncan, *Some Points*, p. 5.

22. A Scottish Working Man (Robert Wilson), *Prostitution Suppressible* (Glasgow, 1871), p. 92.

23. Socialist League Archives, F. 274. International Institute of Social History, Amsterdam.

24. A.A. Bulley and M. Whitley, *Women's Work* (London, 1894), pp. 99-100.

25. Floyd Dell, *Love in the Machine Age* (London, 1930), p. 59.

26. Herbert G. Gutman, *Work, Culture and Society* (Oxford, 1977), pp. 72-4.

27. James H. Muir, *Glasgow in 1901* (Glasgow, 1901), p. 189.

28 *The Evergreen*, 1896-7, Part IV, p. 146.

29. Young, *Radical and Working Class Movements*, pp. 158-60.

30. James D. Young, 'John Murdoch: A Land and Labour Pioneer', *Bulletin of the Society for the Study of Labour History*, no. 19, 1969, pp. 22-4.

31. *Transactions of the Gaelic Society of Inverness*, vol. X, 1884, p. 59.

32. *Ninth Decennial Census of the Population of Scotland in 1881*, Parliamentary Papers, vol. LXXVI, 1882, p. xi.

33. Dr Rorie, 'On Some Scots Words, Proverbs and Beliefs', *Proceedings of the Philosophical Society of Glasgow*, vol. XXXI, 1899-1900, pp. 38-45.

34. A.J.G. Mackay, *History of Fife* (Edinburgh, 1895), p. 261.

35. Geoffrey Wagner, 'Lewis Grassic Gibbon and the Use of Lallans for Prose'. *Aberdeen University Review*, vol. XXXIV, 1952, p. 3.

36. *Eleventh Decennial Census of the Population of Scotland in 1901*, Parliamentary Papers, vol. CXXIX, 1902, p. xvii.

37. *Transactions of the Gaelic Society of Inverness*, vol. X, 1884, p. 59.

38. Hugh MacDiarmid, *Lucky Poet* (London, 1972), p. 17.

39. HH 55/78, Scottish Records Office, Edinburgh.

40. HH 1/128 and HH 1/293.

41. Lord Advocate's Papers, Box 116.

42. HH 1/284.

43. *Proceedings of the Free Church of Scotland*, 1884.

44. William Stewart, *James Keir Hardie* (London, 1921), p. 59.

45. *The Evergreen*, 1896, Part III, pp. 49-50.

46. John MacDonald, 'The Social Condition of the Highlands', *Transactions of the Gaelic Society of Inverness*, vol. X, 1883, p. 240.

47. *Labour Standard,* 13 August 1881.

48. For a critique of the Social Democratic Federation, see James D. Young, 'Democracy, Totalitarianism and the British Labour Movement before 1917', *Survey,* vol. 90, 1974, pp. 132-53.

49. Socialist League Archives, K. 2219/3.

50. Ibid., K. 12981/1.

51. Ibid., K. 1543/3.

52. Daniel De Leon, *Flashlights of the Amsterdam Congress* (New York, 1929), p. 133.

53. Socialist Labour Party Archives, Box 36, Folder 3; Wisconsin State Historical Society, Madison, United States of America.

54. Ibid., Box 14, Folder 4.

55. Karl Kautsky, *The Social Revolution* (Chicago, 1902), p. 100.

56. David Lowe, *Souvenirs of Scottish Labour* (Glasgow, 1919), p. 43.

57. *Falkirk Herald,* 2 May 1896.

58. Quoted in H. Lynd, *England in the Eighteen Eighties* (London, 1954), p. 143.

59. R. Harrison, 'The Land and Labour League', *Bulletin of the International of Social History,* vol. VIII, 1953, p. 183.

60. Tom Johnston, *History of the Working Classes in Scotland* (Glasgow, 1920).

61. *The Gateway,* May 1919, p. 18.

62. See James Leatham's letter pasted into the front page of *The Gateway,* vol. VI, National Library of Scotland, Edinburgh.

63. Papers on Andreas Scheu, International Institute of Social History, Amsterdam.

64. Archibald McLaren to R.F. Muirhead, 16 November 1887, McLaren-Muirhead Correspondence, Baillie's Institute, Glasgow.

65. *Minutes of the Scottish Liberal Association,* 22 October and 22 Novembe: 1889, Edinburgh University Library.

66. Address to the Electors of Selkirk and Peebles, June 1886. Melgund contested an English seat instead of the one in Selkirk and Peebles. Minto Papers, Box 175, National Library of Scotland.

67. *Hamilton Advertiser,* 20 September 1884.

68. H.J. Hanham, 'The Problem of Highland Discontent, 1880-1885', *Transactions of the Royal Historical Society,* vol. XIX, 1969, p. 33.

69. *Scottish Co-operator,* February 1903.

70. James Keir Hardie, *Review of Reviews,* June 1906.

71. T.W. Moody, 'Michael Davitt and the British Labour Movement, 1882-1906', *Transactions of the Royal Historical Society,* vol. III, 1953, p. 46.

72. *Hamilton Advertiser,* 20 September 1884.

73. See the Papers of William Small. National Library of Scotland, MSS Acc. 3359.

74. *Dunfermline Journal,* 27 September 1884.

75. Joseph F. Wall, *Andrew Carnegie* (New York, 1970), pp. 447-8.

76. *Dunfermline Journal,* 11 October 1884.

77. *Glasgow Observer,* 11 September 1886.

78. Ibid., 15 October 1887.

79. See the biographical sketch of John Ferguson, *Labour Annual,* 1895.

80. Obituary notice, *Glasgow Herald,* 7 January 1929.

81. *Scottish Leader,* 21 May 1888.

82. Andrew Carnegie to J. Stuart Blackie, 22 April 1884. Blackie letters, MS 2635. National Library of Scotland.

83. See below.

84. *North British Daily Mail*, 27 August 1888.

85. *Hamilton Advertiser*, 25 January, 23 March and 20 April, 1889.

86. Ibid., 11 May 1889.

87. *Falkirk Herald*, 11 May 1889.

88. Fred Reid, 'Keir Hardie's Conversion to Socialism', *Essays in Labour History, 1886-1923*, Asa Briggs and John Saville (eds.) (London, 1971), pp. 17-46. Reid, I think, underestimates the extent to which William Small was also searching for new ways forward.

89. William Small to Comrade Binning, 2 January 1889. Socialist League Archives, miscellaneous.

90. *North British Daily Mail*, 20 January 1890.

91. Shaw Maxwell to Terence V. Powderly, 27 February 1890. I am indebted to Moreau B.C. Chambers, the archivist of the Catholic University of America, Washington, DC, for sending me a copy of this letter.

92. *North British Daily Mail*, 17 April 1890.

93. Andrew Carnegie on Socialism, Labour and Home Rule, an interview reprinted from the *Northern Daily News*, Aberdeen, 23, 24, 26 and 29 September 1892.

92. Wall, *Carnegie*, p. 573.

95. *North British Daily Mail*, 18 September 1867.

96. Rules and Constitution of the International Cigarette-makers Union, FS 7/99, Scottish Records Office.

97. Rules and Constitution of the International Tailors' Union, FS 7/101, Scottish Records Office.

98. *Arbeiter Freind*, 25 July 1896. I owe this reference to Dr Joe Buckman.

99. *Glasgow Weekly Mail*, 3 February 1900.

100. G.D.H. Cole, *British Working Class Politics, 1832-1914* (London, 1941), p. 100.

101. Fred Reid, 'The Early Life and Political Development of James Keir Hardie, 1856-1892', PhD thesis, Oxford, 1969, p. 199.

102. K.D. Buckley, *Trade Unionism in Aberdeen, 1898-1900* (Edinburgh, 1955), p. 95.

103. *Fiery Cross*, 25 June 1892.

104. J.F. McCaffrey, 'The Origins of Liberal Unionism in the west of Scotland', *Scottish Historical Review*, vol. 50, no. 149, p. 53.

105. Election address of W.G. Scott. Haldane Papers, MS 5904, National Library of Scotland.

106. *Stirling Journal*, 14 September 1900.

107. James G. Kellas, 'The Mid-Lanark By-Election (1888) and the Scottish Labour Party (188-1894)', *Parliamentary Affairs*, vol. XVIII, 1965, pp. 318-20.

108. 'State Insurance for Old Age', *Glasgow Weekly Mail*, 5 December 1891.

109. G.D.H. Cole, *A Short History of the British Working Class Movement, 1787-1947* (London, 1952), p. 253.

110. *Report of the Scottish TUC*, 1897, pp. 29-30.

111. Ibid., 1897, pp. 46-7.

112. J.S. Reid, *The Origins of the Labour Party* (Minneapolis, 1955), p. 86.

113. *Report of the Scottish TUC*, 1899, p. 50.

114. Cole, *British Working Class Politics*, p. 155.

115. *Report of the Scottish TUC*, 1900, p. 38.

116. Ibid., 1897, pp. 20-1 and 1900, p. 27.

117. In *The Social Geography of British Elections* (London, 1967), Henry Pelling ascribes the absence of a Lib-Lab pact in Scotland to 'the strength of Scottish Radicalism'. However, he produces very little evidence to back up his judgment.

118. Cole, *British Working Class Politics*, p. 183.

119. Pelling, *Social Geography*, pp. 411-13.

120. P. Poirier, *The Advent of the Labour Party* (London, 1958), p. 79.

121. R. MacKenzie and A. Silver, *Angels in Marble* (London, 1968), p. 243.

122. These percentages have been calculated on the basis of the data and classifications of candidates given in T. Wilkie's book *The Representation of Scotland* (Paisley, 1885), and information in the *North British Daily Mail*.

123. *Dunfermline Press*, 14 January 1900.

124. D. Lennox, 'Working Class Life in Dundee, 1878-1905', unpublished typescript (n.d., probably 1905), p. 54. St Andrews University Library, MS DA 890.

125. *Hamilton Advertiser*, 22 June 1889.

126. William Nairn, *Scottish Co-operator*, 25 January 1901.

127. Peter Payne, 'The Savings Bank of Glasgow, 1838-1914', *Studies in Scottish Business Studies*, ed. Peter Payne (London, 1967), p. 165.

128. 'A conference of unofficial delegates from all the socialist and progressive districts in Lanarkshire was summoned at Hamilton in July 1917, and as a result of its deliberations the Lanarkshire Miners' Reform Committee was founded and the heads of a Manifesto, of which 50,000 copies were to be printed and distributed at the pits, were agreed upon. It is worthy of remark that a prominent part was played in the conference by Lanarkshire men who had experience as officials or members in the United Mineworkers' Union of America, either in Illinois or in British Columbia. Other Scots-Americans were very active in spreading the movement into the eastern counties. Many features of the new programme were consequently drawn from the practice of the American mine-workers.' James D. MacDougall, 'The Scottish Coalminer', *The Nineteenth Century and After*, December 1927, p. 767.

CLASS STRUGGLE IN 'CANNY SCOTLAND'

Just as the 'cautious Scot' myth is an English device, with
which Scottish Nationality has now been everywhere
inspissated in the interests of Anglicisation, so most of the
debased brands of letters and drama are made in England,
or by Scots enslaved by the ubiquitous and incessant
suggesting of the Sassenach — now become in such a great
proportion of cases auto-suggestion.[1]

As the Scottish labour movement failed to muster effective electoral
support, it frequently succumbed to defeatism, introspection and
sectarianism. The continuous internal shift of population into the
towns and cities between 1900 and 1914[2] was paralleled by the intensification of the myth of the Anglo-Scottish bourgeois elite that the
'canny Scot' only began to acquire civilised characteristics after he
came under the influence of the more culturally advanced English
in 1688. This image of the 'canny Scot' functioned as a perceptional
prison in which even militant socialists could not break out of the
illusions about the Scottish labour movement's cultural dependence
on the English.

Moreover, as distinctly Scottish socialist and labour organisations
were being absorbed by English organisations, it was not surprising
that most Scottish activists and thinkers on the left became very
anti-nationalist. Far from promoting a sense of national identity on
the picket lines, Scottish socialists were forced to operate in a milieu
where the provincial elite had again succeeded in splitting and dividing
the working class by using the Irish immigrants as the scapegoats for
the problems thrown up by capitalism. Besides, as Scottish socialists
themselves began to perpetuate the myth that the indigenous working
class was docile, temperate and well-behaved, they unwittingly shored
up the capitalist system by thwarting the class struggle.

As Scottish socialists usually accepted these metropolitan myths
uncritically, they were forced to portray a docile working class that
was seemingly immune to socialist ideas. As James Maxton, who was
already a leading figure in the Independent Labour Party before the
outbreak of the First World War, put it:

The Scottish worker of literature and history is commonly depicted
as a man dour, dogged, honest, hard-working, and superlatively

thrifty. He is the ideal worker from the Sweater's point of view. His eagerness and capacity for labour raise his productive power to a maximum. His honesty renders the cost of supervision very low, while his thriftiness, frugality, and simple way of life incline his wages to the lowest possible point. Such for a long period were cardinal virtues inculcated from school and pulpit as regarded the working man, and as going to school and attending church were the two principal relaxations with which the Scot used to indulge himself, these turned out to be not merely virtues in precept, but practical assets of considerable value to others.

Far from seizing upon Scottish peculiarities to agitate for the self-government that the Scottish Labour Party had seen as the immediate remedy for the problems facing working people in the late nineteenth century, socialists were now acutely aware of their cultural dependency on the English. This was why Maxton described the Scottish labour movement as 'an offshoot' of the English one without any distinctively national characteristics or even unique problems.[3]

Just as English observers regarded Scotland as 'the country where the independent labour movement' began in the 1880s, so metropolitan socialists like H.M. Hyndman now depicted 'the muddy ways of capitalist Liberalism' into which the Scottish labour movement had since fallen.[4] The Scottish socialists' cultural dependency on the metropolitan socialists, together with their uncritical acceptance of the myths of the Anglo-Scottish bourgeois elite, now pushed them to the right of British working-class politics. Moreover, as they failed to develop their earlier critique of Scottish capitalism, ethnic splits were deepened and the myth of the 'canny Scot' impinged on the consciousness of working people to a much greater extent than ever before.

I

But if there was a dialectical relationship between the fact that Scottish working people were much more indoctrinated than their English counterparts and their oppression within a much poorer and more authoritarian country, the metropolitan bourgeois elite and publishing houses frequently 'flattered' the Scots by promoting myths about their superior behaviour and superior status. For example, in his book, *The Condition of England*, C.F.G. Masterman, a leading English Liberal, falsified the picture of the contemporary British scene by drawing comparisons between the Scottish and English working classes in which he sought to fawn upon the former by arguing as follows:

The new Labour members in the House of Commons are often supposed to reveal the 'working man' at last arrived: to be able to reveal a kind of selected sample of the English industrial population. They may perhaps stand for the working man in opinion. The majority of them are certainly remote from him in characteristics. Many are Scotsmen; and there is no deeper gulf than that which yawns between the Scotch and English proletariat. They are mostly men of laborious habits, teetotalers, of intellectual interests, with a belief in the reasonableness of mankind. The English working man is not a teetotaler, has little respect for intellectual interests, and does not in the least degree trouble himself about the reasonableness of mankind.[5]

However, as the Scots were still consuming at least twice as much alcohol as the English, Irish or Welsh, Masterman was clearly more interested in manufacturing myths than in exposing Scottish capitalism and the enormous gulf between the proletariat and the labour movement in Scotland.[6]

Unlike the English rural proletariat, who were afraid to talk about politics in the public house, the rural Scot was well-known for his verbal radicalism.[7] The myth of the 'canny' Scottish farm labourer was accompanied by the 'flattery' of the metropolitan elite about his superior status as a citizen. This point was summed up by George Broderick in the *English Labourers Chronicle*: 'The humblest member of a Presbyterian congregation in Scotland is made to realise that he is a citizen, but the English farm labourer accustomed to depend on the clergyman in spiritual matters, has to depend on the squire for his cottage, and on the farmer for his wages, and does not feel a citizen'.[8] Instead of attacking capitalism where it was most vulnerable, Scottish socialists like William Diack reinforced these metropolitan myths by arguing that 'unlike the English farm labourer, the Scot voted as he liked'.[9] But in conditions of overwhelming Liberal electoral predominance, where neither Tory nor socialist opposition existed in many constituencies, this 'freedom' was virtually meaningless except at the level of mythology.

It is impossible to understand the process by which the Scottish labour movement was largely reintegrated into the existing social order between 1900 and 1914 without identifying the unique features of Scottish capitalism. As the relationship between the unique features of a harsh, brutal and authoritarian society and what Antonio Gramsci called 'civil hegemony' constituted the mechanism by which the provincial elite was able to minimise social tensions, the application of the marxist concept of hegemony ought to illuminate some of the dark by-ways of the Scottish experience.

In spite of outsider's growing awareness of the brutality, oppression and harshness of Scottish capitalism, the provincial elite who articulated the social attitudes and moral values of the British possessing classes managed to minimise class conflict by persuading the majority of Scottish working men and women to accept their values. The general process by which capital imposed its hegemony on labour was explained by Gramsci as follows:

> The normal exercise of hegemony in the area which has become
> classical, that of the parliamentary regime, is characterised by the
> combination of force and consensus which vary in their balance
> with each other, without force exceeding consensus too much.
> Thus it tries to achieve that force should appear to be supported
> by the agreement of the majority, expressed by the so-called organs
> of public opinion — newspapers and associations . . .[10]

However, as Scotland was an internal colony without its own State apparatus, it was necessary for the possessing classes to depend on ideological indoctrination and consensus to a much greater extent than occured in most other modern, industrial societies.

What kept Scotland stuck in the eighteenth century was the Scot's absolute refusal to admit or acknowledge the existence of sharp social tensions between the possessing classes and the working class. With a much harsher Poor Law, a more savage exploitation of labour and greater social insensitivity than existed in the rest of Britain, the provincial elite assisted their superior counterparts in London to promote the image of a docile, apathetic and contented Scottish working class that had no equivalent in western Europe.

A minority of socialists writers like James Leatham attempted to expose the hypocrisy on which the consensus between the contending social classes rested by depicting John Galt, the early-nineteenth-century Scottish novelist as 'the first of the Kailyarders' who inspired the continuity of propagandist images of Scottish society as a rural idyll remote from strife or class conflict.[11] Nevertheless, the dominance of these images in Kailyard novels, together with the systematic indoctrination of working people in church and school, made it exceptionally difficult for the labour movement to popularise their quite moderate critique of the capitalist system.

Yet there was nothing uniquely Scottish about ruling classes refusing to admit or acknowledge class conflict within their own societies at a particular stage in their social development, for the same pattern was discernible in America until the late nineteenth century. This particular feature of American capitalism was described by Edward and Eleanor Marx Aveling in their book on *The Working-Class Movement in America*: 'But of the American novelists none of repute has pictured for us the New York or Boston proletariat. From a double point of view this seems strange. The American is nothing if not descriptive, photographic; and the society in which he lives cries out to be pictured by him. We have portraits of the "ladies", of Daisy Millers, and so forth. But there are no studies of factory hands and of dwellers in tenement houses; no pictures of those sunk in the innermost depths of the modern Inferno. Yet these types will be, must be, dealt with; and one of these days the *Uncle Tom's Cabin of Capitalism* will be written'.[12] Nevertheless within a few years of these observations being formulated by the Avelings bitter strikes between working people and their employers inspired the socialist novels of Jack London, Upton Sinclair and many others. But in the much older capitalist society of Scotland, where serious strikes disturbed the calm of social life between 1910 and 1914, novelists and social reformers still refused to acknowledge the reality of the class struggle.

As Scotland was an internal colony ruled by a provincial elite who did not quite believe in their own political legitimacy, there were two major reasons for their refusal to recognise a class struggle in their own society. Firstly, the Scottish possessing classes were more socially insensitive and indifferent to appalling housing and other social conditions than their English counterparts,[13] and secondly the 'conditions of Scottish life and society' precluded 'the possibility of a distinctive literary class or caste'[14] functioning at a time when the centralisation of British capital was inimical to the survival of Scottish culture. As 'London rather than Edinburgh [was] the literary and artistic capital of Scotland',[15] it was inevitable that even the Scottish labour movement would be culturally dependent on the metropolitan elite. Outside the labour movement altogether an unrepresentative observer of the Scottish scene attributed the Scots refusal to portray political or class conflict in contemporary novels to the cultural dependency which developed during the Scottish Enlightenment.[16]

Besides, it ought to be emphasised that the absence of an independent literary caste facilitated the imposition of English cultural imperialism. Though the number of Gaelic speakers declined from 6.3

per cent of the entire Scottish population in 1891 to 4.3 per cent in 1911, the provincial elite regretted that there seemed 'little likelihood of Gaelic becoming a dead language for many years to come'.[17] But if the 'chief enemy of local dialects [was] the schoolmaster', standard English was being imposed by means of books and newspapers in the remotest villages as well as in the towns and cities.[18] As the 'universal hastening of the decay of the Scots' dialect'[19] gave rise to an abruptness in the speech of the commonalty,[20] teachers increasingly complained of the 'great difficulty' in getting working-class children to 'speak and express their views'.[21]

II

As this working class was made and re-made, everything within the Scottish milieu conspired to keep working men, women and children inarticulate, docile and malleable. But if the Scottish workers were often inarticulate, they were also very volatile and unpredictable. Unfortunately, this inarticulacy and apparent 'docility' impressed outsiders much more than their *potential* to become politically mature and advanced. Yet outsiders had every reason to observe and deplore the social insensitivity of the Scottish possessing classes who held the working class down with very heavy-handed authoritarian methods.

Indeed, social conditions in Scotland were the worst in western Europe and two German students of the social question who visited Scottish cities argued that they had come face to face with 'masses of ragged, barefooted, unwashed and uncombed people, evidently injured by the misuse of alcohol — women as well as men — such as we have never met with before in our lives'.[22] An English observer noted in 1905, 'in the Scotch themselves it awakens mild suprise to hear a Southron express astonishment that one should see, even in mid-winter, so many naked little feet, not in the streets only, but in the very schools'.[23] Moreover, child labour in Scotland was even more brutally exploited than in England,[24] and the social distance between the provincial elite and the working class was so great that the Scottish Poor Law Commissioners who reported their findings in 1909 could not account for the lower level of old age pauperism. As Mrs George Kerr, who was secretary of the Charity Organisation Society in Edinburgh, put it:

Scotland, we find, is again in a better case than England, as the proportion of old age pauperism relative to population is less by nearly a half. The Commissioners are evidently much struck by

this, and have difficulty accounting for it. They hesitate to say
whether it should be attributed to greater self-reliance and thrift,
or a more wholesome recognition of filial responsibility.[25]

By ignoring a social scene in which it was difficult to practise filial
responsibility, the provincial elite was again attempting to keep the
working classes quiet and docile by 'flattering' them about their unique
thriftiness and good behaviour.

Alongside this self-imposed perceptional blindness to the extreme
poverty which led to mass ill-health amongst school children, the
provincial elite's 'flattery' of working men and women was often
mingled with self-righteous social criticism.[26] Rather than create a
tolerant intellectual atmosphere in which social reformers might have
been stimulated to look for the precise causes of extreme Scottish
poverty and mass ill-health, the representatives of a ruthless and particularly insensitive bourgeoisie attributed every specific social problem
to working-class behaviour. For when James Morton, the clerk of the
Glasgow parish council, was asked to explain the reasons for the appalling housing conditions there, he put the blame on working people.
In a comment reflecting the semantic value judgments of his own
class, he said:

> The working classes spend readily on food, drink, dress and
> amusement, but rent is grudged.[27]

The spokesman for the possessing classes were usually irritated when
outsiders asked them awkward questions about the social conditions
of working people, for their own hegemony rested on their myths and
images of a more docile and superior working class than existed elsewhere in Britain. As they still attempted to reconcile the myths they
had inherited from the Scottish Enlightenment with the intrusion of
the reality of a class-torn industrial society, they emphasised the
presence of the alien Irish who were said to be responsible for the social
problems which could not be hidden from outside investigators and
social reformers. This was alluded to by T.F. Henderson and Francis
Watt when they argued thus: 'As has been already noted, the lowest
industrial positions are but seldom filled by native Scotsmen. To meet
the peculiar demand thus created, there has been an enormous Irish
immigration, and in a great number of towns there is a distinct Irish
quarter'.[28] But if the indigenous working class often believed themselves
to be socially superior to the Irish immigrants, the oppression of

women was a universal trait in most working-class communities.

Hidden behind the myths perpetuated by the provincial elite, the extreme poverty and oppression of working people, whether indigenous or immigrant, frequently culminated in death from starvation or wife-beating.[29] It would indeed have been surprising if wife-beating had not existed in a patriarchal, capitalist society, where not even the minority of working-class socialists treated their wives as equals,[30] and yet Scottish (as distinct from English) socialists rarely mentioned the problem of wife-beating until after the First World War. In a retrospective comment on wife-beating in Glasgow, James Leatham wrote: 'A friend who was for a time in low water had to live in a working-class tenement, and his wife assured me that her husband was the only man in the building who did not give his wife the occasional thrashing'.[31] But the actual experience of working women was at odds with the myths that even some outsiders repeated about Scottish women's superior status by comparison with their counterparts elsewhere.

Nevertheless, the impressionistic evidence shows that wife-beating, though real and tangible enough, was not so brutal in Scottish as in English working class communities; and the comparative absence of the extreme violence against women that was well-known in English communities gave rise to a further mythology about the allegedly superior status of Scottish working class women. For just as Eugene A. Hecker argued that Scotland was 'more liberal' (sic!) than England in the treatment of women,[32] so did Jane J. Christie assert that Scottish working men were too dominated by their 'Celtic imagination' to beat their wives.[33] However, the statistics of wife-beating in the Parliamentary blue books told a different story, and when Margaret Sanger came to study municipal socialism in Glasgow in 1913, the gap between the mythology and the reality could no longer be hidden from the outside world. As she put it: 'Throughout the slum section I saw drunken, sodden women whose remaining snag-like teeth sunk down like fangs and protruded from sunken mouths. When I asked one of the executive officers of the corporation why they were so much more degraded than the men, he replied, "Oh, the women of Glasgow are all dirty and low. They're hopeless". "But why should this be", I persisted. His only answer was, "It's their own fault" '.[34]

On the infrequent occasions when the provincial elite were compelled to face the social problems created by the extreme poverty of working men and women, they responded to criticism in a uniform and unconvincing way by using such phrases as 'It's all their own fault'. But if it was much more common for them to perpetuate their myths about the 'superiority' of the indigenous working class, the superior literacy of Scottish men and women in contrast to the Irish immigrants in their midst and the superiority of Scottish 'democracy' and the educational system, they also took refuge behind what Father Anthony Ross calls 'a type of silent censorship in literature and art'.[35]

In a country well-known for its orthodox zeal for the Presbyterian religion, the silent censorship practised by the provincial elite created the perceptional problems that prevented them from analysing Scottish society with any scientific rigour. For though the socialists occasionally criticised some aspects of the extreme authoritarianism of Scottish society such as the excessive flogging of juveniles,[36] they were still too imprisoned in the myths of the possessing classes to release the pent-up forces of resentment and opposition to capitalism. Moreover, if most socialists doubted the existence of inchoate opposition to social injustice, the annual civil and judicial statistics implicitly emphasised the gap that existed between these myths and social reality.

Yet it did not occur to most socialists that there was an enormous contradiction between what James Maxton called 'the Scottish worker of literature and history' and the reality of social life in an internal colony. A profound failure to expose this contradictory situation contributed to the labour movement's comparative isolation from the vast majority of unorganised working people. This had two important consequences. In the first place, it prevented the socialists from fully mobilising the potential forces of social change by building up a strong, anti-capitalist labour movement; and secondly, it has led present-day historians like Robert Roberts to see Scottish social history as a complete enigma.[37]

But if the 'canny Scot' was often the same militant worker who played an important role in the labour movement, it is not too difficult to see why he was, and is in the eyes of present-day historians, something of an enigma. In marked contrast to other labour movements where there were vocal and articulate spokesmen prepared to recognise the role of national peculiarities in shaping — or sometimes in suppressing — working-class consciousness, Scottish socialists increasingly emphasised their cultural and ideological dependency on the English and the Americans. This was particularly evident in the writings of John Carstairs Matheson, a Scottish university graduate and leading theorist in the breakaway Socialist Labour Party, who asserted that 'the political and economic development of Scotland, particularly after the Union of Parliaments in 1707, was practically identical with that of England'.[38]

Just as the labour movement's earlier agitation for Home Rule was beginning to collapse in 1900, so a bourgeois nationalist movement began to fill the vacuum. Yet it could not hope to impinge on working-class consciousness without rejecting capitalism and the major cultural heritage of its own society, the Scottish Enlightenment. However, the bourgeois nationalist movement that arose in the early twentieth century found its heroes in such anti-working-class figures from the past as Sir Archibald Alison,[39] Francis Jeffrey, Walter Scott and Henry Cockburn. As the Scottish nationalists were identifying with the creators of the anti-socialist, anti-class-struggle myth of the 'canny Scot', they were vitiating their own attempts to forge a sense of national identity. Moreover, by criticising the Kailyard school of novelists and comedians for ridiculing their country and by contrasting them with Scott, Jeffrey and James Hogg instead of seeing that Kailyard literature was the logical outcome of the Scottish Enlightenment, they isolated themselves from the mainstream of Scottish life.[40]

Small and isolated as it was, this bourgeois nationalist movement nevertheless succeeded in 1903 in persuading the Convention of Royal Burghs to support its campaign for the extension of the teaching of Scottish history in the State schools.[41] In the absence of Scottish history textbooks for either the schools or the universities, the nationalists had won an empty victory. Yet they challenged the dominant socialist attitude towards cultural questions and forced them to formulate a 'marxist' interpretation of Scottish history.

As the socialists' own isolation from Scottish life encouraged their sectarian intolerance, it was to be expected that they would denounce the nationalists for their anti-socialist utterances. From their particular socialist perspective nationalism simply consisted of a morbid idealisation of a bloody past in which working people had been exploited and oppressed; and they attacked the Young Scots League and the Scottish Patriots for their open associations with the propertied classes whose role was to discourage the 'untutored discontent' of working men and women with capitalist society from developing into a commitment to socialist revolution.

It is somewhat ironical that the Scottish members of the Social Democratic Federation, who were hostile to the English chauvinism and wine-drinking of H.M. Hyndman and other 'soft' metropolitan socialists, were equally unsympathetic to the agitation for Home Rule. As soon as they broke away from the SDF to form the Socialist Labour Party in 1903, they developed a critique of bourgeois nationalism at a time when left-wing nationalists like Morrison Davidson were criticising the use in the Scottish schools of 'sundry manuals of English history liberally leavened with Jingo imperialism'.[42] But if the anti-socialism of nationalist groups like the Young Scots soon aroused the ire of John Carstairs Matheson,[43] it was their conflicting interpretations of Scottish history which preoccupied both the socialists and the nationalists.

Just as Morrison Davidson attacked the leading Scottish newspapers — the *Scotsman,* the *Glasgow Herald,* the *Dundee Advertiser* and the *Aberdeen Free Press* — for not telling 'the truth about the war against the Boers',[44] so did the SLP lambast H.M. Hyndman and his associates for supporting British imperialism.[45] But when it came to judging the role of British imperialism in the Scottish Highlands, John Carstairs Matheson and the SLP argued that the Highlanders 'were no more part of the Scottish nation than the Sioux are part of the American nation'.[46] As the Young Scots replied to these arguments in the pages of *The Socialist,* Matheson asserted that 'our Scottish nationality had its beginning and its end with the schemes of the ruling class'. As the nationalists had just persuaded 'the Scottish Education Department to institute the teaching of Scottish history in the Scottish schools' in 1910, the SLP felt a strong compulsion to criticise the 'attempts to raise the ghost of Scottish nationality'. Moreover, their particular interpretation of Scottish history influenced the general socialist attitude towards what was still happening in the Highlands. Indeed, when Thomas Johnston and the socialist newspaper, *Forward,* supported the Highland Land League's opposition to the eviction of crofters, the SLP attacked them for associating 'socialism in Scotland with a backward agrarian movement'.[47]

An inchoate nationalism survived in the separate existence of the Scottish Workers' Representation Committee before it was absorbed by the British Labour Party in 1909;[48] but the theorists of Scottish socialism were uniformly opposed to bourgeois nationalism *per se.* John Maclean, the famous Clydeside socialist, who joined the SDF in 1903, was just as hostile to the nationalists as Matheson; and in 1912 he also attacked the Young Scots for their anti-socialist utterances. Yet he also supported the nationalists' campaign for Home Rule without displaying any real interest in Gaelic, the Scots' dialect or the agitation to teach Scottish (as distinct from British working-class) history. As he put it: 'It must be borne in mind that, whatever policy we in Scotland choose to adopt, there is a remote — a distinctly remote — chance of a revival of the Scots Parliament, and, therefore, we ought to be ready to make of it a democratic machine, and to use it for all it may produce'.[49]

As modern Scottish history still lacked its chroniclers, anyway, it is clear that the socialists' frequent and often violent denunciations of bourgeois nationalism were influenced by their uncertainty about how to interpret the Scottish experience from a socialist standpoint. Influenced by a creative rather than a mechanical interpretation of history and ever-conscious of the experience of men and women like his grandparents who had been evicted from the Highlands in the mid-Victorian period by an encroaching capitalist economy, John Maclean thought the Highlanders' plight was central to the struggle for a socialist Scotland. This was why he frequently directed attention to the continuing evictions in the Highlands and in 1914 recommended the readers of *Justice* to buy the re-issue of Alexander MacKenzie's book, *The Highland Clearances*.[50] So far from regarding the agitation for Home Rule as a tactical expedient, he was simply articulating his own awareness of the complex relationship between socialism and nationalism.

Moreover, if the Anglo-Scottish concept of the 'canny Scot' was responsible for 'Scottish denationalisation',[51] Maclean frequently attacked the notion that class conflict could not take place in what he ironically called 'canny Scotland'.[52] In December 1911, after the British Socialist Party had been formed, he wanted the Scottish District Council to be replaced by a Scottish National Council.[53] As he increasingly came round to the view that Scotland was what Michael Hechter calls an internal colony, he developed a critique of the Scots subordination to the metropolitan elite in London. He summed up his impressions of the condition of Scotland question by emphasising the need to break out of the political dependence on the London elite:

> It is bad enough for Parliament to allot only a day and a half a
> year to Scotland; it is worse still to have a British Socialist Executive
> without a representative from Scotland.[54]

However, the far-reaching implications of John Maclean's still nominal support for national self-determination were not worked out until after the First World War. Nevertheless the potential of his pre-war working-class nationalism, though usually inchoate and subterranean, to blossom into a full-scale agitation for national independence was obscured by the unified socialist campaign against the celebration of the Battle of Bannockburn. Within the school boards or management committees the socialist minority challenged the possessing classes' interpretation of the role of Robert the Bruce in Scottish history; and they demanded a socialist interpretation of Scottish history within the

State schools. In Kirkcaldy, Joe Westwood told his fellow members of the local school board that Bruce was a 'murderer';[55] and Maclean depicted the Battle of Bannockburn in 1314 as a battle 'by serfs for the benefit of a few barons'.[56]

Yet in contrast to the majority of Scottish socialists, John Maclean implicitly acknowledged the pernicious influence of the myth of the 'canny Scot' in strengthening the hegemony of the official culture. As he saw the sharpening of the class struggle as the only effective way of developing a sense of national identity among native Scots and Irish immigrants in the trade unions and on the picket lines, he always attempted to accentuate the positive opposition-mindedness of working class Scots whether they were indigenous or immigrant. Far more than any other Scottish socialist in the pre-war years, he encouraged working-class self-activity in strikes against employers and trade union leaders like Robert Smillie as the most effective way to shatter the myths about Scottish 'democracy' and the 'canniness' of the proletariat.[57]

Nevertheless the myth of Scottish 'democracy' in education had a sufficient basis in social reality to make the task of socialists like James Maxton a very difficult one. In a poor, backward, authoritarian country where a minority of working-class children 'made it' to the universities, the 'poverty of many students almost demanded a summer vacation of six months'. Moreover, if they 'managed to earn a portion of the wherewithal to support them during the University session',[58] students who were the sons of 'very poor men' came out on strike when they were employed by the Post Office during the Christmas vacations.[59]

But if there was some sort of basis in reality for the myths of the provincial bourgeois elite, they were often reinforced by metropolitan socialists who engaged in the type of 'flattery' of the Scots that kept them from mounting a fundamental challenge to the status quo. This 'flattery' of so-called Scottish superiority inhibited the socialist movement from developing a far-reaching, radical critique of the unique problems faced by a working class subjected to a complex form of colonialism. Though the Scottish socialists were singled out for their 'superior' knowledge of marxism and their 'superior' command of 'logic' engendered by an allegedly 'popular respect for learning that had no counterpart in England',[60] the social tensions in the schools were actually telling a different story.

As has been suggested elsewhere,[61] the least educated sections of the working class were sometimes the most radical and militant; and beneath the social world occupied by many reformist socialists, class consciousness was, under the growing socialist agitation for the enforcement of compulsory attendance in the State schools, manifesting itself in totally new ways. Most socialists were not interested in the content of what was being taught in the schools, and they simply did not realise that the State schools existed to train working-class children to respond to 'more prompt obedience to orders'.[62] Yet such governmental phrases were constantly appearing in local newspapers. Moreover, the educational system was used to inculcate 'good discipline' into the social consciousness of children, and in many schools 'drill formed a good part' of the social discipline of day-to-day life. However, the diverse responses of different working-class groups illustrated the social distance that existed between the workers and most socialists.

Within the labour movement some trade union delegates opposed the socialist agitation for the enforcement of school attendance on the grounds that working-class parents needed the earnings their children were making;[63] and only a small minority of socialists like James Maxton, John Maclean and Alexander Anderson challenged what was being taught in the State schools. Indeed, with the exception of small sects such as the Plebs League, the Socialist Labour Party and a few individual socialists, the members of most socialist groups agitated for more State education without being particularly interested in what was being taught. In the State schools, where there was a long tradition of using education as a means of social control and where children had long been educated in the correct principles of political economy, temperance instruction was introduced — and unopposed by the labour movement — in 1903.[64] This was in keeping with the social vision that most reformist socialists had of working people as sub-humans who were in need of training in manners and good behaviour.

Day-to-day violence in State schools was comparable to the present-day social atmosphere in America described in such books as *Death at an Early Age;* and the first strike of Scottish school children occurred in the large industrial town of Falkirk in 1889. It was a spontaneous strike which soon involved all the schools in the area, and it had erupted at the same time as a wave of industrial militancy.[65] A man, who was to become a leading figure in the SLP later on, described a strike of school children in Glasgow in the early 1890s:

> Resentment at the cruelty of certain of the teachers led to their being mobbed by the boys after school. More than once I took part in waylaying a teacher, booing and hissing and shouting names at him on the way . . . Finally feelings ran so highly that we organised a 'strike'. [66]

In a study of a series of British strikes of school children which erupted in 1911 side-by-side with mass, trade union militancy, Dave Marson has shown that many Scottish children struck against corporal punishment in the State schools.[67]

As brutality and violence in the State schools occurred in a context where a successful career in teaching depended on the ability to 'crush all initiative and individuality',[68] the Scottish Socialist Teachers' Society campaigned against corporal punishment and compulsory home work.[69] But at the same time as John Maclean struggled to oppose the hegemony of the official culture by using the provisions of the Scottish Education Act of 1908 to get Marxism taught in evening classes for working men,[70] he also attacked the myths of the provincial elite by depicting the alleged superiority of Scottish education as 'a thing of the past'.[71] Besides, in contrast to most of the members of the Scottish Socialist Teachers' Society who largely restricted themselves to struggling against the victimisation of the veteran socialist teacher, Alexander Anderson of Stonehouse, he taught working people the ABC of the counter-culture of socialism and the need for political and cultural independence from the myths of the bourgeoisie.

III

Far from the considerable 'labour unrest' of the period leading Scottish socialists to see the relationship between the myth of 'canny Scotland' and their culture and political dependency on the metropolitan elite in London, they frequently sought to justify their own fatalistic political attitudes by denouncing the passivity of working men and women. In a situation where only the land question and trade union agitation gave the socialists any real leverage on the social consciousness of working people, most socialists perpetuated the myth of the thrifty, cautious Scot who was largely immune to socialist propaganda. At a time when the thriftiness of working-class Scots was visibly on the decline,[72] even a perceptive socialist like John Carstairs Matheson repeated some of the myths about the thrifty Scottish artisans.[73]

As the majority of working people 'looked upon socialism as anti-God'[74] and regarded trade unionism as hostile to their conception of what constituted working-class 'respectability',[75] most Scottish socialists engaged in an abstract criticism of working-class life and behaviour instead of participating in the living struggle between the conflicting social and moral values of the possessing classes and the authentic socialism of John Maclean, James Maxton, Alexander Anderson and James D. MacDougall.

The visit of the American socialist, Daniel De Leon, to the town of Falkirk in 1904 seemed to augur well for a more imaginative approach to the problem of popularising socialism amongst working people. By forcing an engineering employer and leading supporter of Henry George to reinstate twenty victimised trade unionists who had been fired for their open socialist activity, the SLP appeared to be breaking with the sectarianism of the past.[76] But they soon fell back into their old sectarian ways and moralistic attitudinising towards workers who were at least occasionally unruly, rumbustious and rebellious. For in 'An Open Letter to the Employees of J. and P. Coates', they articulated their abstract, defeatist and moralistic criticism of working people:

> I am not flattering you, workers of the Paisley Thread Mills when
> I say that you have a reputation for workmanlike ability and
> speed, general self-respect, habits of thrift, and contentment with
> your lot.[77]

As the 'labour unrest' of 1910-14 challenged the myth of a 'canny Scotland' in which there was no reason for class conflict, the management of J. and P. Coates blamed the dyers' strike at Paisley in 1912 on the activities of 'an English trade union organiser'. Yet they vitiated their own attempts to perpetuate the myth of the 'canny Scot' by prohibiting their workers from belonging to trade unions.[78] However, the Scottish bourgeoisie's refusal to acknowledge the eruption of major labour unrest did not arrest the steady growth of the labour movement.

This steady growth of the Scottish labour movement was the most striking development in a society well-known for its parochialism, silent censorship, thought-control and authoritarianism. The membership of the Fife Miners' Union increased from 5,396 in 1900 to 13,570 in 1910;[79] and the Scottish Farm Servants' Union was first founded on a *permanent* basis in 1912. By 1914 they had 8,000 members in various parts of the country and over 130 branches staffed by men who were now displaying a new interest in radical and socialist ideas.[80] Instead of taking advantage of these new political developments to expose the possessing classes' myth of Scottish society as a rural idyll, George Barnes, a trade union organiser, criticised the women workers at the Kilbirnie net works for the 'individualism' and superstition about 'Providence'.[81]

In 1900 a large number of working men and women were indeed dominated by the myths of the provincial elite. A sense of fatalism kept most working people from challenging the employers' poor wages and tyranny; and in 1901 the Scottish Miners' Federation failed to persuade a majority of miners to strike against a twelve per cent cut in their wages.[82] Indeed, a majority of the miners in most of the pits were opposed to a strike; and most socialists were so surprised when workers struck work spontaneously between 1910 and 1914 that they often responded by repeating the myths of the provincial elite about the docile, thrifty and apathetic Scots. Far from saluting the heroism and encouraging the militancy of workers who were taught to think of themselves as uniquely docile, William Stewart, the veteran of the ILP, wrote thus about a strike of three thousand workers at the Vale of Leven turkey-dye works:

> They were an example of frugality and respectability to the entire world . . . They went to the Kirk on Sundays and won football matches on Saturdays. Scottish thrift found its apotheosis in the Vale of Leven.[83]

As the labour unrest was deepened by workers who were increasingly disaffected from 'canny' Scottish society, trade union leaders such as Robert Smillie attacked strikes and developed a 'Don't Strike' campaign within the labour movement.[84] A wide range of strikes in diverse parts of the country led to serious rioting,[85] and ILP leaders like Stewart argued that the most astonishing aspect of the Singers' strike at Clydebank was simply that thousands of male workers had stopped work in order to rectify the grievances of one dozen women'.[86] And in an article criticising Smillie's comments and role in a bitter miners' strike in Ayrshire, John Maclean used the word *riot* in inverted commas to show that such bourgeois attitudes towards striking workers were retarding the growth of a militant labour movement.[87]

The much more cautious role of full-time Scottish trade union leaders, together with the greater repression of labour within an internal colony, prevented the labour unrest from reaching the same pitch of intensity as was seen in England, Ireland and Wales. For the leaders of the Scottish Trades Union Congress the chief gain of the labour unrest was that it had seemingly forced the Government to push through new legislation beneficial to the working classes;[88] and they were often embarrassed and irritated by workers who were challenging their dependence on Parliamentary legislation rather than on mass struggles.

In Glasgow, Edinburgh, Aberdeen and Dundee strikes were accompanied by unprecedented violence and sustained discontent. The dockers' strike in Leith in 1912 was bloody and bitter, and as happened elsewhere the police felt compelled to make baton charges against striking workers. A simultaneous strike of dockers in Glasgow was described by Edward Tupper:

> Glasgow was in the throes of a dock labourers' dispute which was to become a very bitter battle in which dock sheds were burned to the ground, and serious rioting was always ready to break out.
> There were grave disorders, and many baton charges by the police.[89]

But the most unruly 'riot' in the Fife coalfields sprang from a conflict between Michael Lee, a secretary of the Fife Miners' Union, and rank-and-file miners who were provoked by his elitist remarks into assaulting him. When he told a mass meeting of miners that they were 'hooligans', they articulated a new class consciousness by retorting, 'You forget that it is the hooligans who are keeping you'.[90]

Yet this eruption of class consciousness in labour disputes with employers and trade union officials was not reflected in a mass agitation for Parliamentary representation. In 1906 ten labour and socialist candidates polled an aggregate of 33,000 votes.[91] But if there was not 'a single Lib-Lab in Scotland to compensate, as in the English Midlands, for the comparative failure of the independents',[92] the 'uniform hostility of official Liberalism' in Scotland did not prevent the election of two Labour candidates — Alexander Wilkie and George N. Barnes — in Dundee and the Blackfriars division of Glasgow. Moreover, as Scottish Liberalism was, as G.D.H. Cole put it, 'much more bitterly hostile to a labour movement' which contained a strong left-wing element,[93] the provincial elite's myths about the Irish sometimes kept Scottish socialists from creating class unity between the native and the immigrant workers.

The election of George Barnes for the Blackfriars constituency gave the provincial elite another opportunity to perpetuate the myth of 'canny Scotland' where the *indigenous* workers were immune to socialist ideas. As the Liberals made it known that they would not, if elected, introduce an Irish Home Rule Bill, the local branch of the united Irish League asked the Irish to vote Labour. This gave rise to the fallacy within the labour movement at the time that Barnes owed his electoral success to the Irish immigrants, for as Harry McShane, the grand old man of Scottish socialism puts it in his autobiography, *No Mean Fighter*, 'the Irish voted Labour and Barnes was elected'.[94] But as the Irish voters did not count for more than 1,400 out of a total electorate of

7,300 in the Blackfriars constituency, it is clear that some indigenous working men were beginning to move in a socialist direction.[95]

This is not to deny that an increasing minority of Irish immigrants were beginning to identify themselves with the socialist movement. In 1906 a mob of right-wing Roman Catholic workers burnt an effigy of John Wheatley, who fought for a Roman Catholic's right to be a socialist without being excommunicated from the Church, outside his home;[96] but this incident was a reflection of the Roman Catholic hierarchy's worry over the growing influence of socialists amongst the Irish immigrants. But though a priest asserted that the Young Irish immigrants were 'dying like flies of socialism',[97] the revolt of the Irish Roman Catholics was still confined to a minority who would grow in size and influence later on. Moreover, Kellogg Durward, who published a report of his sociological excavations entitled *Among the Fife Miners,* also perpetuated the myth about the differences between the native Fife and the immigrant miners in Lanarkshire when he asserted that the Fife miners did not 'evince the same enthusiasm for fresh movements that many of his brother miners in some other parts of the country do'.[98]

There was certainly a lack of enthusiasm in Fife for the agitation for either direct or independent labour representation in Parliament; and in 1900 only fourteen out of thirty collieries had answered the Miners' Union's previous questionnaire, 'Are you in favour of a Labour candidate?'.[99] Then in 1906 a majority of the members of the union voted against their leaders' campaign for Parliamentary labour representation.[100] Yet such opposition was not confined to Fife. The Scottish Union of Range, Stove and Ornamental Workers refused to support the Scottish Workers' Election Committee or the agitation for working class representation in Parliament;[101] and in 1911 the Stirlingshire Miners' Union voted against the agitation for Parliamentary labour representation.[102]

Yet a small minority of socialists all over Scotland were preparing the way for the dramatic class struggles of the First World War by undertaking systematic propaganda and socialist education. Indeed, the Scottish miners were particularly prone to riotous drunkenness and they consequently alienated themselves from the middle classes.[103] Besides, in contrast to miners elsewhere in western Europe (including the English ones),[104] the Scots displayed what was often a riotous, though serious, sympathy for revolutionary socialism.[105] But if there was little interest in the Fife coalfields in socialist doctrine during the last two decades of the nineteenth century,[106] Lawrence Storione, a remarkably knowledgeable and highly cultured French anarchist, who lived, worked and agitated in the Fife coalfields between 1901 and his death in 1921, organised militant trade union activity, study classes and a socialist Sunday School for miners' children.[107]

In June 1905, Michael Lee, the grandfather of the famous Jennie Lee, joined the SDF;[108] and he was soon followed into it by miners in Cowdenbeath, where Storione was active, Kelty, Kirkcaldy and Methil. As the dramatic and turbulent growth of the Fife coalfields led to Cowdenbeath acquiring the nickname of the 'Chicago of Fife',[109] where the coal companies gave their streets numbers rather than names, the socialist recruits to the SDF attributed their conversion to socialism to the trustification of the coalfields.[110] But just as working-class women in Glasgow were opposed to State interference in their social life in the form of the compulsory medical inspection of school children,[111] so were many miners throughout the Scottish coalfields opposed to what was being called the Servile State. Even in 'canny Fife' anarchists like Lawrence Storione had little difficulty in persuading many miners to oppose State insurance in an attempt to maintain some freedom for labour. Indeed, some of the branches in Fife disaffiliated from the Miners' Union in protest against the trade union leaders' support for the Government's State insurance scheme.[112]

There were, therefore, already signs of a touch of disaffection from the Scottish Establishment in the ranks of the unorganised majority as well as the organised minority of working men and women in the pre-war years. In a situation of emigration, immigration and internal migration, where the composition of the labour force was constantly changing[113] and illuminating Hannah Arendt's concept of 'lawlessness' being 'inherent in all uprooted people',[114] the Scottish labour movement failed to utilise the potential disaffection of the vast majority of working people. Though not without enormous courage, as was seen when such members of the SDF as John Leslie got into trouble with the authorities for running guns to the Russian revolutionaries in 1905,[115] most Scottish socialists, who were few in number, anyway, alienated themselves from working people by their elitism and advocacy of temperance.[116] And by refusing to analyse the Scottish scene from a rigorous socialist standpoint including the myth of the 'canny Scot' and the importance of the land question[117] in the consciousness of working-class Scots, they isolated themselves from an unruly, rumbustious proletariat that was capable of heroic struggle and self-sacrifice.

With the outbreak of the First World War, the most militant sections of the labour movement would articulate the aggressive radicalism of a hitherto voiceless proletariat.

Notes

1. 'Causerie', *Scottish Chapbook*, vol. 1, no. 4, 1922, p. 90.
2. Anthony Slaven, *The Development of the West of Scotland* (London, 1975), pp. 233-4.
3. James Maxton, 'The Working-Class Movement', *Scottish Review*, Winter, 1914, p. 559.
4. H.M. Hyndman, *Further Reminiscences* (London, 1912), pp. 242-3.
5. C.F.G. Masterman, *The Condition of England* (London, 1911), pp. 122-3.
6. Dr Ebenezer Duncan, 'Some Observations on the Consumption of Alcohol', *Proceedings of the Royal Philosophical Society of Glasgow*, vol. XXXIX, 1970-8, p. 177.
7. Christopher Holdenby, *Folk of the Furrow* (London, 1913), p. 161.
8. Quoted in O. Jocelyn Dunlop, *The Farm Labourer* (London, 1913), p. 93.
9. William Diack, 'The Awakening of the Farm Servant', *Scottish Review*, Summer 1914, p. 252.
10. Quoted in James Joll, *Gramsci* (Glasgow, 1977), p. 99.
11. James Leatham, 'John Galt, the First of the Kailyarders', *The Gateway*, mid-August 1920, p. 17.
12. Edward and Eleanor Marx Aveling, *The Working-Class Movement in America* (London, 1891), p. 18.
13. James D. Young, 'The Condition of Scotland Question', *Bulletin of the Society for the Study of Labour History*, no. 36, 1978, p. 43.
14. J.H. Millar, *A Literary History of Scotland* (London, 1903), pp. 682-3.
15. Robert Laird Mackie, *Scotland* (London, 1916), p. 548.
16. Hector MacPherson, 'Development of the Literary Spirit in Scotland', *The Scottish Review*, 7 September 1905.
17. *Report of the Twelfth Decennial Census of Scotland*, Parliamentary Papers, vol. 2, 1913, p. 156.
18. Sir James Wilson, *Lowland Scots as Spoken in the Lower Strathearn District of Perthshire* (Oxford, 1915), p. 13.
19. T.F. Henderson and Francis Watt, *Scotland of Today* (London, 1907), p. 576.
20. Ibid., p. 148.
21. *Stirling Journal*, 29 November 1907.
22. Quoted in W.J. Ashley, *The Progress of the German Working Class* (London, 1904), p. 50.
23. Robert J. Sherard, *The Child Slaves of Britain* (London, 1905), p. 175.
24. *Annual Report of the Principal Lady Inspector of Factories and Workshops*, Parliamentary Papers, vol. XXIX, 1914, p. 644.
25. Mrs George Kerr, *The Path of Social Progress* (Edinburgh, 1912), pp. 159-60.
26. John E. Gorst, *The Children of the Nation* (London, 1907), p. 68 and J.J. Johnston, *Wastage of Child Life* (London, 1909), p. 8.
27. Sherard, *Child Slaves*, p. 184.
28. Henderson and Watt, *Scotland of Today*, p. 389.
29. 'Deaths from Starvation', *Forward*, 25 December 1909.

30. 'Most of the socialists were just like other men in their attitudes in the home. Many of them had big families and lived in appalling conditions, and it was the women who carried the burden.' Harry McShane and Joan Smith, *Harry McShane: No Mean Fighter* (London, 1978), p. 34.

31. James Leatham, 'Glasgow in the Limelight', *The Gateway,* mid-May 1923, p. 5.

32. Eugene A. Hecker, *A Short History of Women's Rights* (New York, 1910), p. 180.

33. Jane J. Christie, *The Advance of Woman* (Philadelphia, 1912), p. 152.

34. Margaret Sanger, *An Autobiography* (London, 1939), pp. 94-8.

35. Hugh MacDiarmid, Campbell MacLean and Anthony Ross, *John Knox* (Edinburgh, 1976), p. 69.

36. Llewellyn W. Williams, 'Flogging in Scotland', *Forward,* 1 January 1910.

37. 'For some reason there was (in 1911) a remarkable difference in the incidence of petty crime in Scotland compared with other countries of the United Kingdom. In England and Wales the number of prisoners received in local gaols was 621 per 100,000 of the population; in Ireland, 744 but in Scotland the rate of the 'unco bad' stood at 1,489.' Robert Roberts, *The Classic Slum* (Harmondsworth, 1971), p. 60.

38. John Carstairs Matheson, 'The Third Estate in Medieval Scotland', *The Socialist,* June 1904.

39. By Caledonian, 'Scottish Home Rule', *The Thistle,* April 1913.

40. William Keith Leask, 'The Revival of Scottish Nationality', Ibid., March 1910.

41. Harry Hanham, *Scottish Nationalism* (London, 1969), p. 127.

42. Morrison Davidson, *Scotland for the Scots* (London, 1902), p. 19.

43. *The Socialist,* July 1905.

44. Davidson, *Scotland for the Scots,* p. 17.

45. Raymond Challinor, *The Origins of British Bolshevism* (London, 1977), pp. 15-16.

46. John Carstairs Matheson, 'Socialism and Nationalism', *The Socialist,* November 1910.

47. John Carstairs Matheson, 'A Reversion. The Folly of National Sentiment', Ibid., May 1910.

48. Frank Bealey and Henry Pelling, *Labour and Politics, 1900-1906* (London, 1958), p. 297.

49. Gael (John Maclean), 'Scottish Notes', *Justice,* 27 July 1912.

50. Ibid., 23 April 1914.

51. C.M. Grieve, *Albyn or Scotland and the Future* (London, 1927), p. 7.

52. Gael, 'Scottish Notes', *Justice,* 13 September 1913.

53. Ibid., 9 December 1911.

54. Ibid., 24 August 1912.

55. *Fife Free Press,* 13 June 1914.

56. Gael, 'Scottish Notes', *Justice,* 25 June 1914.

57. Ibid., 30 August 1913.

58. Henderson and Watt, *Scotland Today,* p. 52.

59. *Justice,* 27 December 1913.

60. T.A. Jackson, *Solo Trumpet* (London, 1953), p. 65.

61. James D. Young, 'Belt, Book and Blackboard: the Roots of Authoritarianism in Scottish Education', *Scottish International,* September 1972.

62. *Stirling Journal,* 9 November 1900.

63. *Report of the Scottish Trades Union Congress,* 1898, p. 34.

64. *Stirling Journal,* 6 November 1903.

65. *Falkirk Herald,* 19 October 1889.

66. Tom Bell, *Pioneering Days* (London, 1941), p. 17.

67. Dave Marson, *Children's Strikes in 1911* (London, 1973), *passim*.

68. C.W. Thomson, *Scottish School Humour* (Glasgow, 1936), p. 38.

69. *Justice,* 9 July 1914.

70. Notes dictated by James D. MacDougall in 1927. John Maclean Papers, Acc. 4251, File 9, National Library of Scotland.

71. Gael, 'Education in Scotland', *Justice,* 23 May 1908.

72. 'Thrift and the Working Classes', *Fife Free Press,* 30 January 1904.

73. J.C.M., 'Savings Banks and Hard Times', *The Socialist,* February 1906.

74. T.N. Graham, *Willie Graham* (London, n.d.), p. 23.

75. Letter from Thomas Don, the secretary of the Dunfermline Trades Council, to Sidney Webb. Webb Collection, Section A, Letter E, Library of the London School of Economics and Political Science.

76. *Falkirk Mail,* 27 August 1904.

77. *The Socialist,* July 1906.

78. *Glasgow Herald,* 23 July 1912.

79. *Dunfermline Journal,* 23 April 1910.

80. Diack, 'The Awakening of the Farm Servant', p. 252.

81. *Glasgow Herald,* 24 May 1913.

82. Circular to District Committees of the Scottish Miners' Federation, 30 March 1901, Dunfermline Public Library.

83. *The Clarion,* 5 January 1912.

84. Robert Smillie, 'Do Strikes Pay?', *Morning Post,* 15 September 1913.

85. *Dunfermline Journal,* 29 January 1910 and *Falkirk Mail,* 30 March 1912 and 22 July 1912.

86. *The Clarion,* 28 April 1911.

87. *Justice,* 20 April 1912.

88. *Report of the Scottish TUC,* 1912, p. 79.

89. Edward Tupper, *Seaman's Torch* (London, 1938), p. 74.

90. *Kirkcaldy Times,* 6 May 1912.

91. G.D.H. Cole, *British Working Class Politics, 1832-1914* (London, 1941), pp. 281-97 and William Diack, 'Now for the Next General Election', *Scottish Review,* Spring 1919, pp. 40-1.

92. Bealey and Pelling, *Labour and Politics,* pp. 270-1.

93. Cole, *British Working Class Politics,* p. 182.

94. McShane and Smith, *No Mean Fighter,* p. 16.

95. *Scotsman,* 6 January 1906.

96. *Forward,* 9 February 1924.

97. McShane and Smith, *No Mean Fighter,* p. 18.

98. Kellogg Durward, *Among the Fife Miners* (London, 1904), p. 3.

99. *Dunfermline Journal,* 4 August 1900.

100. *Scotsman,* 5 January 1906.

101. *Report of the Scottish Union of Range, Stove and Ornamental Workers,* 1906, p. 16.

102. *Falkirk Mail,* 11 February 1911.

103. J.H. Whitehouse, *Problems of a Scottish Provincial Town* (London, 1911), p. 10.

104. Peter Stearns and Harvey Mitchell, *The European Labor Movement, the Working Classes and the Origins of Social Democracy* (Itases, Illinois, 1971), p. 205.

105. *Royal Commission on Labour,* Parliamentary Papers, vol. 2, 1892, Q.10,035.

106. Durward, *Fife Miners,* p. 41.

107. I have gathered a great deal of information about this outstanding but

largely forgotten worker-intellectual from the late Bob Selkirk, Mary Docherty and his granddaughter, Teresa Breslin.

108. *Justice*, 17 June 1905.

109. George Wilson, 'Paying the Price. The Effects of Coalmining on the landscape of part of West Fife', unpublished manuscript, Dunfermline Public Library, p. 38.

110. *Justice*, 2 September 1905.

111. *British Journal of Nursing*, 21 February 1914.

112. *Kirkcaldy Times*, 22 May 1912.

113. 'Glasgow gained 60,000 persons from Renfrewshire in 1891, and a further 38,000 in 1912; at the latter date Glasgow also added 185,000 persons from Lanarkshire.' Slaven, *Development*, p. 233.

114. Quoted by Herbert G. Gutman, *Work, Culture and Society* (Oxford, 1977), p. 68.

115. H.W. Lee and E. Archbold, *Social Democracy in Britain* (London, 1935), pp. 150-2.

116. For information on the problem of drunkenness in working-class communities, see Henderson and Watt, *Scotland of Today*, p. 189.

117. See the confidential report to the Labour Party in London in 1911, where it was stated: 'We were also asked to pay more attention to rural questions because the Land Question dominates everything else. Scotland has stood by the Liberal Government so solidly because it hates the House of Lords and the landlords'. *The Infancy of Labour*, Library of the London School of Economics and Political Science, vol. 2, p. 218.

7 JOHN MACLEAN, THE SCOTTISH LITERARY RENAISSANCE AND WORLD REVOLUTION, 1914–1931

Keir Hardie became the leader of British socialism (and his Independent Labour Party had its firmest base on the Clyde), James Ramsay MacDonald, the first Labour Prime Minister, and Clydeside became, during the First World War, the synonym for revolutionary agitation . . . The collapse of Scots industry between the wars halted this development, and turned a derelict country in upon itself. This is perhaps most visible in the fringe phenomena of a Scottish nationalist culture, which sought to create a literature in the artificially archaic idiom of 'Lallans', in accessible to most outsiders, and indeed to most Scotsmen.[1]

E.J. Hobsbawm

Scotland is nowhere more Scots, in the sense of being turbulent, than in the Second City: 'Scenes' at Westminster are the natural, spontaneous expression of the national character, and it never had more legitimate reason for flaring up than it has in these days of governmental ineptitude and frank reaction, with, oddly enough, a Glasgow representative at the head of it.[2]

James Leatham

As jingoism was at 'a discount in Glasgow from the very beginning of the war',[3] the Anglo-Scottish bourgeois elite unwittingly unleashed new social forces by pushing up house rents, persecuting John Maclean and harassing trade union militants and anti-war activists. Yet by creating the stimulus for the Scottish literary renaissance, the First World War gave the Scots their first real opportunity to lift themselves out of the eighteenth century rut in which they were still stuck in 1914. For while Clydeside became the synonym for 'revolutionary agitation' during the war, the myth of the 'canny Scot' was shattered by the spontaneous mass militancy and anti-militarism of the Scottish working class.

The anti-war stance of the Scottish labour movement was already evident in 1914; and in Glasgow in 1915 John Maclean told a May Day rally attended by 50,000 working men and women that they ought to fight for 'freedom and liberty at home before going to Flanders to die for it'.[4] At the same time as the Scottish socialists were conducting a vigorous campaign against the war, rent increases, appalling housing conditions and poor wages, the workers who moved into the shipyards, workshops and munitions factories on Clydeside 'turned to Marx, because they found in him convincing proof of their belief in the evil of capitalism and the reality of the class war'.[5] Moreover, as the agitation against the war was intensified, the labour movement grew in size and influence.

In the dialectical interplay between general working-class militancy, the housing agitation, anti-militarism and socialist propaganda, it is important to emphasise that the socialist leaders – for example, John Maclean, James Maxton, James D. MacDougall and Robert Smillie – were just as strongly influenced by the workers' spontaneous struggles as the workers were galvanised into action by socialist propaganda and deeds. The housing question was certainly raised before the war;[6] but the differences between the pre-war and the war agitation was summed up by the Royal Commission on Scottish Housing in 1917: 'Before the war, the demand for better housing had become articulate; today, after three years of war, it is too insistent to be safely disregarded any longer'.[7] Though Scottish housing conditions were the worst in Europe,[8] Patrick Geddes had so little faith in the militancy of the Scottish workers who occupied the one-and two-room tenements that he attributed the initial discontent with their housing conditions to 'the transference of some hundreds of workmen from Woolwich to the Clyde'.[9]

But if the rent strikes on the Clydeside forced the Government to introduce the Rent Restriction Act in November, 1915,[10] the housing agitation was led by the labour movement.[11] Though the labour movement's success depended on the spontaneous militancy of women munitions workers – and the wives and children of soldiers fighting overseas who carried banners bearing the slogan, 'We are fighting the Huns at home'[12] – *Forward* sought to deepen the anti-war sentiments of the rent strikers by arguing that 'the latest offensive of the House-lord class in Glasgow' would not 'kindle "the war enthusiasm" of the people of Scotland'.[13] However, the most important aspect of this mass strike against rent increases involving 15,000 women 'rent strikers'[14] – and a portent of things to come – was the independent activity of working-class women. For Helen Crawford told a mass rally of 'rent strikers' that their 'fight was essentially a women's fight'.[15]

As the labour movement increasingly attracted mass support and sustained a courageous agitation against the war, militarism and atrocious housing conditions in the midst of governmental repression, a sense of national identity was forged in the heat of class struggle by native Scots, Irish immigrants and Highlanders. Moreover, if the 'Celtic strain was already dominant in the Glasgow character',[16] the presence of Highlanders in the munitions factories – where Gaelic rather than the Scots' dialect was often 'the prevailing language',[17] – raised new questions about Scottish history and the relationship between socialism and nationalism. By 1916-19 the Scottish labour movement's consistent agitation against the war and appalling housing conditions contributed to a new sense of national consciousness and the demand for Home Rule.

In contrast to the few historians who have questioned the argument that the labour unrest on the Clydeside constituted a serious threat to the established social order, the authorities soon identified 'the state of irritation which quickly spreads beyond the boundaries of the establishment where the trouble first arose to other works, and frequently from adventitious causes wholly unconnected with the origin or merits of the dispute it becomes elevated into a question of principle affecting all employers and munitions workers generally throughout the district'.[18] Besides, as the socialists who had been influenced by the ideas of Daniel De Leon, the American socialist leader, propagated the doctrine of syndicalism in the workshops and factories, the provincial elite were frightened by the rank-and-file challenge to 'the duly authorised executive councils and district committees of the trade unions'.[19] Moreover, as this propaganda of the socialist minority began to fuse with the struggle against the dilution of labour and the anti-war sentiments of the 'masses', the authorities deported the leaders of the Clyde Workers' Committee, sent spies into the trade unions and socialist groups and engaged in widespread repression.[20]

In February 1916, the ILP organised a mass meeting in the mining town of Lochgelly where resolutions were carried denouncing the war and militarism;[21] and in April John Maclean was imprisoned for agitating against the war. Far from eradicating the labour movement's agitation against the war, the almost simultaneous imprisonment of James Maxton and James D. MacDougall for anti-war activities galvanised their fellow socialists all over Scotland into renewed activity. In September the Highland Land League launched a bitter and blistering attack on the Duke of Sutherland for withholding fishing rights from returned soldiers who had been wounded in the war; and the Scottish conference of the Labour Party called for the repeal of the Military Service Acts and urged the Government to open immediate peace negotiations.[22]

I

As the most important figure in the anti-war movement and the only British socialist who possessed a 'revolutionary will to power',[23] John Maclean's herculean socialist activities have somewhat obscured the general vindictiveness and repression of the provincial elite and the emergence of uncanny mass militancy. For though the Govan School Board failed in their attempt to dismiss Maclean as a school teacher in March, 1915,[24] they finally got rid of him a few months later. Yet even before he was fired, he wrote an article entitled 'Scottish versus German Education' in which he made the following assertion: 'When we come down to management by School Boards, we can find a detestable tyranny, not so open as that obtaining in Germany, but more cunning and therefore more dangerous'.[25] However, socialists who were much less aggressive and forceful than Maclean were also dismissed for displaying any independence of judgement. In June, 1916, the anti-war activities of James Maxton led the Glasgow School Board to fire him, too;[26] and in December Joe Maxwell MA, was dismissed by the Govan School Board because he refused to 'have anything to do with the "boosting" or handling of the War Loan Stock Vouchers in his school'.[27]

But the victimisation of socialist militants simply heightened rather than stifled the anti-militarist resistance of an increasing number of working men and women; and in 1917 the Scottish working class was still further radicalised by the outbreak of the Russian revolution. In June the All-Russian Congress of Workers' and Soldiers' Deputies decided to organise 'an international conference of world socialism' in Stockholm;[28] and the Scottish miners, steel-smelters, railwaymen and shop assistants soon gave 'a solid vote for Stockholm'.[29] In Glasgow 10,000 working men and women could not gain admission to a packed meeting in the St Andrews Hall in support of the Russian revolution;[30] and the annual conference of the Scottish Trades Union Congress carried unanimously a resolution calling for peace negotiations.[31]

Moreover, frequent debates on militarism versus anti-militarism were organised in diverse Scottish towns and cities, and the tendency for the Scots to be more outward-looking than the English labour movement was discerned by men who wanted to give the Scottish labour movement a nationalist orientation. This difference of attitude towards militarism was summed up by the *Scottish Review*:

The strength of the hostility to militarism in Scotland may be
gathered from the fact that the War Party is a discredited minority
in nearly all the Trades and Labour Councils north of the Tweed.
Only in Aberdeen and Edinburgh has it been possible to secure a
bare majority in favour of the policy of the Labour Party in the
Westminster Parliament . . . In all the other Trades Councils, so far
as I have been able to find out, the feeling is strongly anti-militarist
and even pacifist.[32]

As the 'War Party' in Scotland consisted of a few followers of H.M.
Hyndman who were grouped around the National Socialist Party,
they alienated themselves still further from the Scottish labour movement by criticising the anti-militarism of James Connolly and the
Easter Rising of 1916.

As the leading representative of the 'War Party' in Scotland, James
Leslie attacked the Easter Rising in Dublin, the Russian revolution and
the anti-war agitation of the Scots as manifestations of 'impossibilism,
anarchism and pacifism'. Yet he probably unwittingly contributed to
the growth of nationalist feeling in the Scottish labour movement
when he attempted to explain why Connolly took part in the Easter
Rising:

In the most recent conversation I had with him, one could note a
growing Irishness which, while it might not mean a narrowing of
vision, yet showed plainly that if he had influenced Sinn Fein, the
influence had been mutual and reciprocal, and that Sinn Fein had
made its mark on him; but that does not explain everything. I will
venture my own opinion for what it is worth. I have reason to
believe that Connolly did not place a very high estimate upon the
labour or socialist movement there. Knowing the man, I say it is
possible that, despairing of effective assistance from that quarter,
and indeed believing that it would act as a drag upon his efforts to
form an Irish Socialist Party, he determined at all costs to identify
or to indissolubly link the cause of Irish labour with the most
extreme Irish nationalism, and to seal the bond of union with his
blood if necessary.[33]

But just as Connolly's Celtic communism influenced John Maclean
and others, so were most Scottish socialist leaders stretching outwards
to support the world revolution that was being predicted by Vladimir
Lenin and Leon Trotsky.[34]

Moreover, if the Scottish ILP's peaceful co-existence with capitalism before the outbreak of the war had made it difficult for them to attract new members,[35] aggressive socialist militancy and anti-militarism transformed the whole of the labour movement. As the Scottish ILP membership jumped by three hundred per cent and the number of branches increased by fifty per cent between the outbreak of the war and the end of 1917, the whole of the labour movement developed a new self-confidence and sense of national awareness.[36]

In February 1918, when hundreds of engineers met Sir Auckland Geddes to discuss the manpower situation, a resolution was carried calling for an immediate armistice.[37] And then the miners in the Scottish coalfields intensified their anti-war activities under the influence of the socialist minority. As James D. MacDougall put it:

> The victory of the revolution in Russia had breathed new life into international socialism, almost killed by the antagonisms the war had bred. The proposal to adopt the May Day holiday was carried. Despite the protests of the Admiralty and a campaign of calumny in the press, the strike took place. At the huge gatherings held at Hamilton and elsewhere solemn declarations of opposition to the continuance of the war were carried with absolute unanimity.

And in the Lanarkshire coalfields the Miners' Union conducted a ballot on peace negotiations, and 18,767 miners voted for immediate peace negotiations and only 8,249 voted for the continuance of the war.[38] Then when 10,000 working men and women took part in a march from George Square to Glasgow Green to protest against the 'continued imprisonment of John Maclean', *Forward* hailed this demonstration as 'a great victory on the Home Front'.[39]

As the Scots became increasingly aware of the mass support they now enjoyed in contrast to the situation in England, the socialists and nationalists who were grouped around Ruaraidh Erskine of Marr's quarterly journal, *The Scottish Review,* started to agitate for national independence. Inspired by the example of the Russian revolution, the Scottish labour movement, whether revolutionary or reformist, supported the cottars' land raids in Sutherland and Skye as the correct application of 'Bolshevik tactics in the Highlands'.[40] Then in November a giant workers' demonstration hailed the German revolution as the beginning of international socialism;[41] and this new mood of working-class militancy found expression in the votes polled in the general election. Instead of the 33,000 votes polled by the labour and socialist candidates in 1910, left-wing candidates now polled an aggregate of 319,572 votes or approximately a third of the total votes cast.[42] As Erskine of Marr, the second son of the fifth Lord Erskine, identified himself with the land raids organised by the Highland Land League at the same time as *Forward* and many socialists were doing likewise, there was a fusion of socialist and nationalist demands.

In 1916 and in 1917 the Scottish Trades Union Congress articulated the general working-class agitation for Home Rule;[43] and by 1918 they were going beyond 'the milk-and-water proposals put forward in timid and apologetic fashion by the Scottish Liberal MPs on their election platforms' and now demanding separate Scottish representation at the Paris Peace conference. Moreover, the 'active co-operation of the Highland Land League and the Scottish Labour Party [was] a significant sign of the times'; and in a joint appeal to the people they emphasised 'the necessity' for a Scots Parliament and the encouragement of Celtic culture.[44] Then in 1919 a national committee composed of Joseph Duncan, Duncan MacGregor Graham MP, William Graham MP, J.M. Hogg MP, Thomas Johnston, David Kirkwood, Angus MacDonald, Highland Land League, John Maclean MA, Neil Maclean MP, James Maxton, John Robertson MP, Robert Smillie, Alexander Wilkie MP, and Ruaraidh Erskine of Marr[45] issued a manifesto to the people of Scotland in which they justified their agitation for national independence by arguing that the Scottish workers were more progressive and left-wing than their English counterparts.[46]

Yet in contrast to socialists such as Robert Smillie who agitated for the revival of the Gaelic language during the war years,[47] John Maclean's Scottish Labour College was criticised by *The Scottish Review* for 'the absence of any definite place for the study of Scottish history from the national and democratic point of view'.[48] But though Maclean was much slower than Maxton, Smillie and other socialist leaders to come out in favour of national independence, he was assured of mass working-class support by his uncompromising propaganda, socialist education and championship of the Russian revolution. And when he was appointed as the Soviet Consul for Scotland at the beginning of 1918, he stiffened the determination of the provincial elite and their metropolitan allies in the Cabinet to put him back in jail without bothering about the rule of law.[49]

However, the whole of the Scottish labour movement participated in the agitation in support of Irish freedom; and, though he was again imprisoned in 1918, Maclean's popularity in the labour movement was unbounded. While he was still in jail he stood for election to Parliament in the Gorbals (formerly the Blackfriars) constituency with William Gallacher deputising for him on election platforms; and, when Smillie addressed a huge election rally in Glasgow in December, he threw defiance in the face of the Establishment by identifying with Maclean's struggle for international socialism: 'I want you to work to return John Maclean to the House of Commons. (Prolonged cheers). I would like to be sitting there in the gallery the first night that John Maclean, the jail bird, rises to face the enemies of labour, the sweaters and exploiters of labour'.[50]

The labour movement in Scotland was indeed much further to the left than the English one at that time. As S.G. Checkland puts it: 'The political confrontation in Glasgow has always been harsher than in England. The Scottish Independent Labour Party has a strong revolutionary element, whereas the English Independent Labour Party was largely reformist'.[51] This revolutionary element was unquestionably supported by the Irish immigrants in Scotland; and in October, 1919, James Maxton, John Wheatley and Emmanuel Shinwell told a mass demonstration that they had to intensify their campaign to get British troops withdrawn from Ireland.[52]

But while the Clydesiders certainly 'identified with a distinctly Scottish position', there is no evidence to support Kenneth O. Morgan's assertion that John Maclean and 'the later generation of Glasgow socialists after 1917' were parochial, inward-looking Celts who just 'conceived of their socialism firmly within a Celtic context'.[53] Indeed, the strategy of the whole of the Scottish labour movement[54] — not just the Clydesiders — was to deepen the fight for national independence as a step towards international socialism. Moreover, the rank-and-file workers in the factories and workshops, who were imbued with the ideas of Daniel De Leon, attempted to link the struggle for national independence with the agitation for workers' control at the point of production. This argument was summed up in an editorial in the *Strike Bulletin* during the forty-hour strike: 'We have to emancipate ourselves from the dictatorship of the London juntas by building an organisation which will be under our control and function when we want it to function. The workshop organisation should be the unit of the strike'.[55]

As the Bolsheviks believed that 700,000 Scottish workers and delegations of soldiers were, in 1918, demanding 'support for the Russian revolution',[56] this romantic myth persuaded the Bolsheviks that Britain — and particularly Scotland — was on the verge of a workers' revolution.[57] By 1919 the revolutionary tide was on the ebb even before the abortive forty-hour strike got underway, and demobilisation of soldiers and sailors and mass unemployment weakened the self-confidence of workers who had successfully engaged in spontaneous mass struggles. Nevertheless, the labour movement was still strong, radical, confident and outward-looking; and as the reality of the horror and special misery of Scottish capitalism impinged on the consciousness of socialists, it seemed to them that self-government was the only realistic solution they could opt for.

What influenced the labour movement's nationalism was not an ideology based on blood, soil, language or an ethnic tradition, but the peculiarities of the evolution and special problems created by Scottish capitalism. In the utterances and speeches of even the most extreme socialist advocates of national independence, the national question was not allowed to prevail over their commitment to international socialism. However, as Scottish working men and women had been taught before the war to see themselves as 'canny' and 'docile', the provincial elite had often pretended that they did not know anything about the appalling housing and other social conditions. Clearly, they did know, but the 'discovery' of the Royal Commission on Scottish Housing that 'the conditions were even worse than in England', coupled with a comment that 'the conditions ... have never been adequately investigated', is a testimony to their indifference and insensitivity.[58] And as the labour movement became increasingly outraged by the appalling housing conditions in Scotland, native socialists fused national awareness with radical demands. In a meeting organised to discuss unemployment and housing Smillie was expressing the labour movement's comparatively new awareness of Scotland's colonial status when he said: 'The Government idea was that Scotland should have three apartments but that England should have five. The Scottish workers were entitled to as good houses as the English. He was determined, so far as the miners were concerned, that the public conscience would never again go to sleep'.[59]

Most of the socialist advocates of national independence now identified the housing problem with the colonial status of Scottish working people, though they failed to develop a fully comprehensive critique of the peculiarities of Scottish capitalism. For example, in 1916 the Rev. James Barr and other socialists were still advocating the virtues of thrift and temperance;[60] and in 1918 the Scottish ILP voted for the total prohibition of alcohol.[61] This strong 'puritanical bias' of the labour movement dominated the social and political thought of most socialists in the 1920s;[62] and in 1926 Hugh MacDiarmid (C.M. Grieve) depicted James Maxton as a chauvinist for suggesting that

'thrift', 'independence' and 'courage' were uniquely Scottish characteristics.[63] Yet the more orthodox Scottish nationalists in the labour
movement were real chauvinists. Instead of identifying and attacking
the backwardness of Scottish society in 1915-18 when the authorities
refused to bestow the status of political prisoners on anti-war dissidents,
Diack and *The Scottish Review* restricted themselves to criticising 'the
English king' for imprisoning Maclean in Edinburgh Castle without
mentioning the role of the Scottish bourgeoisie in suppressing civil
liberties.[64]

Jailed in 1915, 1916, 1918 and again in 1921, John Maclean fought
from inside his prison cell to expose the brutal, authoritarian nature of
Scottish society. Through his wife Agnes Maclean, he appealed to the
British Socialist Party to get English Labour members of Parliament to
'realise' that Scotland was the 'most backward country' in Europe in
'their treatment of political prisoners'. He was indeed put in a convict's
suit, made to break stones for eight hours a day, and he was not allowed
to read books or newspapers.[65] But though he expressed disappoint-
ment through his wife's letters to the leaders of the BSP about their
lack of any systematic campaign to free him in 1916, they then initiated a campaign for his release 'on the basis of the unsatisfactory
character of the police evidence'.[66] However, the English socialists
were not really interested in the peculiarities of the Scottish situation,
and a prominent member of the BSP in London expressed the view that
he was 'better in a civil prison than in the hands of the military'.[67]

Since Maclean wanted the BSP to initiate a mass campaign to force
his release and to expose his lack of status as a political prisoner, he was
already becoming disenchanted with the English socialist leaders as
early as 1916. But just as the English socialists were unsympathetic
to what he wanted, so did the Scots like James Ramsay MacDonald
and Tom Johnston, the editor of the newspaper *Forward* treat his
imprisonment as a tactical question rather than one of principle.[68] In
1918 MacDonald wrote to inform Agnes Maclean that since there was
'no such thing in Scotland as a political prisoner', the situation could
only be rectified by special legislation;[69] yet he then wrote a letter to
the Rt Hon. Robert Munro, the Secretary of State for Scotland, in a
rather different tone:

> Would it not be possible for you to go a little further with Maclean
> and take him away from Peterhead altogether? There are prisons
> in Glasgow, Ayr and Perth where he could be put and you might
> consider whether some concessions regarding books and newspapers

might be made. After all, his crime relates to the realm of opinion
and you know as well as I do how civilised communities regard
such criminals in due time. Can you not anticipate that judgment
and while meting out to Maclean the internment part of the
judgment, recognise in his treatment the real character of his
misdemeanor and I am sure if you will do this you will not only
be giving fair play to Maclean himself but you will be removing
from the minds of some sections of the community at any rate,
those thoughts and passions which offer hospitality to the opinions
and emotions which helped to make Maclean say and do those
things for which he is now being punished.[70]

But it was Maclean, the Bolshevik 'extremist', rather than MacDonald,
the 'humane' social democrat, who sought to humanise Scottish society
by gaining some recognition for the rights of anti-militarists and dissidents; and when he was released in 1918 due to the pressure of a mass
workers' agitation, he wrote to Sir James M. Dobbs, the Under Secretary of State for Scotland, to refuse the King's free pardon and to
complain of 'your cold-blooded treatment in those infernos, Peterhead
and Perth'.[71]

II

Bearing in mind that the Scottish labour movement campaigned against
such manifestations of a repressive, authoritarian society as the excessive flogging of juveniles before the war, it is somewhat ironical that
few socialists supported John Maclean's efforts to gain the status of
political prisoners for socialist dissidents. Moreover, not only did most
socialists ignore the problem of police spies in the labour movement
beyond publishing a few reports in the left-wing press, but they accepted
Maclean's comments about his cold-blooded treatment in Peterhead
and Perth without asking for any reform of the penal system. In contrast to the socialists grouped around *Forward* and *The Socialist* who
still concentrated on solving bread-and-butter problems at the expense
of social ones, Maclean was determined to take advantage of the opportunities presented by the war to agitate for the enlargement of democratic freedoms.

As Maclean was committed to the enlargement of the democratic
process within a society he identified as very authoritarian, he was
determined to utilise mass discontent to develop a comprehensive
critique of his own society including socialists who minimised the
importance of democratic processes. In 1915 he admitted that H.M.

Hyndman and the War Party were sincerely committed to socialism; but he attacked their vision of socialism since it rested on the need for a 'socialist aristocracy'. Besides, if Tom Johnston, the editor of *Forward*, waited until Maclean's death before he criticised 'his conviction that machiavellian attempts were made to poison him',[72] *Forward* published one of his letters in 1919 criticising the authorities for 'drugging prisoners' food' without comment or criticism.[73]

The labour movement complained in 1924 about militant miners being beaten up in the police cells in Blantyre; and as a result of mass indignation meetings to demand action against police brutality the issue was raised in Parliament.[74] But Maclean's influence was certainly important in galvanising some Scottish socialists into action against the authorities' toleration of police brutality and the use of spies in the labour movement; and his opposition to the attempts of the agents of the Russian Bolsheviks to impose Leninism on the British labour movement sprang from a profound commitment to the democratic process. As he believed that he could get all the money he needed from the workers on Clydeside,[75] he exposed the attempts of Russian agents like Theodore Rothstein to subsidise and thus dominate British socialism.[76]

But though John Maclean was in touch with Leon Trotsky during the war years, this did not contribute to the latter's understanding of Scottish peculiarities. In contrast to the sympathy, insight, understanding and sensitivity that permeate Trotsky's books *My Life* and *Literature and Revolution,* his study of British politics entitled *Where is Britain Going?* was characterised by its failure to understand the Scottish situation or the labour movement's agitation for Home Rule. For at the same time as he criticised the 'British "socialist" gentlemen' for not understanding the similarity of the Scottish and Russian experience in pushing backward countries on 'the road to socialist change', he attacked the Scottish socialist MPs for threatening to set up a Scottish Parliament for which they had, in his view, 'absolutely no need'.[77]

As a growing number of Scottish militants believed that the Scots had moved far to the left of the English working class, they now had fewer inhibitions about agitating for Scottish self-government. As they believed that a Scottish Parliament would be dominated by the socialists, they no longer saw the agitation for Scottish self-government as being incompatible with international socialism. So, when the Scottish ILP met at their annual conference in 1921 they again demanded the setting up of a Scottish Parliament;[78] and at the annual conference of the Scottish Trades Union Congress left-wing delegates justified their agitation on the grounds that Scotland was far to the left of England.

As a delegate from the Scottish Union of Dock Labourers put it: 'There would have been no Triple Alliance failure north of the Tweed if the Scottish workers had been free to decide for themselves'. He complained that the Scottish workers could not move far without the consent of the 'great' people in London. This had created 'disastrous consequences'.[79]

This new mass agitation for Home Rule was quite distinct from the objectives of the bourgeois nationalist movement of Ruaraidh Erskine of Marr and John McArthur; and the labour movement's nationalism was accompanied by an outward-looking, if critical, support for the Russian revolution. Besides, before the labour movement's big electoral breakthrough in 1922, Scottish socialist MPs urged the miners to adopt a 'canny policy' of restricting coal production;[80] and the workers' new social attitudes were reflected in their rejection of pre-war fatalism in relation to such problems as unemployment. For in a whole number of diverse towns and cities the unemployed demanded 'work or full maintenance',[81] and in towns like Falkirk the unemployed carried banners bearing new slogans — 'Unemployed, Don't Pay your Rent' — in most of the May Day demonstrations.[82] And at a time when Falkirk and Cowdenbeath were the only two towns in Scotland where 'the local authorities comprised a majority of the representatives of the working class',[83] John Wheatley appealed to the working classes in Glasgow to break the law if they were threatened with eviction as he would be of 'greater value' to them in jail than if he was 'outside'.[84]

From the war through to the early 1920s working women were in the forefront of the struggles against rent increases and evictions, and a significant minority of working women began to develop new social attitudes towards society in general. The working-class women who took part in the general election of 1922 were, in the opinion of such opponents as Annie S. Swan, the Kailyard novelist, 'better informed than the women still attached to the old-fashioned parties'.[85] Moreover, when Margaret Sanger came to lecture in Glasgow in 1920 on birth control she discovered the emergence of these new attitudes amongst the minority of working women whose husbands were active socialists. As she put it:

> That evening I spoke in a hall under socialist auspices, Guy Aldred acting as chairman. One old-timer said he had been a party member for eleven years, attending Sunday evening lectures regularly, but never before had he been able to induce his wife to come; tonight he could not keep her at home. 'Look!', he cried in amazement,

'The women have crowded the men out of the hall. I never saw
so many wives of comrades before'.[86]

This concern with social and cultural questions was also reflected in the
general election of 1922, though not always in a realistic, socialist
fashion.

For if nothing stood between the Scottish socialist movement – a
movement possessing 'its full share of unemployed and victimised men
and women' – and the 'greed and tyranny of the capitalist class' on the
eve of the general election of 1922,[87] socialist propaganda was the key
to the new challenge to the traditional images of the 'docile', 'passive'
and anti-socialist 'canny' Scots. Though the official labour (as distinct
from the smaller socialist) movement did not raise fundamental cultural
questions in the election campaign, they did put the housing problem
at the forefront of their agitation. The housing question was, as *The
Scotsman* put it, 'used to stimulate the virus of socialism in the community';[88] and even in the countryside, where the socialists' victory
was much less decisive, the major struggle was now 'for or against
organised Labour'.[89]

As Scottish labour increased its Parliamentary representation from
seven out of a total of seventy-four seats in 1918 to thirty in 1922
and 1924, outside observers were astonished by this dramatic electoral
breakthrough which put Scottish socialism on the international map.
But if the outsiders were momentarily surprised by this sudden, dramatic and mass upsurge of militant proletarian socialism, some of the
reformist socialists in the remnant of the Social Democratic Federation
attributed these new developments to the socialist educational work
of John Maclean who had died in 1923.[90] Even so, the now traditional
gap between the labour movement and the majority of unorganised
men and women remained a serious one. For the socialist and labour
candidates were temperance advocates who fought the election on 'a
no-license policy', and they were elected in spite of their teetotalism
rather than because of it. But the most perceptive explanation of their
electoral victory was presented by a special correspondent in the
London *Times* who wrote as follows:

No-one can make even a cursory investigation of the methods of
propaganda pursued by the Labour Party on the Clyde without
discovering in them the real foundations of victory. Year in and
year out, in season and out of season, the Clyde area has been
saturated with socialist teaching.[91]

As the Scottish labour movement had been pressing for self-govern-ment since the war years, it is important to emphasise the influence of Maclean's propaganda for a Scottish Workers' Republic before 1922 if the Scots' subsequent disruption of the business of the House of Commons is to be kept in proper perspective. This influence was seen most dramatically in Fife in 1921 during the coal miners' strike when thousands of miners paraded through the main towns with red flags, cut the telgraph poles, sang the Red Flag and The International, and flooded the pits. At the same time as the left-wing elements flooded the pits, three members of Sinn Fein in Dunfermline started a series of farm fires which led to their arrest and trial in the Sheriff court. Before one of their sympathisers in the court called upon the trio to 'keep the Red Flag flying',[92] the authorities sent in armed marines to restore order in a situation where striking miners — and particularly the ex-servicemen amongst them — were drilling and organising pro-cessions with a 'military appearance'.[93] Certainly, the local newspapers[94] were not in any doubt about the 'widespread revolutionary spirit' inspired by John Maclean, Sandy Ross and James D. MacDougall.[95] As one newspaper, *The Dunfermline Journal,* put it: 'A plot to estab-lish a Scottish Communist Republic was seriously projected, while the Scots were referred to in a leaflet as "bloody tools of the English against our brother Celts of Erin" '.[96]

But while Ruaraidh Erskine of Marr and the Scottish nationalist fundamentalists with their romantic dream of 'Celticising' industrial Scotland denied that working people were interested in either inter-national socialism or even their 'immediate surroundings',[97] the coales-cence of Scottish nationalist sentiments and an aggressive socialism had been motivated by economic factors and a new awareness of Scotland's colonial status as an internal colony. This awareness of the colonial status of the Scottish working class was expressed with pas-sionate clarity by James Maxton in the House of Commons in 1923 when he argued that, in his own district of Glasgow, 'one thousand and thirty-five infants died who *would have lived in English condi-tions*'.[98] Moreover, the Scottish socialists were frustrated by their experience in Parliament at a time when working-class opinion was demanding far-reaching social change. And Maxton told an audience organised by the Scottish Socialist Teachers' Society in Glasgow of the frustrations felt by his fellow Scottish MPs:

It was a humiliating experience to sit in the British House of Commons, one of a majority returned to the House of Commons to push on a policy of fundamental social change for the benefit of the Scottish people, and to find the Scottish majority steadily voted down by the votes of the English members pledged to a policy of social stagnation. It was now over two hundred years since the Union of Parliaments, and although one was perpetually told of the blessings conferred on Scotland by the Union, it was difficult to find many blessings except the somewhat doubtful one of fighting England's wars.[99]

When the Scottish Home Rule Bill was sabotaged by William Adamson, the Secretary of State for Scotland, and Ramsay MacDonald, the Labour Prime Minister, the Scottish socialists created so much disturbance and disorder that 'the Speaker at last found himself obliged to adjourn the House'.[100] Then the Scots articulated an angry, aggressive mood that raised new expectations in the labour movement in industrial Scotland. As Maxton told the Duchess of Atholl that they would no longer tolerate either economic or cultural *'dependency'* and Kirkwood accepted responsibility for 'the beginning of the end of your Parliament',[101] it was clear that something akin to Eurocommunism was already being foreshadowed in 1924. This emergence of the Red Clyde was, indeed, spelt out by William Bolitho in his study of Glasgow, *The Cancer of Empire*:

> Shadowy yet in details, but already crystallised by two phrases as fatal as the motto of the first French Republic, Liberty, Equality, Fraternity, a new socialism, different from, but no less fierce and sincere than the communism of Lenin, evolved on the Clyde. It is Western socialism, an unfatalistic socialism, apt for Western peoples, which the stockyards of Chicago, the thrifty faubourgs of Paris, the conservative miners of the Ruhr, may one day hear and understand.[102]

Moreover, as the Highland Land League had already been transformed into the Scots National League in 1920, a division between the labour movement and the Scottish nationalist fundamentalists was inevitable. This did not, however, dampen the labour movement's passionate concern over the Highland question. A Highland Labour Party was formed in 1923 to carry the socialist message into 'the remote glens and clachans';[103] and at a time when famine was forcing Highlanders into 'the packed baskets of Glasgow every month',[104] Maxton wanted the Labour government to deal with 'the famine conditions in the Western Isles of Scotland' without depending on the 'charity' of bourgeois do-gooders.[105] Then as the agitation for self-government reached a high pitch of enthusiasm in 1924, Maxton told a mass audience in Glasgow of his dream of a Scotland no longer economically or culturally dependent on the whims of the metropolitan Parliament in London.

> He would ask no greater job in life than to make English-ridden, capitalist-ridden, land-owner-ridden Scotland into the free Scottish Socialist Commonwealth, and in doing that he thought it would be rendering a very great service to the people of England, Wales and Europe, and to the cause of internationalism generally.

But far from marking 'an epoch on the road to Scottish self-government',[106] it was actually the beginning of the decline of the mass upsurge of proletarian socialism.

III

During the years between 1918 and 1920 John Maclean was influenced by Ruaraidh Erskine of Marr, John McArthur, H.C. MacNeacil and the other fundamentalists in the Scottish nationalist movement. As Maclean's disenchantment with the soft, compromising political behaviour of the English leaders of the BSP, together with the coalescence of socialism and nationalism in Ireland, heightened his already latent Scottish nationalism, the fundamentalists' interpretation of Scottish history became a catalyst leading him away from the classical marxist ideas he once upheld and propagated. As an exponent of Bolshevik marxism — or what Antonio Gramsci called the revolution against Marx's *Capital* — he was influenced by the Scottish nationalists' historiography rather than their ideology of blood, soil, language and an ethnic tradition.[107]

As Marr, McArthur and MacNeacil supported Sinn Fein rather than the Irish labour movement, they were really interested in Celtic communism rather than Bolshevism.[108] Far from Maclean's new commitment to Celtic communism coinciding in 1918 with 'the conversion to socialism of the country's leading advocate of Gaelic Scotland',[109] the relationship between Maclean and Marr was complex and complicated. For just as Leon Trotsky argued that 'the most radical elements in Britain [were] mostly of the Scots or Irish race', so did Maclean attribute this concrete reality to the peculiarities of Scottish capitalist development.

In the early 1920s the Scottish labour movement as a whole depicted industrial unrest on the Clyde and agrarian disorders in the Highlands as symptoms of the general crisis of international capitalism; and Maclean argued that the land raids in the Highlands were the equivalent of the strikes of industrial workers in the Lowlands.[110] Yet what the Scottish nationalists were committed to was something quite distinct from and even hostile to the objectives of the Scottish socialists. As the nationalist fundamentalists were isolated from the vast majority of the Scottish people, and as Marr, McArthur and MacNeacil gradually realised that they would have to forge a political alliance with the working class if they were to gain support for their dream of a Gaelic Scotland,[111] the Scots National League was founded in 1920.

Ruaraidh Erskine of Marr was 'an old-fashioned radical', and not a socialist in 1918-20.[112] His one consistent objective from the early twentieth century onwards was to 'Celticise the whole of Scotland';[113] and, though he flirted with some 'communist' ideas when he was under the influence of John Maclean, he never believed in the potential creativity of the Scottish working class. Even when he adhered to 'communist' ideas, he made it clear that he did not share Karl Marx's vision of the political capacity of working people to create a humanistic, socialist society. As he put it: 'It is possible, of course, that the Proletarian rule may disappoint in practice the glowing expectations formed of it by its friends, and may show itself to be as little dependable as *medicina animi* as Monarchy, Aristocracy, and government by the capitalist class have proved themselves to be so . . . but . . . apart from the fact that real popular rule is as yet a practically unknown and untried force in political Europe, the dictatorship of the Proletariat, how dismally soever it might fail, could not possibly sin against humanity more deeply and unforgivably than the other systems of government have done'.[114]

When the Scots National League organised a public meeting in Arbroath in September, 1920, to celebrate the sex-centenary of the Arbroath Declaration of Scottish Independence of 1320, John Maclean took the chair. But though John McArthur apologised for the absence of Marr, who was ill, and Maclean and Sandy Ross advocated an independent, democratic Republic, the two latter speakers did not join the League.[115] What appealed to Maclean and Ross was the League's support for the Irish struggle and their interpretation of Scottish history. This was made clear in a report of the meeting in the League's journal, *Liberty*: 'Introducing Mr John MacArthur, he [Maclean] said that *Liberty* was the best paper in Scotland from a Scots standpoint. Mr McArthur was trying in his pages to teach them true Scots history instead of the false and perverted variety taught in the school-books'.[116]

In an article in *The Vanguard* entitled 'The Irish tragedy', Maclean told his working-class readers in Lowland Scotland about his motive for sharing a platform with John McArthur, the editor of *Liberty*, in quite unambiguous language: 'Why did I visit Arbroath on Saturday, 11 September, but to protest the hollow mockery of the centenary celebration of the Scottish Parliament's declaration of independence to Pope John XXII, whilst Scottish boys dressed in the garb of the English government were then and now daring the Irish to set up a free and independent Irish Parliament elected by the overwhelming vote of the Irish people'.[117] But if he was influenced by the fundamentalists' interpretation of Scottish history, Marr's assertion that 'the community' would be 'the ruling power' in the future[118] conflicted with Maclean's conception of a transitional socialist society as a class 'dictatorship'.[119]

In fact there were also constant elements of romanticism and racism, if not fascism, in the social and political thought of Ruaraidh Erskine of Marr and the Scottish nationalist fundamentalists; and Maclean's implicit ideological differences with their orientation were profound and incompatible. When Maclean and Ross were put on trial in Airdrie Sheriff Court in May, 1921, on eleven separate charges including one of inciting the workers to revolution,[120] Marr seized the opportunity to show that, although he was already moving away from his flirtation with 'communism', he still felt a deep hatred of industrial capitalism. Since his hatred of capitalism sprang from the destructive impact it had had on Celtic culture, he was always anxious to initiate and support 'revolutionary' movements committed to the overthrow of capitalist materialism.

But if the imprisonment of the two leading Bolsheviks gave the Scots National League an opportunity to assert their 'special interest' in the two men who had given them 'valuable assistance' at the Arbroath meeting, the latent ideological differences between them were soon articulated by Marr: 'It is not without significance that with scarcely one exception the doughtiest opponents of capitalist rule throughout England's cracking Empire are men of *Celtic blood and Gaelic name,* and not the least amongst them are John Maclean and Sandy Ross'.[121] By March 1922, but before Maclean's Scottish Workers' Republican Party was formed, the national committee of the Scots National League published a statement which made any further co-operation between the two groups impossible:

> The Scots National League is a single-object organisation. It has
> been formed for the sole purpose of securing Scottish Independence:
> consequently it is not *per se* concerned with any other question.
> The League holds that the question of the forms which the future
> government of Scotland shall take is for the Nation, and not for
> the League, to determine, after the former shall have acquired
> sovereign independence.

And at the same time Marr appealed to Scottish communists to follow 'the lead of John Maclean, who like Radek, the spokesman of the Russian government, is a nationalist as well as a communist'.[122]

In contrast to Marr, who was soon to support Italian fascism, Maclean, the champion of the Scottish Workers' Republic, stood as a candidate in the general election of 1922 as 'a Bolshevik, alias a communist, alias a revolutionist, alias a marxian'. His support for the Irish struggle and Scottish independence were designed to overturn the mighty British Empire; and unlike James Connolly, who had supported the Irish Gaelic language movement before the First World War,[123] he always concentrated more on educating the Scottish workers in the fundamentals of marxist economics than on cultural questions. Besides, as a critic of fascism at home and abroad, he was too deeply rooted in the traditions of international socialism to condone literary romanticism or unrealistic attempts to 'Celticise' industrial Scotland.

However, the Scottish labour movement — and not just Maclean, Maxton and the Red Clydesiders — had inherited the Calvinist contempt for art, literary culture and aesthetic activity; and this is why it is difficult to accept Hamish Henderson's argument that the literary renaissance of the 1920s 'cannot be disassociated from the growth to political maturity of the Scottish working classes during World War I'.[124] Moreover, it is equally difficult to accept Hugh MacDiarmid's verdict that the literary renaissance was pushed into life by a situation in which 'an adequate majority of the Scottish people' were shaken out of 'their old mental, moral and material ruts'.[125] For though causal connections between the Scottish literary renaissance and working-class politics are hard to see in the post-war years, there is ample evidence to suggest that the sheer philistinism of Scottish society as a whole was responsible for leading artists, novelists and poets into a posture of literary fascism. So if there was any clear connection between the two, the Scottish socialists only influenced the literary renaissance in a negative way by their failure to promote what Connolly called 'spiritual' values in the sense of 'mental and moral development upward'.[126]

For while Scottish socialism displayed revolutionary tendencies in the 1920s, it increasingly alienated Hugh MacDiarmid, the major figure in the literary renaissance, by its obsessive preoccupation with 'economistic', bread-and-butter questions. A unique, 'unfatalistic' and 'Western socialism' which was quite distinct from Bolshevism notwithstanding Maclean's role in helping to put it on the international map, Scottish socialism had not transcended its social and intellectual origins within a context of what William Power, the literary critic, called 'Gradgrind Calvinism'.[127] Yet in contrast to what MacDiarmid believed about the Clydesiders being unable to rid Scotland of the epithet 'canny' in spite of a new 'dynamic and determined mood' amongst working people,[128] outsiders like William Bolitho were aware of the militancy and socialist sentiments of the Scottish working class.

As a major revolutionary and cultural genius who analysed Scottish socialism with uncanny perception and astuteness, Hugh MacDiarmid invites comparison with Leon Trotsky. A common and constant element in their social thought was the need for a much higher level of human consciousness than existed in capitalist society; and they were both elitists. Just as Trotsky divided humanity into 'the tale-bearers and the envious at one pole, the frank and courageous at the other and the neutral vacillating mass in the middle',[129] so did MacDiarmid assume that 'his native culture was lacking in activities or people of a calibre to extend or match a mind as powerful as his own'.[130] Nevertheless, it was MacDiarmid's elitism and aloofness from the day-to-day struggle in the factories, workshops and industrial communities which allowed him the 'objectivity' to develop his critique of Scottish bourgeois society and the labour movement.

For just as Trotsky wanted a society in which 'the average human type' would 'rise to the heights of an Aristotle, a Goethe or a Marx',[131] so did MacDiarmid want to extend human consciousness through literature and the arts.[132] As outward-looking internationalists, they were both striving for a universal culture in which, as Trotsky put it, the working class would 'take from Shakespeare, Goethe, Pushkin and Dostoevsky' a 'more complex idea of human personality, of its passions and feelings, a deeper and profounder understanding of its psychic forces and the role of the subconscious'.[133] But as MacDiarmid lived in a backward, insular society where cultural dependency on London vitiated the existence of an independent 'literary caste', there was much less awareness of European culture or of the realities of the European cultural situation.

Moreover, MacDiarmid was profoundly ignorant of the aims of the

Bolsheviks and the pre-1914 socialists of the Second International whose objective was to 'render to the proletariat all the sources of culture';[134] and, though he identified with the European thinkers, artists and poets who were reaching out towards a culture for a new age, he opted for an insular and elitist strategy when he joined forces with Ruaraidh Erskine of Marr to launch the movement for a Scottish cultural revival. The elitism was evident in the decision to create 'Scots as a literary language' rather than as 'a language or dialect that was spoken by the man in the street or on the farm';[135] and it was again spelt out in *A Drunk Man Looks at the Thistle*:

> The core of ocht is only for the few,
> Scorned by the mony, thrang wi'ts empty name.[136]

While he was actually committed to universality and what were many of the cultural aims of international socialism, MacDiarmid's apparent ignorance of the heritage of European socialist thought also led him into the trap of attempting to solve the national question by opting for a universal fascism as an agency of social change. What really worried him was the Scottish working-class socialists' incomprehension of aesthetic activity and their hostility towards the creative faculty itself. As he mistakenly identified the particular insularity, parochialism and narrow bread-and-butter outlook and aspirations of the Scottish labour movement as an in-built feature of international socialism, he embraced elements of fascism. Yet wrong-headed and self-defeating as his 'fascist' utterances were, he was nevertheless inspired by the national dimension in the fascist message. He summed this up in an essay he wrote in 1923:

> Official socialism had ceased to be patriotic. It had put theory above the nation. Mussolini reverses the order — that is all. His is an experiment in patriotic socialism, if one may use a vague expression, whose bases are moral, not economic. His is a war of the idealist against the materialist, and the most dangerous forces of materialism are not on the left. That is why the future of fascism concerns Europe so much.[137]

It is, moreover, very important to emphasise the social and political context of the Scottish literary renaissance in the 1920s; for if the Scottish literati were backward-looking romantics, the labour movement was — at least after the death of John Maclean in 1923 — insular, parochial and preoccupied with bread-and-butter problems. As enthusiasm for a Scots Parliament was dampened down after the failure of the general strike in 1926, the labour movement became more, not less, parochial and inward-looking. Throughout the 1920s the Scottish Trades Union Congress ignored European fascism, what MacDiarmid called 'the horrors of the Cheka' and international affairs; and the secretary responded to press reports of fascist activity in Scottish towns by asserting that there was not 'the slightest evidence of the existence of any fascist movement'.[138]

Admittedly *Forward* published only a very rare article on the violence inflicted on socialists and trade unionists by the Italian fascists;[139] but even if they had done more, MacDiarmid was basically interested in Italian culture rather than in European politics or even the international labour movement. As he consistently championed what he called the universality of the human spirit, he wanted Italian culture to be diffused throughout Europe. He made this plain in an essay he wrote in 1928 entitled 'Scotland and Fascismo':

> That anything in the nature of an armed attempt to impose fascism
> on Scotland would be resented and resisted by us to the taking up
> of arms goes without saying; but we have too profound a belief in
> Italian common sense, moderation and humanity to think that
> nation capable of entertaining any so wild and infamous measures.
> On the other hand, a peaceful diffusion of the cultural influence
> of fascismo would be neither resented nor resisted, but, on the
> contrary warmly welcomed, if happily it should be found that the
> doctrine contains cultural elements of abiding worth; and that this
> will prove to be the case we doubt not now that, in his latest work,
> Groce has written so hopefully of the general future of his country
> and people.[140]

But he tried to introduce this new cultural element into a complicated national situation. In an internal colony with a long tradition of ethnic divisions and anti-Irish prejudice, he sympathised with and supported the Irish immigrants against their racialist critics. But the apparent confusion in his social thought between means and ends or agency and long-term objectives led the Scottish nationalist literary renaissance movement to divorce itself from the working class by electing to 'live upon' and be judged by its 'poetical achievement'.[141] Besides, this literary movement was striving to close the gulf between contemporary Scottish consciousness and the 'Kailyard school'[142] at a time when Ruaraidh Erskine of Marr, one of its principal spokesmen, was attacking 'class conscious internationalism' as another 'form of tyranny on an international scale'.[143] Much closer to the literary renaissance than the labour movement, MacDiarmid was also engaging in self-defeating literary postures.

Far from being parochial or inward-looking in the early 1920s, the Scottish labour movement attempted to reconcile the agitation for national independence with internationalism.[144] But MacDiarmid's apparent ignorance of European socialist thought and his isolation from the Scottish labour movement motivated and sustained a literary romanticism and unrealistic assessment of how the Scottish working class was to transcend its bread-and-butter, 'economistic' world outlook. Because of this and because he was not yet aware of John Maclean's role in Scottish politics, MacDiarmid was able to create a myth central to his thinking in the 1920s and to Scottish nationalist historiography today. But though the myth claimed that the Scottish socialists were not interested in the national question until they were elected to the House of Commons *en masse* in 1922,[145] he could nevertheless perceive the reality of their cultural and ideological backwardness when he asserted:

> Scottish socialism has contributed nothing of the slightest consequence to socialist thought. It has taken over its tenets lock, stock and barrel from continental thinkers — but the principle of selection has been Scottish of a sort. The lack of independent thinking of any calibre worth speaking about accounts for the anti-intellectual, 'democratic' character of Scottish socialism — for a wholesale borrowing without making any return is a demoralising process; the morale — or rather lack of morale — of the Scottish socialist movement shows this clearly enough.[146]

As the socialist aspirations of an important minority of working men and women were being suffocated by the general philistinism of Scottish society and the inward-looking parochialism of the labour leaders after 1926, this brilliant and perspicacious critique might have contributed to the labour movement's adoption of a more positive attitude towards cultural questions. But MacDiarmid cut himself off from any possibility of influencing the Scottish labour movement when he appealed to indigenous socialism to contribute to the ongoing literary revival by attempting to develop 'a fascist rather than a Bolshevik *spirit*'.[147] Moreover, though he did not advocate a programme of blood and soil, he did allow the nationalist elements in his thought to prevail over the socialist ones. As he put it:

In Scotland less than in any other country in Europe is Labour contemptuous of culture or inclined to disregard spiritual factors which alone can consummate its programme. In this connection it is particularly noteworthy that already MPs who were formerly all out for economic change of the old type, have become passionately nationalistic with benefit to their internationalist outlook. The Scottish labour movement is already modifying its socialism as Mussolini modified his. It has got out of the rut of mere theory; and takes service as the touchstone of social values. As soon as it ceases to work for 'socialism' and makes its goal 'Scottish socialism', it will have purged itself of the elements which make for false progress and be within measurable distance of complete triumph.[148]

However, though he was the only Scottish thinker to analyse the labour movement with perception and accuracy, he could not bring himself to associate with the common ruck of working-class humanity; and by an irony of history the very parochialism of the Scottish labour movement which led it to reject any interest in cultural questions also immunised it from the virus of fascism.

As historians and literary critics have repeatedly emphasised MacDiarmid's alleged lack of what Christopher Harvie calls 'ideological consistency',[149] it is important to stress the constant elements in his thought and in the poetry where he experimented with technique. As MacDiarmid believed that political power was ultimately exercised through cultural leadership, he simultaneously supported fascism, national socialism and Bolshevism. In 1923 he published a poem evoking the memory of the 'dead Liebknecht',[150] the German communist martyr, and wrote laudatory essays on the role of Mussolini and Italian fascism as a world-wide cultural movement. Then in 1931 he published a major poem entitled the 'First Hymn to Lenin' and praised Hitler's national socialists for substituting 'the principle of race-consciousness' for 'class consciousness'.[151] Moreover, if he believed in what he claimed was 'the inherent leftism of the fascist movement',[152] he could consistently support fascism, national socialism and Bolshevism as expressions of the 'unconscious' forces in history.

With the exception of Edwin Muir, James Barke and Lewis Grassic Gibbon (James Leslie Mitchell), the leading figures in the Scottish literary renaissance movement were devout fascists. Just as Ruaraidh Erskine of Marr and Lewis Spence[153] had become out-and-out fascists who shared none of MacDiarmid's sympathies for the labour movement, so did this pattern persist in the 1930s when Gibbon attacked the 'literary fascism' of *The Modern Scot.*[154] But MacDiarmid was a much more complex figure than the other Scottish nationalists in the literary renaissance. As he saw fascism, national socialism and Bolshevism as enemies of 'materialism' and 'industrialism', he did not hesitate to support the totalitarian forces of the right and left simultaneously. In his view most men were, and are, only men in the 'zoological' sense, and he supported 'the Cheka's horrors' in Russia in his 'First Hymn to Lenin':

> To lessen that foulest murder that deprives
> Maist men o' real lives.

Moreover, there was a very real sense in which Hugh MacDiarmid was, in Trotsky's phrase, unearthing 'the principle of race from a medieval graveyard';[155] and as he always insisted on the power of the 'unconscious' in history, he was quite prepared to use such apparently 'arbitrary' agencies of social change as the Scottish socialists, the Italian fascists, the German national socialists and the Russian Bolsheviks to smash the framework of a 'civilisation' on which industrialism had been erected. In his attitude to politics, language and race he insists constantly on the importance of the unconscious. Thus he campaigned for the restoration of the Scots' dialect or vernacular as a 'vast storehouse' of the unconscious and a 'vast unutilised mass of lapsed observation';[156] and in his second volume of autobiography, *The Company I've Kept,* published in 1966, he attributed John Maclean's 'great power' to the unconscious depths of his racial origins.[157]

In the 1920s Lewis Grassic Gibbon, who was haunted by the fear that fascism might 'sweep through Europe', tended to equate Scottish nationalism with fascism;[158] and Edwin Muir, who realised as early as 1923 that humanity was threatened by something more complex and multi-dimensional than just Italian fascism, supported the agitation for Home Rule. This was how he put the case for Home Rule in a private letter written in 1926:

> When we were in Scotland last time we heard a lot about Scottish nationalism from C.M. Grieve who wrote *A Drunk Man Looks at the Thistle.* It seems a pity that Scotland should always be kept

back by England, and I hope the Scottish Republic comes about;
it would make Scotland worth living in. Grieve is a strong
nationalist, republican, socialist, and every thing that is out and
out. He thinks that if Scotland were a nation we would have
Scottish literature, art, music, culture and everything that other
nations seem to have and we haven't.[159]

However, in the 1930s Gibbon came round to supporting the agitation
for Scottish self-government without abandoning his hatred of fascism,[160] while Muir abandoned his nationalism in conditions where the
fight against fascism seemed to be paramount.[161] But the dramatic
conflicts between MacDiarmid and Muir in the 1930s over Scottish
nationalism and the language question were already foreshadowed in
the pages of *The Scottish Nation* in 1923.

But there is more to 'ideological consistency' than commitment to a
particular political party or ideology. Furthermore, MacDiarmid, Muir,
Gibbon and James Barke, who were the four major literary representatives of the Scottish left in the 1930s, had always been very critical of
urban life *per se;* and, though MacDiarmid, Gibbon and Barke claimed
to be marxists, this triumvirate shared Muir's profound dislike of
urbanism. Far from agreeing with Karl Marx's belief that capitalism
was historically progressive in so far as it 'rescued a considerable part
of the population from rural idiocy', they were always harking back to
a lost rural paradise.[162] Gibbon and Barke were ideologically estranged
from the labour movement through their innocence, faith in rural
virtues and failure to fully accept the industrial proletariat as an agency
of social change.

It is, however, important to emphasise the Scottish labour movement's failure to react to international fascism. As this parochialism
became more apparent from 1928, when the Scottish TUC did not
renew its long-standing affiliation to the non-party Scottish Home
Rule Association, MacDiarmid lost faith in the 'revolutionary and
republican psychology' of the Scottish socialists and put his faith more
in 'great men' whose 'means to ends' were 'greater than themsels
could ken'.[163] But if the 'unsimultaneity' of history or what Trotsky
called the survival of the consciousness of the tenth in the twentieth
century was an important element in fascist ideology, Edwin Muir
already hinted at his growing doubts about the viability of cultural
nationalism in 1923 when he predicted that Scottish writers would
probably be 'fated hereafter to use English'.[164]

Moreover, there can be no doubt that Muir's attitude to the Scots' dialect was influenced by the rise of fascism. Yet he was too clear a thinker and too much of a humanistic Utopian to depict the murderous anti-humanism in literature, art and poetry as simply fascist. At a time when the similar totalitarian tendencies in both fascism and Bolshevism were scarcely perceived by anyone else, he identified D.H. Lawrence, Sherwood Anderson, Hugh MacDiarmid, the German Expressionists, etc., as those who were assaulting humanism and the heritage of Western civilisation. But while the fascists were utilising the forces of irrationalism to destroy existing civilisation, so had men like Victor Serge and John Maclean been prepared to use primordial forces to make the socialist revolution.[165] As this complex political reality was still half-hidden in the 1920s, it is all the more remarkable that Muir, who was just emerging from his parochial experience in the Scottish labour movement to become a European literary critic, could describe these trends with such perspicacity:

> Why or in what manner appeared the unconscious assault on the humanistic tradition which characterises our time would be hard to say. Many people will be disposed to doubt its existence, and among these are some who are being carried mid-stream in its flood. It is a movement which it is difficult not merely to define, but even to perceive; for it is indirect, unconscious, and is to all appearances more human than the humanistic tradition itself. Its chief preoccupation, crude enough when one has disentangled it, is that culture and civilisation stand between mankind and itself; and its main concern, therefore, is with the immediate contacts of life, in which it hopes to find a life beyond that which is expressed in all the activities of man, immediate and general. It uses the note-book more than the inward eye, and the diary more than either. It distrusts theories, it distrusts consciousness; it distrusts everything, indeed, but the instinctive contact with the immediate environment.[166]

However, Muir was now living abroad and his physical and spiritual isolation from his own society testified to the divorce between the Scottish literati and the labour movement. Besides, as the labour movement fell back into a defensive, inward-looking posture after the failure of the general strike in 1926, the ethnic conflict between the native Scots and the Irish immigrants, Scottish inarticulacy and cultural dependency on the metropolitan elite in London created a mood of despondency and pessimism. But the decisive factor in creating this new situation sprang from economic dependency on English metropolitan capitalism in conditions of world slump and economic depression.

Yet there was nothing inevitable about this turn of events at all; and the complexity of the relationship between culture, economics and politics was witnessed in the outward-looking optimism of the Scottish labour movement in the early 1920s when the agitation for Home Rule promised freedom from cultural dependency during a period of mass unemployment. For if 'the most memorable feature of Scottish economic life between the wars was the severity of unemployment',[167] there was also a marked mood of socialist optimism in the early 1920s in contrast to the inward-looking introspection and despondency between the years 1926 and 1939.

Moreover, the unresolved questions of the Scottish labour movement's attitude towards Gaelic, the Scots' dialect and cultural dependency in the 1930s led to the literati's doubts, self-questioning and in-fighting over the cultural aspects of the national question. For at the same time as Gibbon defended Lallans as 'the speech of bed and board and street and plough', he depicted his fears of what an independent Scotland could mean in conditions of world economic depression.

> It will profit Glasgow's hundred and fifty thousand slum-dwellers so much to know that they are being starved and brutalised by Labour Exchanges and Public Assistance Committees staffed exclusively by Gaelic-speaking, haggis-eating Scots in saffron kilts and tongued brogues, full of such typical Scottish ideals as those which kept men chained as slaves in the Fifeshire mines a century or so ago.[168]

But if MacDiarmid responded to the problem of the cultural dependency of the Scottish working class by publishing poetry in Lallans, he was 'defeated' by the lack of an adequate readership rather than by using an 'inaccessible' language.

As Edwin Muir became increasingly preoccupied with the problems created by the 'linguistic division' in Scotland, he identified 'the lack of a whole language' as the major problem which kept the Scots stuck in the eighteenth century.[169] Yet the remarkable perception he displayed in the early 1920s was somewhat vitiated later on by his pessimism about the condition of Scotland question, and he postponed the solution of social, cultural and economic problems until the coming of the Socialist Commonwealth. Indeed, he argued that 'a hundred years of socialism would do more to restore Scotland to health and weld it into a real nation' than anything else he could envisage. But as his analysis was now explicitly hostile to the aspirations of the Scottish National Party and the literary renaissance, he attempted to reconcile socialism and nationalism by looking forward to a socialist future in which linguistic divisions and ethnic conflict would no longer exist.[170] What he ignored was the continuing assault on the Scots' dialect and the decline of Gaelic speakers from 3.3 per cent of the total population of Scotland in 1921 almost to the point of extinction in 1931, and, above all, the problem of reconciling means and ends or agency and long-term objectives.[171]

As a result of their deep attachment to rural life, Muir, Barke and MacDiarmid were unable to identify with industrial society and they articulated their strong revulsion for the ignorance, apathy and fatalism of the proletariat. For though Muir identified and attacked the anti-humanistic trends in European literature and poetry, he found it impossible to regard the working men and women he saw in Glasgow as active, intelligent agents of history. Moreover, the other figures on the Scottish literary left were so hostile to the suffocating provincialism and anti-intellectualism of their own society that they allowed it to obscure the enormous potential consciousness of the working class; and as they were, with varying degrees of perception, aware of the 'important point that poetry in Scots ha[d] still an access, not only to a cultured section but to the working classes, in Scotland, that no English poetry has ever had, or, to all appearances, can ever have', their underestimation of the labour movement was all the more regrettable.[172]

By postponing the solution of Scottish social, economic and cultural problems to a future Socialist Commonwealth, Muir ignored the questions of how and why a hundred years of socialism would solve anything. By implying that the problems of language and the legacy of cultural dependency would be solved simply by improving the economic well-being of the 'masses', he was displaying the same sense of unreality as MacDiarmid had done. For though they both wanted to modernise and Europeanise Scottish society, they tended to portray the wasteland and 'darkness of industrialism' and explored new realms of technique without sketching in the multi-dimensions of a socialist society in which minority cultures and languages would have a place and function. Moreover, while MacDiarmid engaged in a polemic with Muir and put the case for the superiority of 'the vaguest adumbration of what we might have been' over 'any possible development of what we are',[173] he dismissed the common ruck of humanity in *A Drunk Man Looks at the Thistle*:

O gin they's stegh their guts and haud their wheesht I'd thole it,
for 'a man's a man', I ken, But tho the feck ae plenty of the 'aa
that', They're nocht but zoologically men.[174]

But the revolutionary and cultural genius who regretted that he had
to 'feed frae the common trough' nevertheless failed to emancipate
himself from the Scottish provincialism that John Maclean had opposed.
By speaking contemptuously of his fellow men, he was uneasily straddl-
ing the dominant and minority traditions and attitudes of Scottish
society. For at the same time as he shared Trotsky's hope of 'the
average human type' rising to 'the heights of an Aristole, a Goethe or a
Marx', he also allowed his 'murderous streak of "anti-humanity"',
conveyed for instance in the craving to hear the roar of the human
shingle', to cut himself off from the working class he was otherwise
'proud' to belong to.[175] This characteristically Scottish *bourgeois*
contempt for human suffering stood out in marked contrast to the
authentic identification with the victims of injustice that a man like
Eugene Victor Debs, the American socialist, expressed in 1917 when he
was put on trial for his anti-war agitation:

Years ago I recognised my kinship with all livings things, and I made
up my mind that I was not one bit better than the meanest of the
earth. I said then, and I say now, that while there is a lower class,
I am in it; while there is a criminal element, I am of it; while there
is a soul in prison, I am not free.[176]

When Muir's later obsession with the need to break up industrial
societies altogether and MacDiarmid's consistent 'Stalinism' are seen in
the light of Scottish history, it is unprofitable to debate the question
of whether they were socialists or not. For while the relevance of
Muir's socialism to an industrial society was at best dubious,
MacDiarmid's socialism — 'I would sacrifice a million people any day
for one immortal lyric'[177] — was alien to the socialist humanism of a
Debs, a Maclean, a Maxton or the tradition of the Second International.
Since they were at least partly responsible for the literati's failure
to impinge on the consciousness of the majority of Scottish working
men and women, they left a legacy which allowed an American scholar
to comment on the condition of Scotland question in 1970 as follows:

There operates also, in Scotland (as elsewhere), a most important
sociological law, which, though examples of it are not difficult to

observe, I do not recollect having seen formulated in print. And
that is the petrifying but protective influence of great military
defeats on those nations which have nevertheless managed to
survive these defeats. As the Scots are themselves the first to
recognise, the whole cultural and political life of the country is
attuned, basically, to no later period than the mid-or late-eighteenth
century, except in the neo-marxist atmosphere of Glasgow and the
industrial area, which has entirely leapt the nineteenth century,
into the present, owing to the industrial blight.[178]

But artists and literary men have never required to be progressive in
politics in order to show men what they were, how they lived and what
they might become; and at their best Muir, MacDiarmid, Gibbon and
Barke produced imaginative literature which, though restricted to a
narrow audience, offered important insights into the human condition.

IV

As the National Party of Scotland founded in 1928 and the literary
renaissance movement became increasingly absorbed in their backward-
looking dreams of 'Celticising' industrial Scotland, the labour movement was deprived of intellectual influences which might have sustained
its earlier outward-looking internationalism and socialist militancy.
Besides, as the provincial elite were able to blame the severity of
Scottish unemployment on the Irish immigrants,[179] the sense of national
identity which Lowland Scots, Highlanders and Irish immigrants had
forged in the heat of a class struggle was undermined by the competition for jobs. As pessimism and despondency began to dominate a
derelict country which was turning in upon itself, the problems thrown
up by industrial capitalism were blamed on the Irish immigrants who
retreated into their own quarters within Scottish communities. This
criticism of the Irish was carefully expressed before an audience of the
Glasgow Philosophical Society:

Owing to Scotland's geographical position, and the nature of her
industries as these emigrants (the native Scots) depart from our
shores, their places are filled by inferior Irish, who, exploiting the
folly of our statesmen, live at ease and comfort on the bounty of
our laws. Not only so, but these newcomers are responsible for an
undue proportion of serious crime in our land, fill our hospitals,
create our slums, organise no-rent strikes, foment revolution and
encourage violence in labour disputes.[180]

But by the time these prejudices were being formulated the reality was quite different, since mass unemployment had contributed to the prevalence of quietism and apathy.

This apathy was seen in 1928 and 1929 when the National Unemployed Workers' Movement failed to mobilise any real support for their hunger marches outside of the mining communities. Indeed, the few workers who took part in these marches to London to demonstrate the plight of the unemployed were all miners;[181] and the Labour government took active measures to try and drive the Scottish marchers into the workhouse.[182] But the labour movement was badly split and divided as a result of the Communist Party's denunciation of the Labour Party and ILP as agencies of 'social fascism'; and in 1929 a police spy reported to the Scottish Office that 'no action was necessary' as the number of the marchers was very small in contrast to the English situation were police surveillance was an urgent necessity.[183]

As the Communist Party was now hell-bent on pursuing a policy of sectarianism and splitting the labour movement, it took steps in 1928 to form a Mineworkers' Union of Scotland consisting of communist and left-wing miners.[184] In Fife — and particularly in Cowdenbeath and Lochgelly — the labour movement was involved in internecine conflict; and ironically the Fife district committee of the Communist Party vetoed an instruction from their headquarters in London to mount a workers' insurrection.[185] But though the communists in Fife refused to unleash a workers' insurrection, the young pioneers — the communist sons of communist parents — did not hesitate to disrupt the work of the State schools by telling teachers that they wanted 'working-class history' instead of that of the 'boss class'.[186] As social democratic and apolitical teachers were driven to nervous breakdowns as a result of bitter conflict in the classrooms, teachers were taken to court for 'assaulting' pupils. Besides, the Communist Party and the Roman Catholic church fought symbolic 'battles' at the gravesides of deceased communists. Since the latter had been Roman Catholics before they had gone over to communism, both sides fought for the 'soul' of individuals whose alleged death-bed recantations were regarded as very important in mining communities where political polarisation was unimaginably extreme.[187] But if the conflict between the communists and the rest of the labour movement was most violent in Fife, *Pravda* denounced James Maxton and other leading members of the ILP as 'agents provocateurs' and 'lackeys of social fascism'.[188]

As these divisions in the labour movement only reached their peak after Scottish socialist Parliamentary representation was increased to thirty-six in the general election of 1929, this new factor of serious internecine strife in trade unions and working-class communities deepened the demoralisation that had begun after the failure of the general strike of 1926. In 1931 the Scottish TUC rejected a resolution calling for self-government;[189] but it was the labour leaders' response to the severity of the world slump rather than the so-called 'parish pump outlook' of the Home Rulers which helped to turn a derelict country in upon itself. This was summed up by the president when he opened the proceedings a few months before the disastrous general election of 1931: 'Surely no person engaged in industry believes that Scotland could survive as a separate economic unit. We are part of a great Commonwealth, and all we desire is that we should be allowed without handicap to take our full share in the industrial life of the Commonwealth'.[190] So the vision of a brave new socialist world envisaged by John Maclean, John Wheatley and James Maxton and a solid section of working-class opinion was being replaced by a plea for a few crumbs from the table of metropolitan capitalism.

But as this increasing awareness — and, indeed, fear — of economic dependency no longer inspired the socialist aspirations or the self-confidence of most working-class Scots, a bitter price was paid in a number of ways. First of all, the Scots experienced the highest death rate, sickness rate[191] and infant mortality rate in Britain;[192] secondly, Glasgow's reputation for being 'Red' was responsible for 'the loss of industries which might have come to the district';[193] and thirdly, the 'rout of Labour in Scotland' in 1931 gave great comfort to those section of the Scottish bourgeoisie who were infatuated with literary fascism.[194] As what were 'previously considered socialist citadels' were 'successfully stormed' and Scottish socialist representation in Parliament reduced to six seats, *The Scotsman* newspaper looked forward to an era of stability under a National government which had seemingly exorcised political 'extremism' and class conflict.[195]

In reality, however, railwaymen and farm workers were still willing to carry socialist ideas to working men and women in town and country; and though their work of harrowing rather than harvesting was usually conducted in clandestine conditions, they shared a fate similar to the one experienced by their 'defeated' comrades in Austria of whom Joseph Buttinger has written:

> Their socialism lives on, like seed beneath the snow. In every
> country they have brothers, including some of other name, brought
> up in other schools. Everywhere, individually or in small groups,

they search for a new way. Gradually they will be joined by other men, thrust into thought and action by the curse of social disaster. They will not be units of a mighty host in the near future. But even if their spirit cannot prevail in politics for many years, the needs of the time will call them sooner or later. Going his own way, even the loneliest will some day encounter brothers, at home or abroad. And wherever in the world they meet, however different their tongues, they will know and embrace one another, and wonder what made them think they were alone.[196]

Notes

1. E.J. Hobsbawm, *Industry and Empire* (London, 1968), p. 265.

2. James Leatham, 'Glasgow in the Limelight', *The Gateway*, mid-May 1923, p. 2.

3. James D. MacDougall, 'Clyde Labour: A Study in Political Change', *New Statesman*, 5 February 1927.

4. *Forward*, 8 May 1915.

5. W.R. Scott and J. Cunnison, *The Industries of the Clyde during the War* (Oxford, 1924), p. 149.

6. *Forward*, 13 January and 14 February 1914.

7. *Report of the Royal Commission on the Housing of the Industrial Population of Scotland Rural and Urban*, Parliamentary Papers, vol. XIV, 1917-18, p. 346.

8. Patrick Geddes, *Cities in Evolution* (London, 1915), p. 134.

9. Ibid., p. 140.

10. Nan Milton, *John Maclean* (London, 1973), pp. 102-4.

11. John Wheatley, 'Big Struggle Projected', *Forward*, 18 September 1915.

12. Milton, *John Maclean*, p. 89.

13. *Forward*, 16 October 1915.

14. Ibid., 30 October 1915.

15. *Glasgow Herald*, 15 November 1915.

16. Anonymous, *The Scottish Socialists. A Gallery of Contemporary Portraits* (London, 1931), p. 213.

17. Scott and Cunnison, *The Industries*, p. 3.

18. *Report of the Rt Hon. Lord Balfour of Burleigh and Lynden Macassey on the Clyde Munitions Workers*, Parliamentary Papers, vol. XXIX, 1914-16, p. 2.

19. *Commission of Enquiry into Industrial Unrest, Scotland, 1917*, Parliamentary Papers, vol. XV, 1917-18, p. 3.

20. James Hinton, *The First Shop Stewards' Movement* (London, 1973), p. 147 and pp. 157-61.

21. *Forward*, 26 February 1916.

22. Ibid., 30 September 1916.

23. Walter Kendall, *The Revolutionary Movement in Britain, 1900-1921* (London, 1969), p. 133.

24. James D. MacDougall, 'The attack on John Maclean', *Forward*, 27 March 1915.

25. Ibid., 3 July 1915.

26. *The Scottish Socialists*, p. 205.

27. *Forward*, 16 December 1916.

28. Julius Braunthal, *History of the International* (London, 1967), p. 70.

29. William Diack, 'Scottish Trade Unionists and Industrial Unrest', *Scottish Review*, Autumn 1917, p. 336.

30. *Forward*, 19 May 1917.

31. Ibid., 5 May 1917.

32. By a Scottish Trade Unionist, 'The Future of the Scottish Labour Party', *Scottish Review*, Spring 1917.

33. John Leslie, 'James Connolly: An Appreciation', *Justice*, 18 May 1916.

34. John Maclean, *In the Rapids of Revolution*, Nan Milton (ed.) (London, 1978), p. 18.

35. *Labour Leader*, 16 April 1914.

36. 'The ILP Election Policy for Scotland', *Forward*, 12 January 1918.

37. Ibid., 2 February 1918.

38. James D. MacDougall, 'The Scottish Coalminer', *The Nineteenth Century and After*, December 1927, p. 769.

39. *Forward*, 13 July 1918.

40. Ibid., 22 June 1918 and 6 April 1918.

41. Ibid., 16 November 1918.

42. William Diack, 'Now for the Next Election', *Scottish Review*, Spring 1919, pp. 40-1.

43. Harry Hanham, *Scottish Nationalism* (London, 1969), pp. 10-11.

44. William Diack, 'The Future of the Scottish Labour Party', *Scottish Review*, Summer 1918, pp. 168-70.

45. Ibid., Winter 1919, p. 448.

46. Ibid., Summer 1919, pp. 139-40.

47. Ibid., p. 170.

48. William Diack, 'Scottish and Irish Labour Colleges', Ibid., Winter 1919, p. 390.

49. Iain MacLean, 'Red Clydeside, 1915-1919', *Popular Protest and Public Order*, Roland Quinault and John Stevenson (eds.) (London, 1973), p. 223.

50. *Forward*, 14 December 1918.

51. S.G. Checkland, *The Upas Tree* (Glasgow, 1976), p. 37.

52. *Forward*, 18 October 1918.

53. Kenneth O. Morgan, *Keir Hardie: Radical and Socialist* (London, 1975), p. 45.

54. *Strike Bulletin*, 12 February 1919.

55. 'It is a trifle unfortunate, though understandable, that when people outside Scotland discuss Scottish politics they invariably assume that Glasgow and Scotland are synonymous terms. They are not. Indeed, Glasgow is the least Scottish of all Scots cities. One of the misleading effects of this assumption is that the attention of the observer is drawn away from such significant facts that Edinburgh is almost proportionately as much a Labour stronghold as Glasgow'. *The Scottish Socialists*, p. 143.

56. 'Bolshevik "News" and Bolshevik "Representatives" ', *Justice*, 15 August 1918.

57. Kendall, *Revolutionary Movement*, p. 141.

58. Richard Reiss, *The Home I Want* (London, 1918), p. 13 and the *Report of the Royal Commission on Housing*, p. 347.

59. *Forward*, 3 May 1919.

60. Ibid., 10 June 1916.

61. Ibid., 1 June 1918.

62. C.M. Grieve, *Contemporary Scottish Studies* (London, 1926), p. 251.

63. Ibid., p. 254.

64. Diack, 'Scottish and Irish Labour Colleges', *Scottish Review*, p. 384.

65. Mrs Maclean to Albert Inkpin, the general secretary of the BSP, dated 16 June 1916. John Maclean Papers, File 2, National Library of Scotland.

66. Letter from Inkpin to Mrs Maclean, 25 July 1916, Ibid.

67. Letter from Thoreau Whitehead, 7 July 1916, Ibid.

68. *Forward*, 28 June 1917 and 18 May 1918.

69. Letter from James Ramsay MacDonald to Mrs Maclean, 21 June 1918; File 3.

70. Letter from James Ramsay MacDonald to the Rt Hon. Robert Munro, 5 July 1918, Ibid.

71. Letter from John Maclean to Sir James M. Dobbs, Ibid., date not clear.

72. *Forward*, 8 December 1923.

73. Ibid., 22 March 1919.

74. *Hansard*, vol. 176, 1924, p. 3214.

75. James Clunie, *The Voice of Labour* (Dunfermline, 1958), p. 80.

76. 'For the present we suggest that John Maclean's charges should be met, not in the secret conference, but in the open light of public inquiry'. Thomas Kennedy, 'Subsidised "Revolutionaries" ', *Justice*, 27 May 1920.

77. Leon Trotsky, *Where is Britain Going?* (London, 1926), pp. 44-5.

78. *Scottish Home Rule Association News-Sheet*, January 1921.

79. *Annual Report of the Scottish Trades Union Congress*, 1921, p. 64.

80. *Fife Free Press*, 21 January 1922.

81. Ibid., 29 April 1922.

82. *Falkirk Mail*, 6 May 1922.

83. Ibid., 18 March 1922.

84. 'Evictions in Glasgow', *Forward*, 3 February 1923.

85. Leatham, 'Glasgow in the Limelight', p. 8.

86. Margaret Sanger, *An Autobiography* (London, 1939), pp. 267-8.

87. James Maxton, 'Appeal to the Working Class in Glasgow', *Forward*, 26 August 1922.

88. 'The Election in Scotland', *Scotsman*, 17 November 1922.

89. *The Scottish Farm Servant*, December 1922.

90. J.B., 'In Memory of John Maclean', *Justice*, 27 March 1924.

91. A Special Correspondent, 'Socialism on the Clyde', *The Times*, 28 December 1922.

92. *Dunfermline Journal*, 21 May 1921.

93. Ibid., 16 and 20 April 1921.

94. 'Short History of the Miners' Unofficial Reform Movement', *Stirling Journal*, 28 April 1921.

95. *Dunfermline Journal*, 23 April 1921.

96. Ibid., 28 April 1921.

97. R. Erskine of Marr, 'Scottish Nationalism', *Scottish Nation*, 9 October 1923.

98. Gilbert McAllister, *James Maxton. The Portrait of a Rebel* (London, 1935), p. 123.

99. *Scottish Home Rule*, November 1923.

100. *The Annual Register*, 1924, pp. 53-4.

101. *The Scotsman*, 10 May 1924.

102. William Bolitho, *The Cancer of Empire* (London, 1924), p. 16.

103. *Forward*, 14 April 1923.

104. Bolitho, *Cancer*, p. 51.

105. *Hansard*, vol. 169, 1924, p. 194 and p. 274.

106. *Scottish Home Rule*, May 1924.

107. For concrete evidence of the influence of Scottish nationalist historiography on John Maclean's thinking, see his articles 'Irish Stew' and 'Literary Note' *The Vanguard,* September and November 1920.

108. Hanham, *Scottish Nationalism,* p. 139.

109. James Hunter, 'The Gaelic Connection: the Highlands, Ireland and Nationalism, 1873-1922', *The Scottish Historical Review,* vol. LIV, no. 158, 1975, p. 199.

110. *Stornoway Gazette,* 13 August 1920.

111. Hunter, 'The Gaelic Connection', p. 199.

112. Harry McShane and Joan Smith, *Harry McShane: No Mean Fighter* (London, 1978), p. 118.

113. Hanham, *Scottish Nationalism,* p. 124.

114. Quoted in Ibid., p. 137-8.

115. Patriot, 'The Centenary of Scottish Independence', *Liberty,* 2 October 1920.

116. Ibid.

117. *The Vanguard,* November 1920.

118. Liam Mac Gill Iosa (Erskine of Marr), 'Bannockburn and its Lessons', *Liberty,* June 1920.

119. 'The Fiscal, cross-examining, questioned Maclean about what he meant by revolution. Maclean held out both hands, one above the other; he said they represented the two classes in society, the top one being the capitalist class. He then swung his hands round to the reverse position, and said that was revolution.' Maclean, *Rapids of Revolution,* p. 232.

120. John Broom, *John Maclean* (Loanhead, Midlothian, 1973), p. 139.

121. Liam Mac Gill Iosa (Erskine of Marr), 'John Maclean and the Crown', *Liberty,* June 1921.

122. Ruaraidh Erskine of Marr, 'Russian Sovereignty', *The Standard,* March 1922.

123. James Connolly, *Socialism and Nationalism* (Dublin, 1948), pp. 58-64.

124. Hamish Henderson, 'Flower and Iron of the Truth: A Survey of Contemporary Scottish Writing', *Our Time,* vol. 7, no. 12, 1948, p. 304.

125. Quoted in Duncan Glen, *Hugh MacDiarmid (Christopher Murray Grieve) and the Scottish Renaissance* (Edinburgh, 1964), p. 49.

126. Connolly, *Socialism,* p. 72.

127. William Power, *Literature and Oatmeal* (London, 1935), p. 177.

128. C.M. Grieve, 'Scottish Election Results', *The Scottish Nation,* 11 December 1923.

129. Leon Trotsky, *My Life* (New York, 1960), p. 72.

130. David Craig, *The Real Foundations. Literature and Social Change* (London, 1973), p. 236.

131. Leon Trotsky, *Literature and Revolution* (New York, 1957), p. 256.

132. Hugh MacDiarmid, 'Art and the Unknown', *The New Age,* 20 May 1926.

133. Trotsky, *Literature and Revolution,* p. 225.

134. Karl Kautsky, *The Class Struggle* (New York, 1971), p. 157.

135. J.K. Annand, 'The Vocabulary of Hugh MacDiarmid's Scots Poems', *Akros,* vol. 12, nos. 34-5, p. 15.

136. Hugh MacDiarmid, *A Drunk Man Looks at the Thistle* (New York, 1967), p. 12.

137. C.M. Grieve, 'Plea for a Scottish Fascism', *The Scottish Nation,* 5 June 1923.

138. *Annual Report of the Scottish Trades Union Congress,* 1924, p. 74.

139. 'The Fascist White Terrorists of Italy', *Forward,* 1 April 1922.

140. *Pictish Review,* April 1928.

141. Lewis Spence, 'The Scottish Literary Renaissance', *Nineteenth Century and After*, July 1926, p. 126.

142. C.M. Grieve, Foreword to Adam Kennedy's novel, *Orra Boughs. The Modern Scot*, vol. 1, no. 3, 1930, pp. 1-2.

143. *The Scots' Review*, January 1925.

144. Thus David Kirkwood, MP, told a meeting to celebrate the battle of Bannockburn that: 'As an international socialist he wanted Scotland for the Scots; he wanted Home Rule for Scotland'. *Scottish Home Rule*, July 1923.

145. 'The majority of the Scottish Labour members returned to the House of Commons went there as "internationalists". A short experience of Westminster transformed them completely.' C.M. Grieve, *Albyn or Scotland and the Future* (London, 1927), pp. 7-8.

146. C.M. Grieve,' Backward Forward', *The Pictish Review*, May 1928.

147. C.M. Grieve, 'Towards a Literary Revival', *The Scottish Nation*, 18 September 1923.

148. C.M. Grieve, 'Programme for a Scottish Fascism', *The Scottish Nation*, 19 June 1923.

149. Christopher Harvie, *Scotland and Nationalism* (London, 1977), p. 46.

150. *The Scottish Chapbook*, vol. 2, no. 3, 1923, p. 78.

151. C.M. Grieve, 'The Caledonian Antiszygy and the Gaelic Idea', *The Modern Scot*, vol. 2, no. 32, 1932, p. 333. This essay was written before the general election of 1931, though not published till January 1932.

152. T.S.E., 'The Fascist Idea', *The Scottish Nation*, 4 September 1923.

153. Lewis Spence, 'Enthusiasm or Caution, Success or Failure', Ibid., 12 June 1923.

154. Lewis Grassic Gibbon and Hugh MacDiarmid, *Scottish Scene* (London, 1934), p. 167.

155. Leon Trotsky, *The Struggle Against Fascism in Germany* (Harmondsworth, 1975), p. 412.

156. Causerie (Hugh MacDiarmid), 'A Theory of Scottish Letters', *The Scottish Chapbook*, vol. 1, no. 8, 1923, p. 210.

157. Hugh MacDiarmid, *The Company I've Kept* (London, 1966), pp. 147-8.

158. Ian S. Munro, *Leslie Mitchell: Lewis Grassic Gibbon* (Edinburgh, 1966), p. 43.

159. Peter Butter, *Edwin Muir: Man and Poet* (Edinburgh, 1966), pp. 111-2.

160. Munro, *Leslie Mitchell*, p. 189.

161. Harvie, *Scotland and Nationalism*, p. 156.

162. James D. Young, 'Images of Rural "Idiocy" and Labour Movements', *Bulletin of the Society for the Study of Labour History*, no. 24, 1972, pp. 34-7.

163. *The Socialist Poems of Hugh MacDiarmid*, T.S. Law and Thurso Berwick (eds.) (London, 1978), p. 4.

164. Edwin Muir, 'A Note on the Scottish Ballads', *The Scottish Nation*, 10 July 1923.

165. Victor Serge, *Birth of our Power* (London, 1977), p. 41, and Maclean, *Rapids of Revolution*, pp. 162-3.

166. Edwin Muir, 'The Assault on Humanism' and 'The Assault on Humanism Again', *The Scottish Nation*, 4 September 1923 and 6 November 1923.

167. R.H. Campbell, *Scotland since 1707. The Rise of an Industrial Society* (Oxford, 1965), p. 249.

168. Gibbon and MacDiarmid, *Scottish Scene*, p. 165 and p. 123.

169. Edwin Muir, *Scott and Scotland* (London, 1936), pp. 21-2.

170. Edwin Muir, *Scottish Journey* (London, 1935), p. 233.

171. *Preliminary Report on the Thirteenth Census of Scotland*, Parliamentary Papers, vol. XVI, 1921, p. 356, and *Census of Scotland*, Parliamentary Papers,

vol. 2, 1931, pp. xxxviii-xxxix.

172. *The Golden Treasury of Scottish Poetry*, selected and edited by Hugh MacDiarmid (London, 1941), p. xxv.

173. Hugh MacDiarmid, 'The Assault on Humanism', *The Scottish Nation*, 16 October 1923.

174. MacDiarmid, *A Drunk Man*, p. 10.

175. Peter Thirlby, 'The Piper on the Parapet', *The New Reasoner*, no. 8, 1959.

176. Quoted in Guy Aldred, *Convict 9653. America's Vision Maker* (Glasgow, n.d.), p. 8.

177. Hugh MacDiarmid, 'Lewis Grassic Gibbon', *Little Reviews Anthology 1946* (London, 1946), pp. 211-2.

178. G. Legman, *The Horn Book* (London, 1970), p. 365.

179. *Hansard*, vol. 220, 1928, p. 2015.

180. George Wingate, 'The Dole and Unemployment', *Proceedings of the Glasgow Philosophical Society*, vol. LIV, 1927, p. 41.

181. *Scotsman*, 25 January 1929.

182. DD 10/245, Scottish Records Office, Edinburgh.

183. DD 10/245/6.

184. *Scotsman*, 18 September and 20 September 1928.

185. Letter from the late Bob Selkirk, a veteran communist organiser, 8 September 1972.

186. *The School Bell*, October 1928.

187. Interviews with Bob Selkirk, April and May 1972 and letter from Jennie Lee, 14 July 1972.

188. McAllister, *James Maxton*, p. 205.

189. *Annual Report of the Scottish TUC*, 1931, p. 142.

190. Ibid., p. 23.

191. Grieve, *Albyn or Scotland and the Future*, p. 64.

192. Fenner Brockway, *Hungry England* (London, 1932), p. 197.

193. George Mitchell, 'The Trade and Industry of Glasgow', *Proceedings of the Philosophical Society of Glasgow*, vol. LIX, 1931.

194. *Forward*, 31 October 1931.

195. 'How Scotland Stands', *The Scotsman*, 29 October 1931.

196. Joseph Buttinger, *The Twilight of Socialism* (New York, 1953), p. 550.

SELECT BIBLIOGRAPHY

Archives

Elcho Papers: RH40, on microfilm, Scottish Records Office, Edinburgh

Elliot, Arthur: Paper, Acc. 4246, National Library of Scotland

Graham, R.B. Cunninghame: Letters (1887-8), MS 5903, ff.63, 85; Letters (1890), MS, 2638, f. 164; Letters (1893), MS, 4599; Letters (1895), MS, 5142, ff. 76.81, National Library of Scotland

Glasse, John: Letter (1892), MS.3410, National Library of Scotland

Haldane, R.B: Paper, National Library of Scotland

Hardie, James Keir: Letters (1888), MS. 1809, ff. 71-5, Letters (1898-1914), MS. 7198, ff. 122; Letters (1893), Acc. 4494; Letters (1910-11), Acc. 4461, National Library of Scotland

Howell, G: This collection was researched for the letters exchanged between Howell and the Scottish reformers during the period 1865-8

Lennox, D: Working Class Life in Dundee, 1878-1905, (n.d., probably, 1905), unpublished typescript in St Andrews University Library, MS DA 890 D8L2

McLaren, Archibald: Letters to R.F. Muirhead, 1884-1891, Baillie's Library, Glasgow

Maclean, John: Papers in the National Library of Scotland and a few leaflets and pamphlets in the possession of the author

Maxwell, Shaw: Letter to T.V. Powderly, American labour leader, 27 February 1890, Catholic University of America, Washington, DC

Minto papers: National Library of Scotland

Moir, James: Papers, Mitchell Library, Glasgow

Proudfoot, J.C: Letter to the secretary of the Liverpool Trades Council, Liverpool Reference Library

Socialist League Archives: International Institute of Social History, Amsterdam

Socialist Labour Party of America Archives: Wisconsin State Historical Society, Madison, United States of America

Small, William: Personal Papers relating to the Scottish miners, Acc. 3350, National Library of Scotland

Scheu, Andreas: Papers and unpublished autobiography, Institute of Social History, Amsterdam

Minutes of Aberdeen Trades Council, 1876-1920, Aberdeen University Library

Minutes of the Edinburgh Trades Council, 1859-1930, in the office of the Edinburgh Trades Council

Minutes of the Glasgow Trades Council, 1884-1889 and May-December
     1900, in the Mitchell Library
Minutes of the Labour Representation League, 1872-1877, in the
     library of the London School of Economics and Political Science
Minutes of the Larkhall Miners' Association, 1890-1894, MSs 8023-5,
     National Library of Scotland
Minutes of the Scottish Liberal Association, 1885-1895, Edinburgh
     University Library
Minutes of the English Reform League, Howell Collection, Bishopsgate
     Institute, London
Royal Commission on Religious Instruction, 1835, HH, 35-37, Scottish
     Records Office
Scottish Labour Party, First Annual Report of the Executive
     Committee, 1889, incomplete photocopy in Transport House
     Library, London
Statements of the Fife and Clackmannan Miners' Association, 1886-
     1912, Dunfermline Public Library
Statements and evidence in the Criminal Processes of the United
     Scotsmen and the Scottish Chartists are cited in footnotes. It is a
     matter of some concern that so many records dealing with plebeian
     radicalism — and particularly those relating to the Radical War of
     1820 — appear to be missing without anyone being very
     concerned.

Annual and other Reports

Aberdeen Trades Council
British Trades Union Congress
Church of Scotland Commission on the Religious Condition of the
     People, 1889-1896
Edinburgh Trades Council
Edinburgh Working Men's Rest Day Association
Free Church Deacon's Association of Glasgow, 1884-1896
Glasgow Trades Council
Glasgow and West of Scotland Working Men's Protective Association
Inspector of Mines
Medical Officer of Health, Dundee, 1880-1910
Scottish Association of Operative Tailors, 1866-96, HD 6661 c6.75,
     TUC Library, Congress House, London

Journals

Aberdeen University Review, 1944-59

Baillie, 1870-1910
Bulletin of the Society for the Study of Labour History, 1960-79
Blackwood's Edinburgh Magazine, 1830-1920
Catholic Directory for Scotland, 1870-1920
Dundee Year Books, 1881-1900
Economist, 1866-9
Edinburgh Review, 1808-1900
In Memoriam (Aberdeen), 1894-1911
Journal of the Scottish Studies, 1954-70
Labour Annual, 1895-1900
Lancet, 1880-1920
New Reasoner, 1957-9
Nineteenth Century and After, 1920-34
North British Review, 1866-71
Quarterly Review, 1910-31
Records of Scottish Church History, 1951-68
Scottish Review, 1892-1926
Spectator, 1866-9
Universities and Left Review, 1956-9

Newspapers

Aberdeen Daily Free Press
Aberdeen Labour Elector
Aberdeen Press and Journal
Arbeiter Freind (Workers' Friend)
Ardrossan and Saltcoats Herald
Artizan
Ayr Advertiser
Chartist Circular
Commonweal
Dalkeith Herald
Dundee Advertiser
Dundee Courier
Dunfermline Journal
Dunfermline Press
Economist
Edinburgh Evening Courant
Edinburgh Labour Chronicle
Edinburgh Reformer
Exile
Falkirk Herald

Fiery Cross
Forward, 1909-31
Glasgow Courier
Glasgow Echo
Glasgow Examiner
Glasgow Herald
Glasgow Observer
Glasgow Sentinel
Glasgow Weekly Herald
Glasgow Weekly Mail
Govan Press
Hamilton Advertiser
Highlander, 1873-9
Justice
Kilmarnock Advertiser
Labour Leader
Labour Standard
Miner, 1879-80
Miner, edited by James Keir Hardie
National Reformer
North British Daily Mail
Perthshire Constitutional
Reynold's Newspaper
Scotsman
Scottish Co-operator
Scottish Leader
Scottish Standard
Shetland Times
The Times
Trade Unionist
Workman's Times

Pamphlets

A collection of newspaper cuttings on working-class groups, characters, customs, and trade unions in Glasgow (Dundee, 1889), Baillie's Library, Glasgow

Arnot, R. Page (ed.), Unpublished Letters of William Morris (London, 1951)

Challinor, R. 'Alexander MacDonald and the Miners' (London, 1968)

Cunningham, A.S. 'Reminiscences of Alexander MacDonald, the Miners' Friend' (Lochgelly, 1902)

Johnston, J. 'The rising tide of irreligion, pauperism, immorality and death' (Glasgow, 1871)

Leatham, James 'Glasgow in the Limelight' (Turiff, n.d.)

Marwick, W.H. 'The Life of Alexander Campbell' (Glasgow, n.d.)

MacLeod, D. 'Non-Church Going' (Edinburgh, 1888)

McShane, Harry 'History of the Glasgow Trades Council, 1858-1958' (Glasgow, n.d.)

Nicol, J. 'Vital Social and Economic Statistics of the City of Glasgow 1881-1885' (Glasgow, n.d.)

Pratt Insh, G. 'Thomas Muir of Huntershill, 1765-1799' (Glasgow, 1949)

Robertson, Alexander 'Where Are the Highlanders?' (Edinburgh, n.d.)

Robertson, Alexander 'Letters on the Breadalbane Clearances' (Edinburgh, n.d.)

Rorie, David 'The Mining Folk of Fife' (Dunfermline, 1912)

Selkirk, Bob 'The Life of a Worker' (Dundee, 1967)

Socialism in Glasgow (Glasgow, 1918)

The Great Reform Demonstration at Glasgow, 16 October 1866, Mitchell Library

Parliamentary Papers

Report of the Royal Commisson on Coal, 1871, vol. XVII

Report of the Royal Commission on the Condition of the Crofters and Cottars in the Highlands and Islands of Scotland, 1884, vols. XXXII-XXXVI

Report of the Argyll Commission on Scottish Education, 1865-7

Report of the Select Committee on Orange Institutions in Great Britain and the Colonies, 1835, vol. XVII

First Report of the Select Committee on Combination of Workmen, 1838, vol. XVIII

Report of the Select Committee of Inquiry into Drunkenness, 1834, vol. VIII

Select Committee on Emigration and Immigration, 1889

Report of the Royal Commission on Labour, 1891-4

Report of the Royal Commission on Mining Royalties, 1890-1

Proceedings

Proceedings of the Free Church of Scotland, 1866-1910

Proceedings of the General Assembly of the Church of Scotland, 1868-1914

Proceedings of the Royal Philosophical Society of Glasgow, 1860-1931

Transactions

Transactions of the Medico-Chirurgical Society, vol. XI, Edinburgh, 1891-2

Academic Theses

Bell, A.D. 'The Reform League from its Origins to the Reform Act of 1867', DPhil thesis, University of Oxford, 1961

Crowley, D.W. 'Origins of the Revolt of the British Labour Movement from Liberalism, 1875-1906', PhD thesis, London School of Economics and Political Science, London, 1952

Dunsmore, Michael R. 'The Working Classes, the Reform League and the Reform Movement in Lancashire and Yorkshire', MA thesis, University of Sheffield, 1961

Fraser, W.H. 'Trades Councils in England and Scotland, 1857-1897', PhD thesis, University of Sussex, 1967

Kellas, James G. 'The Development of the Liberal Party in Scotland, 1868-1895', PhD thesis, University of London, 1966

Reid, Fred 'The Early Life and Political Development of James Keir Hardie, 1856-1892', PhD thesis, University of Oxford, 1968

Young, James Douglas 'Working Class and Radical Movements in Scotland and the Revolt from Liberalism, 1866-1900', University of Stirling, 1974

Books

Arnot, R. Page *A History of the Scottish Miners* (London, 1955)

Bagwell, P.S. *The Railwaymen* (London, 1963)

Barke, James *The Green Hills Far Away* (London, 1940)

Barker, C.A. *Henry George* (New York, 1955)

Bealey F. and Pelling, H. *Labour and Politics, 1900-1906* (London, 1958)

Beer, Max *History of British Socialism* (London, 1919)

Bell, G. *Days and Nights in the Wynds of Edinburgh* (Edinburgh, 1849)

Bell, Tom *John Maclean. A Fighter for Freedom* (Glasgow, 1944)

—, *Pioneering Days* (London, 1941)

Best, G. *Mid-Victorian Britain* (London, 1971)

Blackie, J.S. *The Scottish Highlanders and the Land Laws* (Edinburgh, 1885)

Blake, G. *Barrie and the Kailyard School* (London, 1951)

Blake, Robert *Disraeli* (London, 1966)

Borland, F. *An Introduction to Religious Sociology* (translated and introduced M.J. Jackson), London, 1960

Bowley, A.W. *Wages and Income in the United Kingdom since 1860* (Cambridge, 1837)

Briggs, A. and Saville, J. (eds.), *Essays in Labour History* (London, 1967)

Brown, P. Hume *History of Scotland to the Present Time* (Cambridge, 1910)

Buckley, K.D. *Trade Unionism in Aberdeen, 1878 to 1900* (Edinburgh, 1955)

Burn, J.D. *Commercial and Social Progress* (London, 1858)

——, *Glimpse at the Social Condition of the Working Classes during the Early Part of the Present Century* (London, 1868)

——, *Autobiography of a Beggar Boy* (London, 1855)

Campbell, R.H. *Scotland since 1707. The Rise of an Industrial Society* (Oxford, 1965)

Carswell, D. *Brother Scots* (London, 1927)

Challinor, R. *The Origins of British Bolshevism* (London, 1978)

Chalmers, T. *Problems of Poverty* (London, 1927)

——, *The Christian and Civic Economy of Large Towns, 1821-1826* (Edinburgh, 1852)

Chambers, R. *Domestic Annals of Scotland* (Edinburgh, 1878)

Chesney, K. *The Victorian Underworld* (London, 1970)

Christie, O.F. *The Transition to Democracy* (London, 1954)

Clark, H.E. *Memorials of Elgin Place Congregation Church* (Glasgow, 1904)

Clegg, A.H., Fox, A. and Thompson, A.F. *History of British Trade Unionism since 1889,* vol. 1 (Oxford, 1964)

Cole, G.D.H. *The Common People* (London, 1938)

——, *British Working Class Politics, 1832-1914* (London, 1941)

Cunninghame, A.S. *Mining in the 'Kingdom' of Fife* (Dunfermline, 1913)

Davidson, M. *Annals of Toil* (London, 1910)

Davie, G.E. *The Democratic Intellect* (Edinburgh, 1961)

Davies, W.J. *History of the British Trades Union Congress,* (London, 1910)

Dollan, P.J. *The History of the Kinning Park Co-operative Society* (Glasgow, 1923)

Dowse, R.S. *Left in the Centre* (London, 1966)

Drawbell, J. *The Sun Within Us* (London, 1963)

Dron, R.W. *The Coalfields of Scotland* (Edinburgh, 1902)

Encyclopaedica of the Laws of Scotland (Edinburgh, 1932), 20 vols.

Ewing, W. *Annals of the Free Church of Scotland* (Edinburgh, 1914)

Ferguson, W. *Scotland: 1689 to the Present Day* (Edinburgh, 1968)

Foster, J. *The Members of Parliament for Scotland* (Edinburgh, 1882)

Gillespie, G.F. *Labour and Politics in England, 1850-1867*
(New York, 1927)

Gillet, W.M. *Edinburgh in the Nineteenth Century* (Edinburgh, 1901)

Glasier, J. Bruce *William Morris and the Early Days of the Socialist Movement* (London, 1921)

Greaves, D.C. *The Life and Times of James Connolly* (London, 1961)

Groves, Reg *But We Shall Rise Again* (London, 1938)

Haddow, W.H. *My Seventy Years* (Glasgow, n.d.)

Haldane, E.S. *The Scotland of Our Fathers* (London, 1933)

Hamilton, H. *The Industrial Revolution in Scotland* (London, 1966)

—, *The Economic Evolution of Scotland* (London, 1933)

Hammerton, A.J. *Books and Myself* (London, 1920)

Handley, J.E. *The Navvy in Scotland* (Cork, 1970)

—, *The Irish in Modern Scotland* (Cork, 1947)

Hanham, H.J. *Scottish Nationalism* (London, 1969)

Harrison, Royden *Before the Socialists* (London, 1965)

Harvey, C. *Scotland and Nationalism* (London, 1977)

Hobsbawm, E.J. *Industry and Empire* (London, 1968)

Humphreys, A.W. *A History of Labour Representation* (London, 1912)

Hunter, A.J. *Problems of Poverty* (London, 1912)

Inglis, K.S. *Churches and the Working Classes in Victorian England*
(London, 1963)

Kellas, J.G. *Modern Scotland* (London, 1968)

Kendall, W. *The Revolutionary Movement in Britain, 1900-1921*
(London, 1969)

Lee, W.E. and Archibold, E. *Social Democracy in Britain*
(London, 1935)

Lowe, D. *Souvenirs of Scottish Labour* (Glasgow, 1919)

MacArthur, J. *New Monkland Parish* (Coatbridge, 1890)

McBriar, A.M. *Fabian Socialism and English Politics, 1884-1918*
(Cambridge, 1966)

MacDiarmid, Hugh *R.B. Cunninghame Graham* (Glasgow, 1952)

—, *The Company I've Kept* (London, 1966)

MacDougall, Ian *The Minutes of the Edinburgh Trades Council, 1859-1873* (Edinburgh, 1968)

MacLaren, A.A. (ed.), *Social Class in Scotland* (London, 1976)

Mackenzie, A. *The History of the Highland Clearances* (Glasgow, 1883)

Mackie, A. *An Industrial History of Edinburgh* (Edinburgh, 1963)

Maclean, John *In the Rapids of Revolution* (London, 1978)

Marwick, W.H. *Economic Developments in Victorian Scotland* (London, 1963)

Marwick, W.H. *A Short History of Labour in Scotland* (Edinburgh, 1867)

Mavor, James *The Scottish Railway Strike of 1891: A History and a Criticism* (Edinburgh, 1891)

Mayor, S. *The Churches and the Labour Movement* (London, 1967)

Mechie, S. *The Churches and Scottish Social Development, 1780-1870* (Oxford, 1960)

Middlemas, R.K. *The Clydesiders* (London, 1965)

Millar, H. *My Schools and Schoolmasters* (Edinburgh, 1954)

Milton, Nan *John Maclean* (London, 1973)

Mitchell, A. *Political and Social Movement in Dalkeith* (Dalkeith, 1882)

Myles, J. *Chapters in the Life of a Dundee Factory Boy* (Dundee, 1951)

Nairn, Tom *The Break-Up of Britain* (London, 1977)

Ord, J. *The Bothy Songs and Ballads* (Paisley, 1930)

Palmer, E. *The Story of North Woodside United Free Church, 1876-1936* (Glasgow, 1936)

Paton, D.N., Dunlop, J.C. and Inglis, E.M. *A Study of the Diet of the Labouring Classes in Edinburgh* (1900)

Payne, P.L. (ed.), *Studies in Scottish Business History* (London, 1967)

Pelling, H. *Popular Politics in Late Victorian Britain* (London, 1968)

—, *The Origins of the Labour Party* (Oxford, 1965)

—, *The Social Geography of British Elections, 1885-1910* (London, 1967)

Pollard, S. and Crossley D.W. *The Wealth of Britain* (London, 1968)

Pope, L. *Millhands and Preachers* (Yale, 1942)

Postgate, R. *The Builders' History* (London, 1923)

Robertson, A. *The Reformation* (London, 1960)

Saunders, J.L. *Scottish Democracy* (Edinburgh, 1950)

Scotland, J. *The History of Scottish Education* (London, 1968)

Short, L.B. *Pioneers of Scottish Unitarianism* (London, 1960)

Simpson, P.C. *Life of Principal Rainy* (London, 1967)

Sinclair, A. *Fifty Years of Newspaper Life, 1854-1895* (Glasgow, 1895)

Smillie, R. *My Life for Labour* (London, 1954)

Smith, Joan and McShane, Harry, *No Mean Fighter* (London, 1978)

Sommerville, A. *Autobiography of a Working Man* (London, 1956)

Stewart, W. *James Keir Hardie* (London, 1921)

Strawthorn, J. *A New History of Cumnock* (Glasgow, 1966)

Torr, D. *Tom Mann and His Times* (London, 1956)

Thompson, E.P. *William Morris. Romantic to Revolutionary* (London, 1956)

Tschiffeley, A.S. *Don Roberto* (London, 1927)

Tsuzuki, T.C. *Life of Eleanor Marx* (Oxford, 1967)

Turner, A.C. *Scottish Home Rule* (London, 1951)

Urquhart, A.R. (ed.), *Auld Perth* (Perth, 1906)

Veitch, J. *George Douglas Brown* (London, 1952)

Vincent, J. *The Foundation of the Liberal Party* (London, 1966)

Watt, H. *Thomas Chalmers and the Disruption* (Glasgow, 1943)

Webb, S. and B. *History of Trade Unionism* (London, 1965)

West, H.F. *R.B. Cunninghame Graham* (London, 1932)

Whitehouse, J.H. *Problems of a Scottish Provincial Town* (London, 1905)

Wilkie, T. *The Representation of Scotland: Parliamentary Elections since 1832* (Paisley, 1885)

Wilson, A. *The Chartist Movement in Scotland*

Younger, J. *Autobiography* (Kelson, 1881)

INDEX